Praise for Pau[...]

"Authentic, straightforward truth strai[...]

—Deepak Chopra

"One of the most sought-after psychics ..."   —*Nightline*

Praise for *The Book of Innocence*

"The book is incredible.... Absolutely impeccable ... one of the most important perspectives we can hold to guide us in this time."
          —Aubrey Marcus, *New York Times* bestselling author

"Throughout every historical epoch, the universe speaks to us directly through exceptionally sensitive individuals. Paul Selig is one of those individuals. *The Book of Innocence* is the latest gift in his series of intriguing channeled teachings."
          —Dean Radin, MS, PhD, chief scientist for the Institute of Noetic Sciences and author of *Real Magic*

"Highly attuned and deeply thoughtful ... [This] is an important book."   —Shaman Durek Verrett, bestselling author, activist, and thought leader

Praise for *Beyond the Known: Realization*

"This book is the most audacious of the Guides' teachings to date. It describes how anyone who chooses can claim the true expression of who they are."   —Aubrey Marcus

Praise for *The Book of Mastery*

"What moves Selig's *The Book of Mastery* into the status of a classic is its spiritual insights into the Divine Self relevant to the fundamental questions human beings have asked about the nature of existence since time immemorial."
          —Michael Bernard Beckwith, author of *Spiritual Liberation*

A WORLD MADE NEW

A CHANNELED TEXT

The Manifestation Trilogy: Book Three

PAUL SELIG

ST. MARTIN'S
ESSENTIALS
NEW YORK

First published in the United States by St. Martin's Essentials,
an imprint of St. Martin's Publishing Group

www.stmartins.com

Library of Congress Cataloging-in-Publication Data

Names: Selig, Paul, medium.
Title: A world made new : a channeled text / Paul Selig.
Description: First edition. | New York : St. Martin's Essentials, 2024. | Series: The manifestation
  trilogy ; book 3
Identifiers: LCCN 2024016759 | ISBN 9781250833815 (trade paperback) |
  ISBN 9781250833822 (ebook)
Subjects: LCSH: Spirit writings. | Spirituality—Miscellanea. | Forecasting—Religious aspects.
Classification: LCC BF1301 .W859 2023 | DDC 133.9/3—dc23/eng/20240531
LC record available at https://lccn.loc.gov/2024016759

Our books may be purchased in bulk for promotional, educational, or business use.
Please contact your local bookseller or the Macmillan Corporate and Premium Sales
Department at 1-800-221-7945, extension 5442, or by email at
MacmillanSpecialMarkets@macmillan.com.

First Edition: 2024

10   9   8   7   6   5   4   3   2   1

Contents

AUTHOR'S NOTE

There are now twelve books in print with my name on the covers that I didn't write. I've been serving as the spoken stenographer for the Guides' work for thirty years now and receiving the lectures that comprise their published teachings for the last fifteen.

I may never fully understand how this came to be. I had been a writer with a crippling case of writer's block for much of my adult life, and the irony that the books that are spoken through me are delivered fully formed over a matter of days is not lost on me. The transcripts of the teachings that comprise the Guides' books remain unedited with only a very, very few words corrected that I either stumbled over or mispronounced during the extremely rapid dictation.

The Guides have said that this book is the culmination and completion of the teachings that began with the dictation of their first text, *I Am the Word,* which was delivered in a little over two weeks of sittings in 2009. They also say there are more books to come, and that they are preparing me to serve as the channel for what comes next. I am happy to be the man who sits in the chair for this, and I am also somewhat astonished at the ways my life has been upended and transformed as the result.

It is an ongoing journey, and I thank the readers who have joined me. The Guides speak to us as passengers on a ship moving across a tumultuous sea to a new shore. I am grateful for the company, and glad to be sharing this journey with you.

Paul Selig
Maui, Hawaii
September 28, 2023

The following are the unedited transcripts of channeling sessions conducted by Paul Selig between July 27, 2023, and September 8, 2023, before students in Berkeley, California; Boone, North Carolina; Maui, Hawaii, and in online seminars.

Introduction

TRUE IDENTITY

What stands before you today, in an awakened state, is a new responsibility—to claim a world made new.

Now, your idea of a world stands in the way—what you think a world should be, based on the presupposition of what it has been or how you have known it. To know is to realize, and the world that you have known is in all ways a construct, a manifest construct, born in tone and vibration, solidified in language, and claimed through decree: "I will build a bench," and hence a bench is made. The idea of who you are within this construct holds several ideas, the idea of identity—"my name is such and such, this is my occupation"—and the idea of what it means to be present in a field with other human beings who are also claiming identity.

Now, identity is not what you think. The personage you walk around as is also a construct, born in most ways through the idea of history—what happened to you yesterday, or perhaps in your youth, or perhaps in a past life, if you wish to go there. The truth of your being, we say, is something really rather different. The vibrational echo that you are, the aspect of God come as you, claims itself in form, or vibration in form, and claims identity as a way to accrue information and experience that the soul utilizes for its progression.

Now, the manifest being you are operates in tandem with all other things in form. You know yourself in the field of the world, or the idea of the field of the world, the manifest plane that comes as all things that you see and experience. "It's time to go to school," "to the office," "to my wedding night," "to my death"—all ideas of who you are in agreement with a manifest world where there are churches and deathbeds and employers and employees. These are the things you learn through, yes, but they are all vibration, and in almost all ways agreed upon by the collective. "This is what a death is." "This is what a wedding night is." And "this is what a job looks like." You are always in confirmation of your idea of what is through the collective field that you have chosen to learn through.

Now, your true identity, as we have always said—and we will call this teaching "True Identity"—is the Divine, or the aspect of God come as you, experiencing itself through you in agreement to all things. Underline the word *all*. It's incredibly important. *All* things. Not just the things before you, but all things that have been and will be, all you can see and imagine. You have come to experience the *all*, and the manifest being that you know yourself as is now coming to terms with its true nature. "I am of Source, as Source, and in Source all at once."

"Now, what does that mean?" you may ask. Well, your true identity—we will call it the Monad or the True Self—has always been here, can only be here, and can only be elsewhere as well because it is not bound by the idea of time and space as the productive personality would utilize it. Now, as you understand yourselves in agreement to others, you have a shared construct of a world. But the True Self that is you expresses both in this world and well beyond it—again, not bound by the idea of time and space.

Now, we said *idea* intentionally because all things are ideas, and then claimed in form or made manifest in form—what you call the weather, what you call the globe, what you call your sister or the building you work in. These are all ideas, held in vibration, codified through language, and understood by you in this collective field. But the True Self that is you, while it perceives what is and can know itself in form, also exceeds form or expresses beyond form. And the aspect of you that knows this is the very aspect of you that is charged—and we say that word intentionally, *charged*—with claiming a world anew.

Now, the manifest reality that you exist in now, the vibrational echo of a world that you see, has been contributed to by all who have ever lived here. Every idea made in form—a raindrop, a thimble, an earthquake—all ideas of what has been, inherited by you, claim a realized world or a world known by you as a construct with its own architecture that you all agree upon. The seasons of the year, even the orbit of the planets, all of these things agreed upon by you and held in a certain way as identical.

"What does that mean," he asks, "*held as identical?*" Well, you all understand what a sunrise is, and there is an identical sunrise experienced by most of you wherever you be on this plane. You are in a shared construct, dancing to music that you are very used to. But we will tell you this now: The music has changed. The tempo has increased. And you are still dancing as if you are listening and adhering to the slow beat, the idea of what was, when the new is upon you, increasingly so. And the vibration it claims, it sounds as, is so vastly different than what you have known, it is in most ways releasing the old structures that cannot be sustained at the high octave, the high tempo, the high vacillation that the new is coming as. This very simply means that the world itself is shifting so rapidly that the old structures, born in old ideas, in old collective agreement, are moving so quickly that they cannot adhere to the old, which seeks to come forth as a world made new.

Now, you are ambassadors of this change, whether or not you like it or know it. And by *ambassador* we mean an emissary of this change. The challenge for most of you, if not all, is that all of your training—underline, again, the word *all*—in personality was born in a lie: that you are separate from Source, and that all are separate from Source. It is the great lie that you have been in confirmation of in a collective way and claimed as what is, or as manifest, and then confirmed by your very experience because it's what you've known, it's what you expect, and you get what you expect each and every day you wake up and you see that sunrise. You know what a thimble is, or a raindrop, or a bridge, or an occupation, born in the old idea and the old conditioning that you have utilized to experience this reality through. But this reality is altering. And by the time most of you are gone it will be quite different than it is today, and then different again and again—and in useful ways, we suggest.

Now, by *useful* we don't mean what you wish. Some of the

challenges ahead, all of your own making, are rather challenging and difficult to the idea of self that you have utilized to maintain an identity and collective language in a world that you have been conditioned to know by way of separation. But what is happening, we would suggest, is not only useful, but a requirement for the species as you lift in vibration and claim the new as a whole.

"What will the world look like?" you ask. You cannot even imagine it yet because even what you would imagine is born in your idea of what can be, and that is always presupposition based upon what was or what was expected by yesterday's actions, yesterday's beliefs, yesterday's language. We will discuss language later in this text, and the importance of language, and how language itself is about to be altered to move to a level of thought where even the idea of words becomes secondary to the impulse of being. How this is translated in thought is something that you will understand by experience, and we intend to instruct you in this.

The teaching that is before you is about who you are, who you have become, and who you are about to become in a new way of experiencing the self in a world made new. And, indeed, that will be the title of the text, although Paul would regret having spoken the words. He would like something other, but we are here to remind him and you that this is the text we write. We are indeed the authors. And we sit before you now with a great smile and a great heart that is here to embrace you all as you set forth on a higher wisdom, a higher counsel, than you have known thus far.

Every text we have written thus far has been an energetic transmission, and these will continue to be so as long as we are allowed to teach through Paul. But the text that we write now is the pinnacle of the past teachings, and the culmination of them as a vibrational echo that will actually not only work with you, you who embarks on the teaching, but the manifest world you engage with. As we said, you are ambassadors. But the work of the ambassador is always to share, and in this case deliver the other country, the other tone, the other world— the Upper Room, if you wish—that you have come to know yourself through.

The gift of this teaching for some of you will be a remedy to old pain. But for many of you it will be something other. It will be the awareness of what has always been true that has been denied and ignored and refuted through your agreement to a belief in separation that was never so. Simply put, the world that you see before you, the product of conscious thought and collective agreement, claimed in separation, will be moved—again, altered—again and again by the increase in tone, velocity, vibration, and song that all of you will be holding. Not just you who read these texts, but all who incarnate in these times of rapid, rapid change.

We sing your songs for you so that you may learn the words. And as we teach, we remember you each in your true lineage, your true heritage. And we offer the inheritance that has been overlooked by you in favor of the small things, the things of the world, that you seek to possess and to know so that you may feel special. We are supporting you well beyond those needs because the gift of these teachings is always the Kingdom. And what we say the Kingdom is, again and again, is always so: the agreement to the manifest Source—you may call it God, if you wish—as all things. Underline the word *as*. God *as* all things.

We thank you for your presence. This is part of the introduction of the text. Stop now, please. Period. Period. Period.

(PAUSE)

Sit back, please. We would like to continue.

The velocity of the tone you hold is actually your expression. The expression you hold in vibration alters all things that it encounters. This is true even at the dense level that you are operating at as the small self. Consciousness is always impactful, and you are always claiming a world into being at the level of tone that you hold. The level of tone that you hold is accrued in many lifetimes, but is altered through the basis of your expression here. The challenges you have faced, what you believe should be, is actually out-pictured for you because you are always entrained or in co-resonance with the reality you experience. The teachings that you receive through us, one and all, are about altering the field or incarnating as the vibrational echo that *is* the Christed Self, or the Monad or True Self.

Now, the aspect of you that thinks she knows all things is actually not the Monad. It is the personality, who has been indoctrinated, in most ways, to an idea of self that is sovereign. But the personality self is not sovereign. It thinks it is. The only aspect of you that is truly sovereign is the Divine—that knows itself as free, beyond birth and death, and beyond any logic that the personality structure would utilize to claim an idea of who she is, or who he should be, in this manifest world.

When the Monad begins to express as you, there is a challenging aspect of you that is discovered: the one who says, "No, I must be in charge. I must have my way. I must be the king upon the throne, the queen upon her throne, at the cost of all others." As we once said through Paul, and we will say again, freedom comes when the throne relinquishes its king. And the true king, or queen, if you prefer, is the Divine Self or the Monad or the Christ that is incarnating as you.

Now, we use the word *incarnating* intentionally. The Divine as you, expressed as and through you, comes at the cost of the old, the old idea of what was and also what should be. It is not dominated by the remnants of history. It is not bound by language or the small self's inheritance, what's important in the world, what one should aspire to be or to get. Because the Divine as you knows the Source of all things, it does not operate in lack, but claims its place in great benefit because its inheritance is the Divine.

Now, the manifest Divine that is actually all about you has been ignored and precluded through damnation, and what is damnation but the denial of the Divine? What you damn, what you put in darkness, damns you right back. And the co-resonant field that you operate in works in separation because the Divine has been precluded or ignored or chosen to see as somewhere other, beyond the idea of self that can know God. Once you understand that your true expression *is* the Divine and you begin to operate in full force *as* this expression—while the personality self, still present, succumbs to its true role, the aspect of you that has experience, that learns through things, that makes small choices—you will have a world that is suddenly in co-creation with the Divine that has come as your expression. The manifest Divine, come as you, claims a manifest world that is also of Source. And the cobwebs and the shadows and the detritus of old—all these things that obscure the Divine—are quite readily moved because they cannot be held in the high octave that we call the Upper Room, where the tempo is so high the shadows are banished before they even arrive.

Now, this is not a wonderland. In most ways, it's the world you've known, but from a very different viewpoint and a highly different experience. Your experience of all things is greatly diminished, far more than you can imagine, through the boundaries that you have erected between yourself and God, or, if you wish, the Source of all things. You understand yourself in location through body whereas consciousness operates beyond location, and well beyond body. The field that you hold, in its truly expressed state, the high octave of the Upper Room, is more vast than you can imagine. And everything it touches will be lifted through this presence.

As we said prior, the vibrational echo that you hold as a small self, the consciousness you utilize, is already informing everything that you experience, inclusive of war or of suffering or of poverty. You are party to all these things, and these are all creations born through a belief in separation. When you lift to the higher and you begin to demonstrate as such, the world itself is re-known—underline the word *re-known*—made new, reclaimed, resurrected, in the octave of expression that is the manifestation of the Christ.

Now, the Christ is not a man. Indeed, the Christ may be all men, all beings, all expressions of Source once realized. Underline those words: *once realized*. The one you may know

of as the Christ who lived before you, a manifestation of the
Monad, sought to show the way. But even those teachings were
corrupted and distorted by those who would seek to control
the outcome of them on the manifest plane. The true Divine
comes as each of you seeks reclamation, seeks to resurrect and
to re-know—and, indeed, will re-know, once the act of the
Divine, in a cumulative affect, is upon this plane.

"What does that mean?" he asks. Well, the act of expression,
true being, the escalation of tone that you are now enabled to
hold and to claim for yourselves, seeks to operate through you,
as and with you, for the benefit of all. You are not overtaken as
much as you think. You are simply reclaimed as you have been
prior to the indoctrination through separation that you have all
been experiencing as self in a diminished way. Understand this,
please. The Divine Self is who you truly are, the aspect of the
Divine come as you in its experience. Your humanity is trea-
sured. It is cherished. It is of you, and how you chose to learn,
and it does not come at the cost of your inherent nature. Your
humanity is as divine as anything you can imagine as celestial.

When we teach through Paul, we comprehend his need to
follow the teaching at a level he can say, "I think I understand."
We are going to invite him now to stop understanding, to simply allow the tone, claimed through language in his being, to
be transmitted as it wishes to be transmitted without any interference at all. Our alignment through the man before you
exceeds what he suspects or thinks he can hold. And the same
is true for all of you—as you say yes, as you say yes to your true
inheritance, to your true nature, to your expression as being of
God. *As* and *of*—and, indeed, *in*. God as all things, including

your lips, the sound of your voice, the touch of your fingers, all things you might touch, imagine, and experience.

We are here for you as you wish us. We will continue this teaching when we are ready. This is not the end of the introduction. This is but a pause. We will take two minutes for Paul. Then we will resume this teaching as we are allowed. Period. Period. Period.

(PAUSE)

We would like to continue. The reason you incarnate is not to become better people or more spiritual. It's to re know yourself as who you have always been. And the offering of this text—if, indeed, you wish it—is not only an amplification of the divine presence that you are, but an escalating understanding of how the world operates as a structure, with architecture that can be understood, and, indeed, altered, by the transmission that you hold. A world made new is not theoretical. It is the action of the texts. And as ambassador you become the actors—the one accepting and then expressing your true nature—to the high order that is the Upper Room. When all things are lifted to the Upper Room, all things are in escalation.

Now, you may understand what we said prior: All things are in vibration and vibrating at a higher tone than you know. But your ideas of self, still so diminished by past history, would seek to refute this. So we come in a way that will support all of you in a true recognition, not only of your birthright, but the shared idea that you are all one, have always been one, and indeed can only be. Truth is truth, whether it's not what you wish to hear. And individuation, the raindrop, if you wish, is still of the storm, and the storm is still of nature, and nature is still of Source. These are ways that you discriminate, that you label, that you name things—to high use, in some ways, and to your detriment in others. It is true you are a man, or believe yourself to be a man, while you operate in a body—or a woman, if you prefer, or a child, if you prefer. It doesn't really matter. But these are ways of knowing the self in limitation in expression. Your divine expression exceeds gender, exceeds age, exceeds ethnicity, although you may experience yourself through all these things. The true experience of being that we will promise you here—underline the word *promise*—is that you have come to be who you have always been. Underline *always*. The one who knows, the one who sees her knowing, who sees her expression, as Source in amplification and transmuting or altering all that has been held in shadow. "Behold, I make all things new."

We welcome our students now to this final text of this trilogy: *A World Made New.* Blessings to you each. Stop now, please. Period. Period. Period.

DAY TWO

What stands before you today, in a realized state, is a new permission: to transcend any idea of limitation that you have utilized to deny the Divine.

Now, you make God something other than what it actually is. The idea of God, as you have used it, is of a being who decides for you, sends the flood, gives the victor the wreath, decides who should be and who should not. That is not God. That is an idea you utilize, a hierarchical idea that is highly confused.

Now, *hierarchical* is important to understand in this equation. The Divine, as we speak to it, is high—but high tone, high velocity, the one note sung expressing as all things. The idea of an individuated God, a God who will help you in crisis, is utilized well because it gives you access to the Source of all things that indeed does love, indeed does know. But you have personalized God to be something other than it actually is. You have given it a personality, sometimes a beard, sometimes a throne, sometimes a son, sometimes something other, to give you an opportunity to have a relationship with it. To have a relationship with God is actually to be in God, as God, and of God. You are not the great I Am. You are not the great one on the cloud. But you are of the great one on the cloud, of the one note sung. In fact, any idea of God you hold, whatever is your God, you must be of it, because the consciousness you utilize to claim that idea of God is of you, and consequently you are in tandem with it. To realize God, to truly know God, is to step into God and allow God to step into you concurrently—as you and with you.

Now, this is also confused for most of you. "Let me be a vessel for God, and forget that I have responsibilities." "Let me be of God, but not of that relationship." "Let me be of God, as long as I get what I want and God appeases my every need." The infantile sense of self that you utilize in these relationships gives you a structure that may be useful. "Our Father,"—if you wish, Mother—"who art in heaven" is actually highly useful in some ways because you are claiming your inheritance through your relationship with the I Am, the God that is all things. To know God as Father or Mother is to know yourself as of it, but also to understand that your realization of this does not need to inform your idea of what is through prior bias. "Well, my mother was an alcoholic. My father wasn't a very nice man. I don't want a parent like that. Let's refute God entirely."

The idea of structure, the idea of God in a structure, may be useful for some of you. "Let me climb the ladder to God." We have offered a mountain to God in a prior text. But this mountain was simply an escalation of tone or your vibrational field. As you lift beyond the old structures you have utilized to define yourselves, your understanding of yourselves through these texts supports you in a realization, first and foremost, of what you are not, which is in fact separate, and indeed what you are, which is of the whole. Underline the word *of.* The pigment in the paint is *of* the paint. The cloud in the sky is *of* the sky. The teardrop on your face is of all the tears ever shed in this field. You are one of all in a construct that you confirm through the senses you operate with.

Now, when you know who and what you truly are, the definitions you have utilized to confirm the old reality begin to diminish. They somewhat fade, or become translucent. You understand the wall that was erected. You don't deny the wall was there. But you also understand that the idea of the wall, that which separates you from Source, was merely an idea that was codified in vibration, claimed as manifest, and then confirmed by your senses, by your neighbors, by a collective agreement to what a wall should be. To realize God, which is to know God, is to know the wall as God. And when the wall is known as God, it ceases to be wall, but it becomes the vibration that was named as wall prior to the thought of wall.

Everything in thought that has been made in form once was in the ethers, once was in vibration only, beyond the

idea of structure. When something is claimed as structure—
underline the word *as*—it becomes firm, and your elasticity,
or belief in your elasticity, is a reflection of the form that you
have undertaken to know yourself through. In other words,
the body as form, the wall as form, is in equation. The physical
body you walk around in every day, in its density by nature of
its vibration, confirms the very density of all things it encounters. When you lift to the higher in tone and field, everything
that you encounter is also lifted through co-resonance because
the light that you are begins to inform what you encounter
and claim it as of itself.

"What does that mean?" he asks. Again, God sees God in
all of its creations, and the one who knows who she is perceives the wall, not as form, not as firm, but as God expressed
as wall. Underline, again, *as*. When all things are understood
as the one note sung in vibration, and when you lift to what
expresses in the higher tone—what we call the Upper Room—
your abundance, your ability to create, is made known through
your encounter with the physical realm that has lost its form
or the density that it has been prior endowed with.

"Please explain this," he asks. We are doing our very best,
Paul. The one who sees the mountain confirms the mountain
and all the properties of the mountain. The mountain is only
moved when the tone of the mountain in its first state as of God,
the one note sung, is met in vibration by the one who is also of
God. You meet the mountain in tone. It is no longer mountain. It is God expressed as what you have known as mountain. And the very idea of mountain—the letters that form the
word *mountain*—are re-known in a higher scale. "What does
that mean?" he asks. Well, everything is in tone. In vibration

and tone. And as you are lifted to the higher, as the form you have taken is lifted and expressed in the higher, what aligns to you at this level is beyond the old form, beyond the old rubric or architecture that you have utilized to know what a world is.

"What is a world?" you may ask. Everything you see before you has been claimed by those who came before you. The word *mountain,* the idea of a pedigree, the idea of entitlement, in all ways is born in prior prescription and in a hierarchy of what you should or expect to see all around you. When you understand that you are moving beyond the old, you are actually releasing the very investment that you have been entrained with in what things should be, how they should appear, or what they must be known as. The requirement for this text, and there is one requirement, and this is as follows: to understand the self as beyond what you have known to re-create the life you have expressed through in the higher octave as who and what you can only be in truth. Now, this sounds like a high order, but it is not. It is a challenge for the personality structure. But what you are actually doing is reclaiming the identity that you have utilized to know yourself, first and foremost, prior to the construct of personality, prior to the naming of the land you have expressed in. You are coming to terms with what you truly are: the one note sung, the Monad, if you wish, in expression, come as form, come as vibration, come as sound for the sole purpose of realization.

Now, realization, as we often say, comes at a cost. And your adherence to the old in almost all ways is what stops your progress, what stops you on the walk forward, what you decide must be more important than what is actually before you, the mandates of history, the ideology of old, the tenets of religion, the ideas of what can and cannot be, the very things that you have created that stand in the way of your reconciliation with your true nature.

This is a text of deep reconciliation of matter and vibration, known and known anew as what it has always been. The recalibration of the physical form in its alignment must indeed be part of this teaching, although we have addressed this in prior texts. The manifest form you have taken, the embodiment you have known yourselves through, is actually shifting to accommodate the accelerated tone that we spoke of yesterday. The tempo is increasing, and the body must acclimate to the new sound, the new vibration, in order for it to adhere and align to what stands before it. And what stands before it is realization in the high octave that is indeed the Upper Room.

Now, the body itself is only an aspect of what is re-known. The senses that you utilize to discern what is what, what should be, what a thing looks like, are also recalibrated and re-known, and consequently inclusive of a much higher tone than you have known thus far. In order to access this tone, you must release the attachment to what things have been, how they should seem or even appear. The appearance of the mountain, through human eyes, is what the human eyes see, with the colors in the landscape that the human filters have utilized to discern what reality should be. But in fact a mountain is energy, and that energy is God, and to know God as the mountain is actually to see God.

Now, when one sees God, one sees what is, what has always been, and what can only be. Reality as you've known it is merely a shadow of what actually exists. Imagine there is a piano, and there are a few keys in one octave that are played again and again and again. You become accustomed to these tones, you expect these notes, and you ignore what exists either in the lower realm or the one beyond it, the higher realm, the Upper Room. The Upper Room, as we often say, is the octave above the common field that you have utilized to know who and what you are, in being, in personality, in structure, as others have known you. To escalate to the higher tone, to align in the higher tone, is not to abandon the personality. You understand the lower notes and the old sequence. You've known them all your lives. But you have transcended them. You may appear as you have been. You may have your friends as you've had, your occupation as you've known. But you begin to exist in a world that is inclusive of far more—underline that: *far more*—than you have been able to discern, able to see, able to experience, and consequently able to know.

Realization is knowing. Knowing is not an intellectual act. The tone that you hold as the form you have taken, in agreement with all tone that exists in a similar scale, is having one issuance of experience based on the octave and alignment it has accrued through history. As you shift to the higher alignment, the basis for what you have known is in fact altered and lifted with you, and that is a world made new. You must understand, first and foremost, that you are not separating yourself from an old world. You are reclaiming what was held in shadow in the high light, the high tone, that is the octave of the Upper Room, where indeed all things are made new. You must underline *all*. Few of you wish to. You only want the pretty things to surround you in what you call the Upper Room. But death, as you understand death, is of God, as all things are. And to comprehend your bodies as truly holy does not mean you transcend death. It simply means you comprehend the body as of its Source, and its Source is nonnegotiable. It is unchangeable. God is God, whether it be known as mountain, as farm, as ocean, or as what you think you are.

Now, what you think you are is often quite limited, not because you expect that, but because you can't imagine anything other. To move beyond the old is to move to an elasticity of possibility, an expansion of what can be. As we have often said, nothing is claimed by any of you until it is first known as possible.

We are here to say now this is a practical text. This is not imaginative. This is not a blueprint as you would have it. But it's a simple way forward to a realization of matter and form in an escalated state that we suspect—or, in fact, know—will be experiential for those who apply these teachings to the world and what they see or have expected prior. When you understand that your idea of *blue* is limited to a scale of color, you miss everything else that might express as blue beyond the singular idea you have held. When you expect God to be on a cloud, you miss God that comes as the frog in the forest, as the tree beside it, as the wind that blows through the trees and through all humanity—again, underline *all*—that can only be of God because how could something be outside of it?

Your demands for God to be what you want it to be, enshrined in religious doctrine or fallacy or wishful thinking, simply grant you an experience of limitation, a fairytale God or an angry God or a God that might love you when you are behaving well, but will cast you into the pit when you have an indiscretion. The morality you utilize to decide what God feels—"Oh, God must be angry today, look at what they did"—is purely named after the structures of personality that you have utilized thus far to express as. You name your dog after your favorite actress. You name your father *good* or *bad* based on the idea of good and bad. You decide what things mean based upon the names that they have been given by you, and you choose these names through the ideas of history.

We stand before you today with very good news. You Have Come. You Have Come. You Have Come. You have come to be re-known and to be re-seen.

We will continue after a pause for the man in the chair. Period. Period. Period. Stop now, please.

(PAUSE)

We thank you each for your presence as we continue this dictation.

The reality you know, comprised of thought, thoughts that have been given names and enshrined in form, are claiming you in an identity that you believe is resolute. "The mountain can be nothing but a mountain, and I cannot be anything than the man I am or I have believed myself to be." You understand yourselves through the rules of science. You understand yourselves through the ideology of religion. You understand yourselves through the relationships that you've accrued and how you have perceived yourselves within them. And these have been your experiences. We do not make them wrong. They are simply a part of who you are. They are not who you are, nor in fact have they ever really been.

The realization that you are more than you think must come to you now *as* realization, not as a new idea that you can play with, but a simple knowing. "I am more than I thought. I am more than I believed. I am more than I was taught. I am more than I believed could be, beyond what any idea was that I ever believed about who anyone could be." To understand yourself beyond the old limitations has come in an attunement that we have offered you in prior texts: "I am free. I am free. I am free." But what, in fact, are you free of but limitation, or the old ideas of what reality is, or what God can or should be, that have kept you in a shadow life when what awaits for you is in fact splendorous. And we say *splendorous* intentionally. To realize God as who and what you are does not make you special. It makes you of the thing that you have always been of. It makes you of the whole that in fact you cannot not be a part of.

We are not deifying the personality, not encouraging you to become saints or to pretend that you are holier than you are. You are perfectly holy as you are. You just don't know it. Your idea of holiness—"I should wear white, I should carry a staff, I should pray for the ones that pass me, and be who I'm supposed to be as they would have me be"—all of these ideas, enshrined in personality, have very little to do with these teachings. The who and what that you truly are, the infinite Divine come as you, means you are one of many, and in fact one of all. To be of God simply means that you are the air that is the wind, and the wind knows itself as the air that it moves through. You know yourself in body. The body is part of how you know yourself in incarnation. But it is not the entirety of you. And when the body is re-known as of God, it moves to a new alignment. You begin to perceive the Divine that is nature, that are the ones beside you, the Divine that has come as all in its perfect ways.

Underline *perfect*. What is perfect is God. How you understand yourselves in your infirmities, in your fears, is less than perfect because you've claimed yourself in separation. But even these things that you believe are sinful must be of God and must be re-known in God, because nothing is brought to the light that is denied the light. And if you deny the light in yourself, in the body you have taken, in the actions of your past, you will deny God in yourself always. And in denying God, you put yourself in darkness. Who you put in darkness, what you put in darkness, calls you to the darkness. And that may be your body, or your idea of sin, or your belief in yourself as less than others. God is perfect, and to know the self in perfection does not mean you don't have a blemish on your skin. It means the blemish is perfect too. God as all things. God as the sky and the sun, the earth below, and everything you see that has been known in form.

When a world is made new, the transit is difficult because the architecture that has been utilized in the dense field, known in fear, seeks to claim itself again and again. You can't imagine a world without war, so you perpetuate war. You believe yourselves to be sinful, and perpetuate the idea of sinfulness. All sin is, if you really wish to know it, is the denial of the Divine. And when God is known where the sin is, the idea of sin is, it is also re-known or redeemed. We are not speaking about good or bad behavior. We are speaking of what you think you are, believe others are, how you judge yourselves and your fellows, how you would put a whole human being in a pit of shadow because of your spite for him or her, whereas the aspect of the being that you find so distasteful can be reclaimed or re-known in the high order of the Upper Room. What you have cast along with the person is the God within, and when you deny the God within another, you deny it in yourself as well.

Each of you before us today, each of you who hears these words, is about to be taught what it truly means to be in benefit, to be in receipt, to be reclaimed in the high order of the Upper Room. And as we sing through Paul, we sing through all of you. If you would imagine now, only for a moment, that you are a flute, and the sound that we sing moves through the flute, and plays the flute, and sings as the flute that you have always been, you can allow the bodies you've known, the identities you've utilized, to be reclaimed, and in fact re-sung, in the high tone of the Upper Room.

We sing your songs for you so that you may learn the words. And as we sing through Paul now, we rejoice that this book, this text, this teaching, is commencing as we anticipated. And we are in benefit for your presence as student, as reader, as listener, as you awaken to your true natures.

On the count of three, Paul.

Now one. Now two. Now three.

[The Guides tone through Paul.]

Allow. Allow. Allow.

Be. Be. Be.

And say yes, as you say yes, to the new possibility that will unfold through you by your agreement and accord.

Stop now, please. Indeed, this is in the text. Period. Period. Period.

DAY THREE

What stands before you today, in an awakened state, is a new requirement: to release an idea that things cannot be, or will not be, that you did not believe could be possible. The requirement for this is very simple. We are about to take you on a journey well beyond what you have known, and the infrastructure of reality that you have utilized to know the self through must be altered as part of this passage.

Now, infrastructure is important. You need to know where you go, where the door frame is to hang the door, to enter the door. You need to know where these things are. But the infrastructure that we are speaking to is really rather different. It's the operative system, the way of knowing, that you have utilized thus far.

Now, *the way of knowing* must be understood. The filters that you utilize are highly prescriptive. "This is what the color blue is. That is what a sky is. A sky must be blue." You understand yourselves through a great legacy of deep history, and we use the word *deep* intentionally. While you walk on a planet and you see what's on the crust of the earth, the landscape before you, you don't remember how deep the earth is, how far down it goes. You look at the surface level of everything, but you don't really understand that this surface is informed by all things that came before it. The legacy that you have inherited, known in separation, claims each individual in one requirement: to relearn the who that they are beyond the old self that has been utilized to navigate the small self and its reality.

"What does that mean?" he asks. Well, the small self is utilized. It operates as who. But it is not the True Self, and the

True Self has a mandate and a requirement—that it will not be limited by the old, that it will know the self beyond the simple systems that the small self utilizes, that it will claim itself in its rightful place as an inheritor, one who inherits the Great Divine. Now, this does not mean to sound grand, but the Great Divine is indeed all things made new, all things seen and re-seen in the high order that is the Upper Room. When the manifest world begins to alter in ways that can be experienced, the idea of self is re-known because the aspect of self that can indeed experience these things is not operating in limitation, is not operating through an old system of prior prescription based on inherited legacy.

Now, true legacy, the Monad, if you wish, the Divine as you that is come as you and expresses through you, calls all things to it in divine order. Underline that phrase: *divine order*. In perfect order. As the requirements of the individual must be met in experiential ways, any true teaching must be borne out in experience, any true teaching must be learned experientially. And our intention here is to call you forth, one and all, with your permission, to what expresses beyond the old—the old system, the old legacy, the old way of comprehending the who that you have never truly been. Once you know the full meaning of the claim "I know who I am in truth" and its realization operates through you, you are claiming the Kingdom— because it is this who, the Divine Self, the True Self, that is the inheritor. The small self inherits a small kingdom, born in history, born in a legacy of forefathers, operating in the denial of the Divine. To refute the denial of the Divine is not so much an act of will, but a way of being. When the essence of your being is operative at this level, the transformative aspect of expression maintains itself in a continuum. Imagine a hum, a vibrational hum, that is always present. And what this hum is doing is actually altering what it encounters, claiming what it encounters, in right accord. *Right accord* can simply be understood as expression from the Upper Room.

Now, in the Upper Room, there are levels of expression. When we invite you to the Upper Room and invite you to maintain the expression here, we comprehend the difficulty that you encounter because so much of what you have created was created in fear and you are bound to your creations—"that difficult separation," "that very hard childhood," the things you chose as a result of those things. And how you maintain an identity in the Upper Room cannot be contingent on past creation. A claim that we have offered you in prior texts— "Behold, I make all things new"—is the claim of recalibration, and, indeed, re-knowing. And to be re-known is to be made new. And the act of being re-known has been discussed again and again in prior texts, but we will say it again here: The Monad as you, the Divine Principle operating as you, is what does this work. It is the claim of freedom as expressed through the being you are.

Now, your identity, as you have utilized it, has its manner, has its choice, has its ways of understanding. And you relinquish some of these things as you move up the scale in manifestation, and for one simple reason: What was created in fear cannot be held in the high octave that is the Upper Room. And the translation of the song of your expression, the transposition to the higher octave, is the process you undergo through the reading of these texts and the applications of the teachings. Realization comes at the cost of the old, and it is only your attachment to the old which stands in the way of what awaits you beyond this doorway to the Infinite.

"What does that mean?" he asks. Well, if you understand a doorway, a portal of entry, it must be chosen. We will take no one here who is not prepared for it, or who is unwilling to let go of the very things that would dampen their light or hinder their true expression. The great *yes* that is required here is a *yes* at a level of personality. "I am willing to be re-known and of the True Self who commandeers this change." The aspect of self that ushers you through this process may be seen as the soul, and its alignment and its claim is what promises you that the good that awaits you has been prepared and is yours for the receiving. Notice we said *receiving*. Yours for the receiving. Don't be greedy here, friends. Allow it to come as it can be held. And what will be held through the reading of this text is a level of tone that you have not known yet, that Paul has not known yet, and that we are working with now in triumph over the old.

What this means is very simple. The sound that is present, and awaiting you to encompass you, will support you at a level you don't know, will not know, nor can know until it is experienced. The process of being prepared for this level of tone has been the work of prior texts. But it is also the work of this one. And we must ready the new student, as well as the seasoned one, for what she can manage, what he can adhere to, and what may be allowed and aligned through the great I Am principle that seeks its expression through you.

We will explain this for Paul. Each text has been an affect in vibration or tone that has supported the student at a new level of alignment. When the alignment is present, the lessons that can be claimed at that level of alignment are received. As they are met by the initiate, the initiate progresses through a cycle of realignment where she may be known, and then re-known as she has always been. Underline *always*. You have not always been this age, this gender, this idea of self that you are operative in. When you know who you are and you are realized at this level, the aspect of you that has access to all knowing, all truth, is present and expressed.

Now, what does this mean in a very practical way? You are not the sage. You are not the oracle. You are operating in tandem with True Mind. You may capitalize *true*. You may capitalize *mind*. True Mind. Not the small self's idea of mind, but divine intelligence that may be aligned to and received, and then received again and again as it is required by you. Knowing only happens in an instant. God is only experienced in an instant. And it is always an instant if an instant is now. To align to this level of receptivity is not only a challenge. It's a choice. And the choice must be made by the initiate who is willing to forego an idea of self that she has outgrown, that he has utilized but is no longer in abeyance to. We will not allow the initiate to step over this threshold until she has been prepared at the level of soul where she may be of true benefit for it. You are not escaping reality or renegotiating your old one. You are simply claiming the Divine Self, True Mind, that is your inheritance at a level of tone that you have not been present for while maintaining form.

Now, the Upper Room can be comprehended as Christ consciousness, and we will describe it very simply. It is the highest level of awareness, presence, and being that one may maintain while holding form. There are levels to the Upper Room, some of which don't demand form, and there are levels that exist beyond the Upper Room, where the idea of form is merely a memory, something you knew, experienced, understood, and learned through, but is no longer necessary for your learning. You say yes to what you can manage, and you agree to what you can hold. You may say yes now to what you can manage and what you can hold, and move to a receptive state where you are supported in a recognition of what you can maintain at this level of tone and vibration. To maintain the level of tone that is the Upper Room is less a challenge than a choice. It is a choice to say yes to what exists in the high octave and comprehend that you have learned through the old, made choices, had requirements there, but your learning is now progressing at a higher level of strata and your experience must reflect the choice that has been made.

We will explain something for Paul. He is in the background seeking to translate this teaching to something that he can maintain and comprehend. You still think, young man, that the idea of self is what maintains the Upper Room. The idea of self that you utilize—we call it small-self personality structure—is not what maintains vibration at this level of accord. The knowing of who you are—"I know who I am in truth, what I am in truth, how I serve in truth"—in expression is the Monad expressed. It is not the new and improved, less worried, less frightened, less angry personality. It is the Divine that expresses and utilizes the personality structure to its benefit. The one who sings in a lovely voice will have her song invoked in high praise. The one who dances with such grace will move through the world as grace. And it is this song, it is this movement, that is utilized from the Upper Room to bring forth the Kingdom and the entrainment to the high level that you have incarnated as.

Now, the expression of this teaching—and this must be understood—is how you be. Underline the word *be*. How you *be* beyond the idea that you would utilize of what *be* even means. To trust the Divine Self to express as you claims you in its accord, and it is its accord that supports and responds to what is required, not only for the individual, but for all that the individual encounters. God expresses as God through all of its creations. The denial of the Divine, which precludes your experiences of your true natures, is what must be addressed. And it is, indeed, first an act of will, and then an agreement to the Divine Self to support its own alignment as and through you.

You seek to justify who you have been. You seek to reinforce the choices of your prior experiences. You seek to demonstrate your intellect at the cost of your innate knowing. Your innate knowing cannot fail you. It *is* the Divine, knowing as and through you. To move to True Knowing, which will be part of this teaching, will support you in an agreement to respond and not to decide. "What is the difference?" you may ask. The one who is in response to its True Knowing is not fixing, is not juggling, is not determining. It is. It is. It is. And it is knowing, and knowing is realization.

How does this operate in the manifest world that you are still party to? As wisdom. As grace. And as action informed through wisdom and grace. You are not perpetuating an idea of self that you once utilized that you would seek to put on a pedestal and bow to others with. You must understand that who stands before you, that is you in a higher expression, is who you have always been, that you are encountering—finally, finally—as what can only be in truth.

We said *who stands before you* intentionally because, as we continue with this dictation, you will not only be merging with the idea of self that can be claimed in the highest accord, but you will be knowing the manifest Divine that seeks to express through you. And to know, to realize, is not only of benefit to the individual student, but to the world the student expresses through.

We will take a pause for the man in the chair. We will return and speak some more. Thank you for your patience. Period. Period. Period.

(PAUSE)

We would like to continue, if we are allowed to speak as we wish.

The trajectory of this teaching, which will take place over the next five weeks, will be as so: Each student present who reads these words will be attended to by those of us who support the alignment that can indeed be held. Each of you who speaks the attunements will be accompanied by us as we speak them with you. We are seeking to bring you into entrainment with the level of tone that we occupy. If you understand this, we are supporting you in elevating, and responding in an elevated state to the attunements that are for your benefit.

Now, when we speak with you, don't expect sound. Each attunement that we have taught is vibration encoded with language, or utilized with language, to support the vibrational

intent, each intent described by the offering of the intention
itself.

We will go forth as follows. You may say these words after
we speak them:

*"I am Word through my body. Word I am Word. I am Word
through my vibration. Word I am Word. I am Word through
my knowing of myself as Word. Word I am Word."*

The attunement to the Word is the basis for all teachings
that have followed. And the Word, as we have spoken, is the
energy of the Creator in action come as each of you. "I am
Word" is not a deification of the personality structure. It's the
expression of the Monad, known as the Word, come as and
through each of you, in form, in vibration, and identity.

The attunement that follows (you may speak this when you
read the words)—"I know who I am in truth, I know what I
am in truth, I know how I serve in truth; I am free, I am free,
I am free"—is the agreement to the Monad that knows itself
as and through you. Realization. "I realize who I am, what I
am, and how I express," how you serve in truth. When you
claim, "I am free," you are invoking the true liberation that
the Monad knows itself as and through. The Divine Self is not
bound by time, by space, by law, or anything that might govern
expression. The Christed Self, the Monad, the universal truth
within you, is unbound and free as it knows itself in fullness.

When you speak the following claim, "I am in the Upper
Room"—you may say this as you wish—you are aligning the
energetic field to the level of tone or the octave that presents above the common field. "I am in the Upper Room." The

claims that follow, simple claims and claims of truth, are as such: "I Have Come, I Have Come, I Have Come," the Monad announcing itself as present and expressed; "Behold, I make all things new," the Monad expressing what it is, as and through what it encounters; the lifting of all manifestation to the Upper Room, "It will be so"; "God Is, God Is, God Is," confirmation and agreement.

"I am in the Upper Room. I Have Come. I Have Come. I Have Come. Behold, I make all things new. It will be so. God Is. God Is. God Is."

Each attunement has been prepared to support the individual in moving to a higher level of tone, alignment, and agreement to their true natures. As you say yes, we say yes with you. As you agree, we support you experientially in your agreement. As you comprehend, we see with you the world that can be known by the one who knows who she is, what he is, and how he serves.

We will say that this is the end of the introduction to this text. Thank you for your presence. Period. Period. Period. Stop now, please.

Part I

1

ONE STATE OF BEING TO ANOTHER

DAY FOUR

What stands before you today, in a realized state, is an awareness of what has been, or at least what you believed to be. What you believed to be is actually an artifact of prior consciousness, prior agreement. "I agreed to be this or that" was amply true at the level of creation it occurred. But where you stand today, in a new way, is with the grand permission to reclaim the identity that knows itself beyond form, and can claim form because it can be as all things.

Now, for those of you who are new to the teachings, the process we engage you in is in amplitude, increasing amplitude, so that you may actually hold the higher without becoming frightened or running from yourselves as you might truly be. To regard the process as arduous would be challenging for you. To preside in this process as the one being gifted through this process would support you well. To tell the self that you are not where you are supposed to be will leave you in a place you do not wish to stand. To comprehend the self as being where you are required to be to withstand the changes that come will support you in a higher way. To agree that where you stand is the perfect place to claim your true identity will support the alignment to the higher so you may hold it.

Now, when we say *hold*, we don't mean covet. We simply mean align to. When you align to the Divine, you are simply moving into congruence with what has already been, but has been denied, or had been denied, through the prior construct of what you believed to be so. Underline *believed*. What you believed has claimed you in a reality that conforms to your ideas, your beliefs, of what should be. When you understand yourself in change, what is actually being changed is what you believe, because what you believe will always claim you in a reality that supports it.

Now, the identity that you have utilized thus far, with its highs and lows and in-betweens, has its own place. You regard yourself as separate from the ones beside you and from the Source of all things, not because you don't know why, but because you believe why—that it cannot be so, or could never have been so. And as you are challenged by these teachings, as you agree to them, you move beyond the old structure, born in separation, and hold an amplitude where the new is not only present, but is claimed by you. Underline the word *is*. "It will be so." The manifest Divine that seeks expression through form is already present, but you must align to it.

Now, the trajectory of this teaching for some of you will be what you say it is. "I want a hard road. I trust the hard road."

You will have the hard road. Those of you who say, "It must all be easy," perhaps will have an easier time. But the challenges that anyone incurs on this path are always present, have always been present, and will always be so. And the challenges are such: You have created worlds in systemic beliefs to an idea of reality that has been claimed through fear, realized in fear, and then chosen again and again in fear. To withstand these changes is to simply say, "I am no longer in agreement to what I once believed." But the process of disengaging with what you once believed is highly challenging when you have created a world in support of a belief in separation. To align to the higher in a singular manner still requires you to confront your own creations, the things you have held in darkness, and the beliefs you have held that would support separation.

Now, you are not being changed as much as aligning to change. Just as the wall of rock erodes by the sea's presence, you are changed by the supplication to the inherent Divine that you are now in allowance to. This is not a hardship. It's a tremendous gift. But the realization of the gift must come in stages, lest you understand yourself primarily through the difficulties and not through the splendor that is actually awaiting you. When you are choosing in challenge again and again and again, you receive challenge, expect challenge, and the magnitude of challenge will only increase as you decide that you can withstand more. When we instruct, we call you forth at the level you can hold, and only at the level you can hold. And once you can hold it and enjoy it and understand yourself in a higher degree of expression, you will move to the next. And this is a process that you engage in through will, agreement in will. "I am willing to know. I am willing to be new. I am willing to release the ideas of self that I have utilized to keep me in separation."

Some of you say to us, "Will I get what I want? Will I have this alignment in my lifetime?" What you will have in this lifetime is what you can hold. Now, imagine you have a lightbulb that can hold so much electricity. When you support the lightbulb in expanding to hold more, perhaps it can. But when you decide it should be flooded, more than it can hold, you move into a level of fear or confusion that is actually not a requirement of these instructions. Your realization of the manifest Divine as who and what you are, as and through you, is received in tone, vibration. And the realization that occurs as a result of this will happen in the perfect way that you can hold it. Now, the choice is yours. If you've decided already that you must have the highest and nothing else will do, you are chasing an ideal. If you trust instead that you are being called forth as you can manage it, you will be supported, not only every step of the way, but through the process of integration that is highly essential here.

Now, understand yourselves in several ways. You operate in a physical realm. You are conscious beings. You are co-creating a reality, not only in a singular way, but through a creation that is a collective ideal, what it means to be a human being in a manifest plane. Your realization of who and what you are that expresses beyond these ideals must be assimilated by you in a way that you can walk through or walk with. To trust the self in this process is to understand the self as being in one requirement, and one requirement only: "I am being led in my realization, and I am assuming what I require that can be held at this level of tone."

The idea of self as separate still has a requirement. You need to know whose toothbrush to use, perhaps whose shoes to put on in the morning. It helps to know whose desk to sit at at work. You are not releasing these things. But the who that experiences them is quite altered. She experiences herself in two different realities—the reality that she has known, which is present for her to experience, but this reality has been transposed and is actually operating with her in a higher regard, a higher attention, a higher alignment to the Source of all things. You see God in all you see. You understand yourself as of Source and in Source while going about your daily work. You are privileged, in some ways, to hold a level of experience of being in the world but not of it.

Now, to understand what that truly means is to understand that the form that you have taken, while in most ways elastic to vibration, still has properties. And the conformity of the physical self to a material realm that must also be in change must be understood. The one who climbs the mountain too quickly may get dizzy at the new altitude. The one that swims too deeply in the ocean may not hold the breath that she is required to to carry herself through the ocean waves. As you understand yourselves as moving in this process, you will also understand that the physical reality you are utilizing to operate with and through must be altered, and your presence is what alters it. As you are aligning to the Upper Room in manifestation, as you are stating the I Am presence in all you are and what you experience, as the level of vibration you hold is accrued in experiential ways, the manifest world begins to operate in tandem with you. Some of you say, "I feel so alone in my work. I am so special in my work." You're not very special.

You've simply chosen a path to work with to be in support of the world. You are one of the whole. The belief in separation may also be translated to mean you are not understood or you are not valued. When you know who you are in truth, the requirements of your experience on this plane are altered to support what you require to learn through. And the justification of old behaviors must be understood by you as something that must pass. It was a creation of a lower form of identification. It's what you thought you were, believed yourselves to be.

Now, we will say this for Paul, who is struggling. Indeed, this teaching is in the text. We are working with you carefully and modulating your frequency to be able to withstand what is coming through you. The instructions you are receiving at an individual level are simply to be and to allow, and to allow the work that we do to move through you for the benefit of those who read the words. The level of articulation or the rapidity of speech is actually your choice. You keep up with the dictation as you think you should. If you allow the dictation to speak as and through you without resistance, it becomes a much more graceful act.

He instructs *us* now: "Why is this different and how is this different? Tell me what I am supposed to know." All you are supposed to know is that this is the accumulation of prior teachings, the culmination of them. And the responsibility we hold as the true teachers of these texts is to ensure that the student will be met in perfect ways. That is our work, and your work is always the same. And understand yourself in this way: You are the receiver of the broadcast. You are not the instructor, nor the editor, nor the one that decides. And we are privileged for your presence, as we are privileged for all our students' presence.

As we continue, we wish to talk about one thing we have not—the decision that is being made to parse the teachings as you would like them to be. This is for all of you. When we say we make all things new, or the claim "Behold, I make all things new," the *all* must be understood as essential to the equation. You are not cherry-picking. You are not deliberating on what can be in God and what must be eschewed. To begin to work with the *all*—all that is and all that is manifest— will actually support the manifestation of these teachings in a very radical way. What interrupts you is the idea that you are in selectivity. "I will lift this one to the Upper Room. She seems to be having difficulty. But that one can fall on his own sword." You make these decisions. You say, "Well, I'm human," and, indeed, you are. But the Divine operating as you loves all equally, is not holding a preference for who is admitted and who is not. All are welcome. And finally, we have to say, all will be welcome in the Kingdom.

Now, the Kingdom, again, is the realization of the inherent Divine in matter, in all manifestation, in all things seen and unseen. It is a new equivalency. And this is the text where your equivalency is not only challenged, but moved, to be in support not only of a new world, but of a new idea, a new creation. "Behold, I make all things new."

We will stop this teaching. Thank you for your presence. Stop now, please. Period. Period. Period.

(PAUSE)

What stands before you today, in a realized state, is a new understanding: that everything you chose was based in a concept of what was not only possible, but what could be. Underline *could*. The possibility that *could* holds is generally held in a basis of old ideas, comprehension. "The puddle must hold these properties. You can splash in a puddle or watch it dry up in the sun." Your understanding of what's possible, in most ways, is claimed through the collective. You think that one has an idea that alters the face of the world. In fact, many have the idea because the idea is actually present in the collective field. And some will attain it, will respond to the call for it. Others will say, "That cannot be so."

Now, what is happening at a level of the collective now is that the requirements for change have been imposed in practical ways upon the lives of most of you. You understand the nature of war and what it might cause. You understand the degree that you've withheld appreciation for the planet you stand on, and the results of that are all around you. You understand that the basis of separation is more and more challenging through the kind of polarization you experience in varying cultures. Because you've all agreed at a higher level that things cannot go on as they are, you are claiming a new potential, have claimed a new potential, that will be enacted upon.

Now, some will resist the change. They will deny the change is required. They are actually governed by a terror that if they are not singular and separate that they will not exist. You don't understand that the idea of community that supports the whole can actually extend to the entirety of your species. You don't lose the individuation, but you have a common cause, a common care, indeed a common love, for all that lives and all that abides in God.

The transition that is occurring now, and will continue to occur for several generations, will not be without acrimony. There will be difficulty. But when these difficulties present, they are being shown, or are present to show how they operate so that you may choose differently. When you understand how you contribute to all that you see at a level of varying consciousness, you understand that you are all party to what you see in varying ways. The one who makes the thing may take credit for it, but you are all party to the creation as you perceive it or decide about it. A world made new, not a new world, but a world made new through the alignment of vibration and consciousness that is actually present and can be claimed—again, the potential—can be claimed and now must be claimed.

You are not only way-showers through your realization of this. You become in some ways the barometer, or the tone of vibration, that receives and then transmits itself to all that it encounters. You justify the old: "This is what was." But then you understand that the new can and will be born. You stop requiring the old to be what it was and you perceive the new potential that has always been implicit but has been denied by most.

Now, why do you deny the Divine? Because you did not know that you could do other. The child who believes in fairies, or believes that she sees things that others don't see, is generally amused when others say, "I can't see them at all," but then will lose faith in what she believed was so. The idea of God, entrenched in religion, has become standardized in many ways so that you may have standardized opinions in relation to them. "That is not my God or how we pray or what we do or what we believe to be so." The choice to align to the Source of all things—underline the word *Source*—as a basis for expression, without deciding what this Source must look like or behave as, is a fine start. But, finally, it's the experience of being in and as Source that will answer your questions and allow you to serve at the level of expression that is your True Self. The True Self knows. It knows who it is, what it is, how it serves. And it also knows God, or whatever it wants to call God, as all creation.

To perceive the world through the lens of the small self is to claim the artifacts of history, claimed in old beliefs and rendered as such by those who came before you. To perceive the world with the eyes of the Christ, the eyes that do not judge or fear, is first to become inclusive in what you see, and then to truly see, to truly see what matter is comprised of. When you begin to do this, you become the alchemist who can re-see what was held in shadow anew in light. And once anew in light, what was before you is indeed made new.

The challenge for some of you now, as we continue these teachings, will be your need to justify the old—the old bias, the old hatred, the old law of separation that you have utilized to work through and to create from. If you don't have that, you say, "What becomes of me and my great desires, my need for this or that, that is independent from the others?" You are still operating in separation. You still believe that if you are not the one being rained upon you must be favored. And then the next storm comes and you say, "Oh, well, I guess it was not what I thought."

Your realization of the All That Is can be known in your experience the moment you say it can be, the new possibility—"It will be so"—confirmed by you as manifest, and the realization of it: "God Is. God Is. God Is."

DAY FIVE

What stands before you today, in a realized state, is the great awareness that you choose well when you operate in your knowing. When you are abdicating your choices to what once was, you will always claim what you have had. But your knowing, you see, your innate knowing, does not prescribe things through historical patterns. It knows itself in the ever-present moment that it experiences, and can claim you in that awareness with it.

Now, your knowing is distinct from you in some ways. It operates with you, but its parameters exceed the idea of self that you utilize in your day-to-day lives. When you move towards knowing and begin to inhabit knowing, your expression is increased and you have access to those things that exist beyond the small self and what the small self has accrued by way of information. You idealize the old—the best dinner you ever had, that wonderful date you had when you were fifteen, or that party you attended—and you describe a parameter, what a good date should be, a fine meal should be, based on your prior experience. What awaits you is beyond these things, outside of the old structure, the old prescription. But they will not be experienced until you align to them. The idealized self, your idea of who you are in a higher octave, is in some ways utilized to carry you here. But what will finally bring you here is True Knowing and your expression as the one who knows that can access what is, has always been, and can only be.

You ride on information. You expect information to carry you from one thing to the next, and you confuse information for True Knowing. Now, if True Knowing expresses through you, and your realization of this knowing expresses through you, how you experience yourselves, what you encounter, those beside you, are all altered because knowing does not hold the blemish of the old ideas. It is not held in separation. True Knowing operates in confirmation of the inherent truth that must always be. So when you are aligned in knowing, you are aligned not only to the aspect of you that truly knows—the Divine Self or the Monad—but your experience of self exceeds the limitations or parameters that you have used to justify the old, the old expectations, the old ideas that you claim in form and mandate be your experience of reality.

Now, reality is being altered now in many different ways. Your comprehension of who you have been is what is being addressed right now, because the idea of who you have been in a world you have known is in fact releasing to make room for what it has prepared for. What it has prepared for is a level of realization that cannot exist within the old template. And the old template that you have utilized as a way of knowing the self is actually moving from you, and this is frightening for many of you who demand to be seen as you were seen yesterday, have your relationships reflect the way they were yesterday, or your idea of government or commerce or gender or experience be what you have known, when what is waiting for you actually holds the new, and the new will not be born as you cling so tightly to the old. Why do you cling to the old? For the same reason you expect the old. It's what you have known, and even in its misery it is predictable. "I know what a war is. I know what it's like to be hungry. I know what it's like to be afraid. These are predictable aspects of life and I will confirm them in my experience."

Imagine you were standing before a curtain, and a painted curtain, and the curtain begins to lift and what the curtain first reveals is actually discordant with you. You cannot align to it. You cannot even understand it. What is being withheld from you through this curtain of reality that you have known is what exists beyond it, and what exists beyond it is all things. What informs the manifest world, how thought operates, what your false history has been, based on prior doctrine—all of these things begin to unfold. And there is some apt confusion that is experienced by most of you. Imagine you thought you lived in a country where there were certain rules and one day you awaken and those rules are no longer present. "What country am I in?" you might ask. That is what is occurring now.

The challenges for most of you are very simple—the seeking to confirm the world that you have known through action and through intention. "I expect to do this the way I have. I seek to confirm what I have known." If you allow yourself to release the desire or the claim of past experience and allow the self willingness to hold a higher experience aligned to what's behind the curtain, you are actually encouraged as such. Your willingness, you see, is a prerequisite for what is waiting for you. You will be claimed by it regardless. The curtain is continuing to lift. But if you keep resisting what is waiting for you, you will find yourself in a quandary—seeking to turn your back upon the new and pretend the old is still operative.

A world made new. A world beyond what you have known. You seek to decide how the world should be, and the questions you have for us are generally about how to hold the world as you have known it. "My child's wellbeing, my sense of occupation, how I perceive the world to be" seeks confirmation through these teachings. We cannot offer them anymore in the way that you would wish. What is before you is the new, and the teachings are culminating in this realization: "I Am Known. I Am Known. I Am Known."

Now, to be known in fullness is to be expressed in one's knowing by the aspect of all things that you might call knowing. The claim "I Am Known" is a claim of realization. To be known is to be realized. You do not realize yourselves. It's quite impossible. The small self cannot set out on a journey towards self-realization that would not seek to hold the small self as the one in charge. It is when the old is released, when the mask is abandoned, when the shell that has been accrued, the template of reality that you have chosen to learn through, is released, you may begin to experience what has always been but has been precluded by that curtain, that painted curtain, that you have claimed as reality.

The challenge for you now, as we continue these teachings, is to actually give the permission that is required of you. And this is permission granted by you and for you, both, to surrender the aspect of self that would decide in limitation, that would decide what can and cannot be through the historical data you have utilized to decide what can be so. If you were to choose a preposterous thing to believe—"perhaps I may fly like an airplane without wings," "perhaps I can dance upon the stars"—you would recognize folly. But if you were to ask yourself something other—"I may know myself beyond all things I may have known, I may experience myself in tandem with Source"—you would also seek to refute that. But that is the gift of this teaching, if you so choose it—to merge at a level of recognition or resonance that you may know, and in your knowing you may act in support of the manifestation of the Divine that is present here to be claimed. Underline that phrase: *to be claimed.* The Divine is here to be recognized.

Imagine each time you cast your eyes upon something it was altered through your sight. Imagine each time you entered a room the room was altered, and the idea of room even was altered, through your presence. Your realization, your inherent knowing, your manifest being, is what alters this reality because the level of tone that you are holding must in fact reclaim what it encounters in tandem with itself. The choice to do so, to embody at this level at the cost of the old ideas of what can and should be, is what is being offered. Now, some of you believe that this is about abandoning your lives. It is not about abandoning anything. It is about releasing an attachment to what has been as a way to inform what can and will be.

Now, you ask about the Upper Room—"how do I maintain myself here?"—as if you were balancing a teacup upon your knee at a tea party. Any Upper Room that would demand that of you would be an awful place to stay. The Upper Room, in fact a level of tone and resonance in a field that can be experienced, may be held as foundational by the one who has claimed her true identity. The True Self expresses as manifest in the Upper Room. Or the resurrected Divine as you does not seek to balance itself here—it simply expresses here. If you stop making this a juggling act, you will find yourself far more comfortable in this process. That doesn't mean you have to behave well, never lose your temper, nor does it mean that you have to apply the teaching at times when you feel you cannot. When you are being most challenged, you may be realizing yourself through an aspect of self that has been prior denied. And when you do this, you actually give great permission to release the aspect of self that has been prior denied, and lift it to be re-known in the Upper Room.

Imagine you are sitting on a rock as if the rock isn't even there. "No one will ever see this rock I sit on. I sit on it so firmly it will not be moved." Well, until you fall off the rock and the rock is seen, it will not be transformed because your decision has been to deny the light from the aspect of self—in this case, the rock—that would align you to the higher expression. To align to the higher expression must be inclusive of the rock, not hiding the rock, not denying the rock, but reclaiming the rock, the boulder, the pain, the challenge, in the high light that is the Upper Room. When you understand that realization comes at the cost of what you thought was so, but not what is truly so, this is far less arduous a task. Realization comes at the cost of the idea of separation. And all the things accrued in separation that you would seek to confirm in the common field through historical data are what are now being moved.

Imagine, suddenly, that you lived in a plane where things were suddenly lifting, bumping into each other as the vibration raises, and what you seek to do always is grab on to the teacup that is floating in the air, sit down on the chair that seems to be wafting away in order to try to keep it in place. To release these things to the changes that are seeking to be seen through them is simply to allow what is to become present in what was. And your idea of what was—your idea of what things are, have been, and should mean—is what is being discussed here today.

"Now, I decide who I will let into my little world, I decide what will be and what cannot be," says the small self in its jurisdiction to be the empress upon her petty throne. And we say *petty* for a reason. The one who would exclude another from her world decides in advance who should be allowed. And that *should* is always based in a belief that some are better than others, some are more worthy than others, some have the right to be, and some should never have incarnated at all. When you operate at this level you actually claim an idea of sovereignty in the smallest way imaginable, because it is exclusive, the private club that you would seek to hold the membership for. When you understand that all have the right to be, just as they are, you become inclusive to that. "I have the right to be, as everyone does. I don't have to suppress the aspects of self that I would seek to deny. I have to allow them to be re-seen, re-known, and lifted. And I may allow the same for others as well."

The one who knows who she is knows who others are, realizes who others are, claims who others are, less so through intent but through presence and being. To claim the realization of another is to not override his or her free will. It is to know them. And to know someone, truly know, is to gift them with the experience of knowing. There is no gift in return for this. You do not have a magic wand. You are not tapping the heads of those you wish to awaken, and then take a nice bow at the end. You are simply expressing at the level of the Monad or the Christed Self. And the Christ or the Redeemer, the implicit Divine in each of you, is what does this work and calls forth what is required in the energetic field of those that you would encounter to support their own realization. The matter is then out of your hands. To know another is to gift another. To gift another is to release them to their highest expression, not the mechanisms of change that you would seek to employ through the old strata of experience.

When you understand that the new is before you and seeking to be born through you, you will stop directing what should be and start allowing what can be and what will be so. The claim "It will be so," the manifest Divine experiencing itself as all you encounter, "God Is, God Is, God Is," the experience of that claim as manifestation, will support you and all that you encounter at a level of realization that you could not imagine as a small self because the small self does not hold the directives to align at this level. When we say this—*directives to align*—we simply mean that the small self does not have the manual for realization. It is not present at the level of the egoic structure. There have been many teachings that seek to support an individual in his or her awakening or enlightenment. Many are valuable. But the challenge with most of them is they seek to experience the individual as the one making the change. And that is not, finally, what happens. The individual is changed through its release of the reliance on the personality structure to become the one who changes things. The Divine within, if you wish to call it that, is what does the work.

Paul interrupts. "Is that that phrase 'Of myself I am nothing, the father within me does the work'?" Yes and no. Of yourself you are still Paul, and utilized at that level and having an experience of life at that level. That is not nothing. That is quite wonderful. You are all quite wonderful. Never for a moment think that we are making the small self wrong. But what we are doing is receiving you and claiming you at the level of Monad, which is the Divine within—you may call it father, mother, whatever you wish, but the Source of all things in its expression as and through you, in its splendor and magnificence and its act of reclamation. And it is this aspect of you that is the transformative act that you experience yourself in and through. The basis of this teaching is remarkably simple: the Word, the energy of the Creator in action come as you, experiencing itself as and through you, and then through all. The expansion of the Monad, inclusive of form, inclusive of will, inclusive of the level of consciousness that it may be held through, is not only a benefactor, but a gift to the world it experiences itself through.

Now, the manifestation of the Monad in physical form will be addressed in this text in different ways. We have taught this in prior texts, but the very simple claim "I know what I am in truth," which is eternal truth, means that the Divine Self also expresses as form, and what makes the form, form is in fact the Divine. You are simply distilling the realization of Source in an inclusive state to define the physical self and all things that are held in manifestation. God is the tree. God is the ocean. God is the fingertip, and the tongue that speaks, and the eyes that see. When the eyes that see are in fact aligned at this level, and the eyes that see are released from their shade of distortion, the lenses that have been accrued through separation, the eyes that see or the being that perceives can claim the world beyond the illusion of separation because it is no longer experiencing it. When the Divine Self as you is released from the fear of being separate that you have utilized to know yourself, when the Divine as you has released the fear of being in union—which it cannot hold, but the small self utilizes well—you will know the self beyond the old structure of identity and perceive all things made new.

Paul interrupts the teaching. "Did I say that right? Did I get the words correctly?" The Divine Self as you does not hold separation. The personality structure demands separation as a way to hold to its sense of safety and experience. The True Self, operative with the small self, reclaims the small self in a unified state, and the small self, finally, is known in and of the Source of all things. It may still be operative, prefer this tea to that one, this idea of something to do to that one. But the will which is utilized at this level will support high choice, high agreement, high wisdom—and ultimately, we suggest, True Knowing—which is what will deliver you all from what you have created in fear.

"What does that mean?" he asks. Well, if you understand the template of reality that you are utilizing now and the things that humanity has chosen to learn through, they have been chosen in most ways through what we call the denial of the Divine. War is not an act of God, murder not an act of God. You have chosen to experience these things, you decide what they mean, but you do not kill what you know to be holy and you realize God beyond any idea of separation that any indoctrination through history has supported you in. To come to terms with what it means to know is to become responsible as a species to your creations. The days of pointing a finger at another—"those people," "that man," "those things that happened once upon a time"—and to try to create acrimony through them will not support you well in the coming times. What will support you well is realization and knowing of what is, True Knowing of what is, so that you may choose in a high way and release the need and the predisposition to war that you have been utilizing since one man first threw a rock at another.

We say this now as we complete this lecture. Indeed, this is in the text. We are grateful for your presence. When we return next, we will teach you some more. Blessings to you each. Stop now, please. Period. Period. Period.

DAY SIX

What stands before you today, in an awakened state, is a recognition of past acts, past choices, that have accumulated momentum and are now playing out on a broad stage. It can be a palace toppling from infidel rule. It can be a forest burning from lack of attention to the needs of the planet. But all things are playing out as they must, and you are accountable to your choices individually and collectively.

Now, when the stage is set and the action is not what you wish, how do you attend to your life? When your husband is not doing what you want, when your home is no longer there, when your place of business is closed, how do you attend to the realities the manifest world presents? You ask yourself, "How am I to participate in this? How am I to recognize my own actions as they are presented before me in outcome? How do I make a choice when I am confused and don't know my way?" The answer is a simple one. Know who you are.

Now, the aspect of you that does know—the Divine Self

or the Monad—is not confused, nor is it frightened, nor is it attached to where it lives or where it does its business. The personality structure is useful, but it aids its own discomfort through attachment, through a desire to have what was, be. And the times that are before you—indeed, rapid change and acceleration of tone—need not herald disaster. But change comes as it is required, and the one who chooses not to see how she participates in a world will be forced or called or given the opportunity to see how she has been party to what is before her.

Now, you understand yourselves primarily through what you've done. You understand your own actions and the results of them. But what you don't understand is how consciousness claims identity and replicates ideas in the common field that were useful, perhaps once upon a time, but have no place anymore. Imagine you sulk when no one attends your birthday party or you didn't get the train set that you thought you were promised. Imagine the child that was once disappointed carries her disappointment into the common field, expecting more and more of the same. Perhaps the child who was taught that if he didn't win he was worthless becomes confused when there is no game to play or the rules are not what they were. Who is he then? Who are you today in the midst of great change, and how do you attend to the creations that are before you? Indeed, know who you are.

Now, knowing is realization, as we have said. But to become realized is not to become recognized as the one who knows. To be realized is to become the perceiver who is no longer masking herself, and consequently sees unadorned how she has partaken in any act that supports fear or claims the self in fear in ways that she must now see. We are not blaming people, saying that they were party consciously to the business failing or to the fire burning. But what we are saying is that when you deny what is before you, refuse to see what is being presented, it will call you to its attention in the loudest way it can.

Now, some of you say, "I don't want drama. I just want a peaceful existence." Perhaps you will have that. But the level of attachment that you hold to what you have known yourself through will be moved regardless. The drama is how you are attached, how deeply you are attached, to your own ideas of what should be and what should have been. When a world is made new, the very foundation that was once faulty is exposed so that the new foundation may be built. When a world is made new, what you chose in fear and sought to anoint with great importance, decided should always be, must be seen and reconsidered or re-seen in a different way. All creations claimed in fear are about to be moved.

Now, what is a creation claimed in fear? You may do this at a small level as the personality self. "If I don't love someone I must not be a good person. If I am not loved back I must not be lovable." And you carry these fears of being loved or lovable into the common field, and you play them out upon a stage with others who have operable agendas as well. But a larger construct of fear would be: "If there is not enough, I must have mine first." "If only some will survive, it better well be me." The desire to be the one on top at the cost of others below you is actually treacherous. The bottom will give out far more quickly than you think. And those who have sought to rise to the top at the cost of others' well-being will become disempowered as this year continues, as these times move forward.

The recognition, however, that you have all been party to these creations, deifying some, slandering the other, must also be considered as an act of consciousness—how you have seen and chosen, how you've sought to claim a God that would prefer one over another, or deny the good to another while fostering blame for their lack. The desire to see some win and some lose, some be punished and some exalted, must also be understood as fear operating in a contaminating way. "Why do you use that word," he asks, "*contaminating?*" Because it does so. Imagine you have a rash, and a contagious one. You scratch yourself. You touch the one next to you. She carries the rash now. Now, fear is far more covert. It's insidious in most ways. It denies that it is fear. It parades as self-righteousness. It parades as the right thing or the right people doing what must be done. Once you understand that any politics that disavows the value of any human being is libelous, is wrong-minded—and in most ways a denial of the Divine—you will cease doing so. But you invest in these things. You find them entertaining. It's nice to have a squabble over who was right, or who should be in this position of power and who should be put under a train.

Your lack of awareness for your own inherent value is in most ways the cause of this. If you actually understood self-love, which can also be understood as self-value or self-worth in a very simple way, you would understand what it means to truly value another without utilizing an old criterion—"she is the most famous," "he is the most supplicatory and prays to a God as I would see it," "she is the one who gets her way always"—and mandating that others' behavior be seen in an equation of worth or lack of worth. As you continue these patterns, you continue to deny the Divine in yourself. To know the self as holy or worthy of God at its most simple level—"I am worthy of being"—is to know the same must be true for the ones beside you and those on the other side of the stream who pray differently than you, vote differently than you, claim an awareness of who they are in a way that you would seek to deny.

The useful tenet in this teaching is being. "I am being. I am not being right. I am not being wrong. I am simply being." And in your being you will know. And to know who you truly are, to recognize the God within, is to release the idea that you are the only one, better or worse than the one beside you. As the times are upon you—rapid change, as we have said—you prepare yourself in some ways for the worst when in fact the opposite might be more instructive. To prepare yourself for the best, the best opportunity that can come out of the end of the marriage, the end of the employment, or the fire itself, a world may be made new. You may certainly bemoan the loss. You may carry the pain of the lost ones or the ones you will never see again. But you go forward in an awareness that "God Is, God Is, God Is."

Now, the simple claim "God Is" refutes the denial of the Divine. It does not fix the thing you wish fixed because perhaps the thing that you think needs fixing needed to be altered or had outgrown its old form. Two human beings who decide to marry and vow to never leave the other may grow in distortion without the space between them that allows them to reach a higher level of potential than they could have together. Then you may separate, and you may do so in love. To decide who another should be to you, to demand that they behave as you want, is always the small self.

Now, people choose things for very different reasons. "I

chose to go on this journey for what I may get from it" or "I chose to go on this journey for the wonderful companion I have that I will learn with" or "I chose to go on this journey because what I had prior known is ready to be moved beyond." It really matters not why. It simply matters that you be. And in this experience of being you allow the one beside you to be as well. And you learn from the journey when you don't mandate the outcome. If you mandate the outcome—"it should be as I say"—you are pretending to know. You are simply replicating an idea that you've had that you wish to see in form. A world made new is not a world that you strategize. It is what is unveiled when the detritus of history, the old forms, the old attachments, the old laws, and the old rules are disabled or falling away. Imagine the prow of a boat and the barnacles falling from it. You finally see what you have been traveling in, and in this awareness you recognize the Divine that has always been there, can only be there, and must always be, in spite of appearance.

Now, Paul asks a question. "But what do we do, in practical ways, in situations as I find myself in or as my neighbors do?" You feed your neighbor when he is hungry. You house your neighbor when she requires shelter. And you listen to the ones who need to cry with a deep compassion that comes from an awareness that she is still learning through the crucible she faces. Do not deny her pain. Do not deny his learning. Hold them to your heart if you can, and bless them in their way. You do what you can with your hands. You have been given hands to work with to hold the hands of your fellows, to offer them food or embrace. However, what you don't do is turn the other eye, assume someone else will do this for you, or that the government will fill the role, when you have ample to give.

When you understand that those that are facing change are facing themselves first and foremost in changed circumstance, the compassion you may have for them will be enormous. Now, prayer is useful, yes, but not sanctimonious prayer. Yes, indeed, pray for those who've lost their homes. Yes, pray for the widow who lost her husband. Yes, pray for the children who lost their school, lost their father, or lost their belief to believe in God because of the circumstances they find themselves in. But to know who they are, truly know, realizes who they are and can only be in truth. The recognition of the inherent Divine in anyone, in anything, will actually alter the fabric, the physical form and energetic body, of the one being seen at this level of tone.

You may say these words after we speak them:

> *"To all who know pain, I know you in love. To all who know fear, I know you in courage. To all who know deceit, I know you in truth. And to all who know famine, I see you in plenty. I know who you are. I know what you are. I know how you serve."*

We thank you each for your presence. This is in the text. Period. Period. Period. Stop now, please.

DAY SEVEN

What stands before you today, in an awakened state, is a new permission: to release the idea of separation that you have utilized to support yourself in independence. "I must have it my way. It must be as I say, and as I say it will be." The truth of your being, in a higher octave, is as expression. "I am expressed. And who I am at this level of tone is the Divine expressing as the one I think I am." Now, who you truly are, as has been said, is not the personality structure, not the idea of self that you parlay, seek to benefit from, seek to find your way with. The divine nature, the divine essence, that has come as you is now expressing more fully than you are even aware of. And its expression is what claims the world anew.

Now, the trials before you—and indeed there are trials—are the manifestations of past choice in a new encounter with the higher octave where all things are made new. A structure that will not stand in the higher tone will seek to fail, will find a way to move itself, so that it may be reborn and re-known in a higher expression. The truth of your being, as has been stated, the Monad or the Divine Self, is the aspect of you that escorts you through this process, or escorts the idea of you through this process, of recognition and realization of your true nature. The Divine as you, in its encounter with reality, reclaims reality beyond the old ideas that you have utilized to support an idea of what reality should be.

Now, your idea of reality—the manifest world, if you wish—is intractable in your mind. "There will always be a sunset, there will always be an ocean, there will always be a man and a woman, and we will benefit through what we have known through our ideas of who we are or have been." What is encountering now, what is being created now to be seen and encountered, is actually beyond what you've known, and consequently you have very little format, very little idea of frame, to hold the ideas that seek to come to you. So we recognize this, and as we dictate through Paul we seek to offer you the ways that you may comprehend in a new encounter with a manifest world that is in change.

Now, the change you are undergoing at the level of structure is inclusive of form and even the idea of form—what a body should look like, what a body should be. The idea of *should* in all ways is based in a false premise: what once was must always be. But you don't understand that the process of realization is in some ways a re-encoding of the entire being, form and field, to apply itself to a level of velocity that what you know of as the world is in a new encounter with. In other words, if you live under the ocean you must sprout gills. If you live on a mountaintop you must be able to breathe the refined air. If you understand yourselves at a level of elasticity—"who I have been has been interesting, but who I am becoming is not what I have known"—you will withstand the changes well.

Now, you encounter the changes within the selves, the idea of selves that you parade around in. "My name is such-and-such. Call me by the name I say. I understand myself in this way and I demand you encounter me in the way I say I should be seen." These are ideas of self that you play with, that you parade in, that you are actually moving beyond. The tenets you have utilized to support identity are actually falling away, what it means to be a man or a woman or a citizen or in a body. When all things change, all things are being lifted, but you have to align to the level of tone or vibration that the lifting aligns you in.

Now, alignment is important to understand. The collective or common field is operating at a level of alignment that you are in congruence with. The manifestation of change that is upon you now in an accelerated way is moving your ideas of what reality has been and should be to create a way for the new to be born. And in this acceleration, the realization of what was, how you've corrupted the world, denied the Divine in yourself and your fellows, must be encountered. If you don't wish to encounter these things, you will be deeply challenged. You will say, "We had it this way, it must be that way again." It will not be that way again because it cannot be. The level of vibration in acceleration is actually moving the density of the earth. And you are of the earth, which means the bodies themselves, in an altered way, are being supported at a level of alignment to withstand the changes that are upon you.

Now, Paul interrupts the teaching. "What are the changes?" Look around you, friends. It is all changing. The masquerade is ending, but you are still wearing the old costumes, playing with the old party favors. The idea of who you have been is still present, but in most ways it is a shell. It is not lasting. What occurs when this happens is a recalibration of the idea of self. You have to have this, you have to move with this, in order to maintain any kind of balance or sanity in the midst of great change. When you go to your home and your home is no longer standing, what is your home? If you are no longer the executive who runs her business, who are you then? And if your business is no longer required, what are you to be if you have only known yourself through the trajectory of occupation or career?

The manifestation of change in some ways breeds contempt for the new. "We will not see this change. We will not undergo this trial." But when the trials are upon you, you are being asked to grow and you are saying yes because you cannot say no. When you go to your home and it is no longer standing, you understand yourself beyond a structure that you utilized to hold the self safe, and then you discover what safety is beyond the idea of home. You understand the degree of worth that you hold through your experience of being, not through what you have attained, how others see you, or how you demand to be seen. You are moving as a whole to a level of resonance where who and what you are is simply expression.

Now, to be in expression does not mean you don't do. Actually, far from it. In your expression you are very active. But you are moving in a very different way because the paths that were laid for you of old are being moved. The ways you've known yourselves through sex, gender, race, identity, are all being changed, and in this great change the challenges occur. You seek to restore the old. You seek to confound the new. You seek to blame others or blame the selves. You cannot blame, but you must understand. Humanity has chosen to align at a higher degree of tone. This is a universal principle. Nothing stays the same, and entropy will not be allowed at a level of tone. So you break beyond the old structures, the old legacies, the old ideas that play out as law or as the basis of religion. You release the structures that have been inhibiting.

Now, some of you say, "Well, this sounds awful, or chaos." It is not either. It is simple change. You are not only prepared for this. You actually came for this. You incarnated at this time to be party to a process of acceleration that will support the generations that follow you. This is not all about you, you know, and the idea of who you should be or the relationships you prize. It is about legacy. And the legacy that is being left by those of you here, who are at the basis of this transition, is the legacy of grace, new possibility, and what can be claimed when you become willing to release the old. In three generations, the awareness will have risen. In four generations, it will be cemented in a very practical way in the energetic bodies of all who incarnate. In other words, the promise of the Monad, which is the Divine within you, in its flower, in its expression, will claim all things because the level of consciousness that will be aligned to at this level will support the changes that are required. If you think of yourself as the seed pushing up against the earth and the earth being moved by your presence, that is where you sit today. But the flowers that come after you, and the scent of the flowers, will claim the entire world in a higher tone.

"Now, what does this higher tone look like?" you ask. Well, a higher tone is not something you see, but you may see the fruits of it. Consciousness expresses as form, and everything you have created in fear surrounds you now. Every idea of separation that you would seek to utilize to reinforce the idea of separation must now be understood as being moved. And the consequence of this, in some ways, is a collapse of structure, but only so that the new may be born. Again, the seed pushing its way past the surface of the plain, moving the earth as it goes. The disruption is required for the flower to grow.

Now, some of you sit before us in an awakened state, and what we mean by this is very simple. You know you are not who you were. You know you are more than you were. But you don't understand what it means. The process of becoming awakened is not a process of becoming holy or deified. It is a process of recognition that occurs in stages. You cannot handle it any other way. You would seek to run back to the dark shadows from which you were reared, you would seek to return to the old pains you knew, instead of seeking the new, if it came too quickly. You are prepared for these teachings in each text we author, and the gradation of tone in acceleration that each text presents supports not only the body and the energetic body, but the idea of self in re-formation. That's a lovely word, isn't it? *Re-formation.* To be made new is to be re-formed, not to better behavior, not to a higher way of thinking, but a higher way of expressing. The thinking follows in the level of alignment that you hold.

Now, some of you want a world that resembles your idea of nirvana, your idea of Eden. These are false ideas. You may still go to work in the morning. You may still play with a puppy, bathe your children, feed your family, appreciate the sky, feel the breeze on your face. But you will operate from a place of knowing that is beyond what you've known. And the simple knowing that occurs—"I Am, I Am, I Am"—aligns you to a level of fluidity so that your thoughts and actions are actually operating in concert with the Divine that has never been apart from you.

Now, imagine you are part of a river that is always flowing. Indeed, you are. But you perceive yourselves as obstructions, and what you perceive as obstructions are simply born in the idea of separation that the flow that you seek, or may actually encourage, cannot be experienced by one as you. The Divine has authorship, and the personality structure, once subjugated or moved to a level of alignment where it is not demanding to be known through separation, can claim itself in fruition through you. Underline the word *through.* Some of you prefer *as.* "The

Divine has come as me." But the independence of the *as*—"I am the one as the Divine"—still holds an idea of separation through the language you utilize. When you begin to understand that the Divine flows through you, and *then* as—*through* and *as*—the idea of expression becomes more simple. You don't need to demand anymore. You need to say yes. You don't need to grapple and to seek. You need to receive and discover. To be in a place of discovery is to move towards true illumination because you realize that every moment is an experience of the Divine that can be claimed by the one who knows who she is.

We are not eradicating the world. The world is not being eradicated. If you wish to use a word like Armageddon, it's an apocalypse of the small self, first and foremost, the aspect of you that believes herself to be God or believes himself to be the ruler of all things. When you realign in the octave of the Upper Room, you have access to higher mind as you flow in it. Now, higher mind is not separate from you. The idea that it is somewhere other that must be sought is confounding for all of you because you are always seeking, and rarely in a position to receive. The one who sits in meditation is at least in allowance. But she still seeks to come to a level of awareness, or holds a practice that heralds the idea of outcome. We do not herald the idea of outcome. We herald the idea of permission, so that you may be a supplicant to the Great Divine and participatory in action with it, not separate from it and seeking to benefit from it in the dribs and drabs you allow. The recognition of the Divine as you—"I know who I am in truth"—is an inclusive act of expression. "I know who I am" as expressed as of the whole.

Now, the manifest whole, or the world you see, is indeed

made of separate parts that actually operate in some ways of independence, but they are also operating in complete alignment at a higher level. Imagine the stars and the planets in their own movement. They are of the cosmos and moving in their perfection. The higher you align in vibration, the higher the level of perception you align to. And what you see and how you see is the innate perfection that is in manifestation as all things. Underline *all*. It's terribly important you understand this. *All* things. *All* manifestation. *All* levels of vibration in perfection.

Now, at the low tone or the low vibrational scale you have terror and agony and fear. Are these things of God? These things are the product of the denial of the Divine, and the claim of the denial of the Divine holds a very dense field. The idea of separation is the basis for this, and as you contend with the idea of separation you move beyond it because you have become willing to face it. If you are unwilling to face the belief that you are separate, have thought yourself as separate, operate in a belief in separation, you will not claim your true inheritance, which is unification.

Now, some of you believe still that if you claim your unity you are dead, you disappear, you are gone as you have known it. In fact, that is not true. You are re-known, reborn, or reclaimed in a higher octave of thought, of expression, and manifestation. The manifest world is an expression of consciousness. The consciousness that has been applied to the manifest world that you have been reared in is entirely tainted by a great lie that you are separate from the Source of all things. Everything claimed at this level of tone holds a bias and demand to replicate separation. When you move beyond this, the structures begin to change. When you move to a unified sense of self—"I am of Source, I am of the whole, I am a distinct perfect expression of the Divine, as is everyone else, as is all, capital 'A-L-L'"—you understand that the totality of the Divine is inclusive of all matter, all thought, because nothing exists without it. Nothing exists beyond it. There is no vacuum where God cannot be. However, because you have free will, individually and collectively, you can create a hell on earth and think that's the best you are allowed. You deserve so much more than you even know. You are only beginning to see the promise of the Divine that awaits you.

Now, when we say *awaits you,* we don't mean somewhere other. We mean right where you sit, God as all—inclusive of the air, inclusive of the sky, inclusive of the things known through pain or discord. When all things are known anew, all things may be claimed anew. When something is claimed, it is restated. It is seen anew as fact. The idea comes first, the idea of potential. Nothing can be made in form until it is first a potential. But the receipt of the potential is made in claim. You confuse manifestation with what you get or think you should have or should be. You are already in manifestation. Your life is a manifestation of thought. The collective mind undergoes great process and then you have collective outcome. As the species aligns to a higher level of tone and velocity, the requirements of the species integrate into the manifest world. In other words, when you need something, the potential for it can exist. When the potential for it exists, it can and will be claimed.

To operate in Divine Mind does not mean you are not creative. Your creativity *is* God, an expression of God, as is every other aspect of you. The body, the tongue, and the words the tongue speaks—all expression of the Divine come as and through you. Each of you. And, again, all. All of you. You are one of many, and your idea of many is still so limited. You have no idea how amazing the experience of being in unification is, and can be known as, when one says, "Yes. I Have Come. I Have Come. I Have Come."

The relationship you have with the manifest world is what is being discussed first in this text so that you have an understanding of the changes that are upon you. The first third of this book will focus on the manifest world, and after that we seek to show you who you have been, and can only be, in an experience of transformation. A world is made new through expression. And your expression is what catapults the world, well beyond your idea of self and personal need, to a level of tone where the Kingdom can be known. And, again, the Kingdom is the realization of the inherent Divine in all things. All things made new.

Thank you for your presence. Period. Period. Period.

(PAUSE)

What stands before you today, in a realized state, is a new permission: to decide for yourselves what mandates you require. "What does that mean?" you may ask. Well, you are in agreement to many of them. "This is how time works and how I must abide by time." "This is what things should be because I was told they should be that way." When you relinquish the need to be decided for, you move into an opportunity to what was held in abeyance by your own disbelief or your own sense of what could be possible. The requirement for this is very simple.

"I am willing to accept what is without the precepts of what should be. I am willing to receive myself as I truly am without the requirements or the mandates that I have adhered to thus far." When you say yes to these things, you move to a level of velocity where you may be met by the new. Underline the word *met*. What if the new seeks to meet you? What if what is there for you simply awaits you, and awaits your alignment to it?

Now, to be in alignment to something means, very simply, to be in agreement to it. If you are in agreement with it, you are aligned to it. The reality you see you are in deep agreement with. "This is the color of the ocean." "That is what a true love is." "That is what a good school is." "That is an inferior person." You have all these mandates, constructs, that you abide by without even realizing it. When you lift to the new, what you are doing is granting permission to realize the new, which means to know the new and then move into alignment with it. But you have choice here. You can say, "Yes, I am willing to receive the new. I am willing to claim my participation in the octave above, the higher realm, the Upper Room. I am willing to say yes." Or you may choose to sit in the old, with "my recrimination, my jealousy, my idea of who I should be" mandating the old show itself again and again.

The mandate of the old is always the old. When you have outgrown a form, you release the form. When the body no longer serves you, you release the body. When the marriage is no longer serving you, you may choose to release the marriage. When the idea of self that has been bound by history and legacy is constricting, it is actually inviting you to claim what exists beyond it. What exists beyond it is everything else, imagined and unseen, that you may participate in.

Now, when change occurs, the first impulse is always to re-store the old. "Dear God, let the marriage work. Let my child be well. Let the business not fail. Let me be who I say I am, lest I lose face with my neighbors." The requirement of the old requires maintenance, and much of your time is spent main-taining an idea of who and what you should be at the cost of what would be brought to you.

What is being brought to you now—underline the word *is*—is your own potential, your own gift, your own true expres-sion, which has always existed in participation with you. But you have obscured it by your agreement to the mandates of old: "what this should be and who I should be within it." Each of you says yes at the level of participation that you are willing to receive. Did you hear what we just said? You say yes at the level of participation that you will receive. As you say yes to these teachings, you are not asked to do, but participate in them in an experiential way. The mandate of these teachings is very simple: that you know who you are, what you are, and how you serve, which is your expression come to flower, come to claim a world made new. The agreement of this happens both at a soul level and at the level of structure or personality. The personality is involved in this because you must agree at a certain level to participate in what is before you. You choose to get out of bed every morning, whether or not you know this. You choose to wash the body, feed the body, have relations with others. You are always in choice. The agreement to be—underline the word *agreement*, which means in coherence with your true being in full expression—is a choice made.

Now, the claim you spoke earlier—"I Have Come, I Have Come, I Have Come," the mandate of the claim of vibration as Monad—supports you in a realization of the who, the Divine Self that has indeed come as you at the cost of the old. And that is an important choice one makes, the claim "I Have Come." "I have agreed in participation to a new way of being." The affect of the claim is actually what follows, which is the realization of self, as the Monad explicitly chooses itself to be made manifest by way of your agreement. Nothing happens without your consent at this level.

Now, when we said soul is participatory, we are telling you something very important. You have come with lessons with which to learn through, and you will learn those lessons regardless of the state of resonance that you accrue through these teachings or align to through these teachings. Your way will be made for you, but your mandate or lesson will be given to you at the level that you can hold. To choose these things, to grow beyond the old, is in support of the growth of all. This is not selfish work. This is work you do for all because you are becoming participatory to the manifest Divine through the relinquishing of the old. And the relinquishing of the old is what supports the Divine in full expression. All that is being released is what has stood in the way of your true nature.

Now, some of you would say, "Well, I'm a cranky old man. I enjoy being a cranky old man." Enjoy it all you wish. If your idea of self is not inhibiting your true participation in the sovereign act of resurrection—which participates in universal resurrection, one and the whole at once—have a nice time with it. We are not denying you your pleasures. But the moment you decide that you are the only one of value, the only one that matters, the only one whose opinion matters, you have claimed yourself in the lower floor, in the low octave, yet again. Enjoy your predilections as you wish, but don't deny the Divine either in yourself or in another. To call a man a fool is to make the self foolish. To deny the Divine in another is to deny it in yourself. To praise the Divine who is come in another is to praise the Divine in all things.

Now, praise is not worship. It is the elevation or the lifting of the thing to its true nature. To praise it is to say yes to its divinity. The true claim of being—"I know who you are, what you are, how you serve"—is in fact high praise, not at the level of personality, but at the level of the Monad, the Divine that is always there seeking its expression and manifestation as and through all of you. Again, the word *all*. To say yes to your participation is to release the old legacy and the abiding to the old laws that you have been party to.

Now, if you take one moment now and you ask yourself twelve things that you believe should always be there, you may be surprised to understand that they need not always be there, but your presupposition preserves them in some ways, or preserves the sense of safety that you require, entrusting that what was, yesterday, will be there tomorrow. We have to say, in the years that come much will be changed, and even the maps of the world will have differentials than what you see today. And this may be seen in a high way as progress as you release the idea of what was to what seeks to be born. Underline that: *seeks to be born*. What is awaiting birth. The new manifestation of the inherent Divine that will be revealed will be re-seen, that which has been hidden will be unveiled, and your vision is participatory to its manifestation.

"What does that mean?" he asks. Well, how you perceive anything claims the thing in form by nature of your agreement,

both individually—"what a lovely ring"—and collectively—
"what an ugly ring or a worthless ring"—because you abide
by standards or shared constructs that you utilize daily. When
you release the need to decide what things should mean based
upon what they have meant, you open yourself up to a new
potential, a new visual awareness of the inherent Divine that
has not been labeled and weighted down by the legacy of prior
meaning. *Prior meaning* very simply means the meaning it has
been endowed with by those who came before you, which is
how you know things as valuable or useless or worthwhile,
how you know a man as beautiful or homely, all based in past
construct of what these things should mean. When you truly
perceive the beauty in another, you are seeing beyond the flesh.
Not denying the flesh, but seeing what creates the flesh, the
beauty that is inherent inclusive of flesh, inclusive of form, and
all of those things that exist beyond form.

Now, the trials that are before you today, for almost all of
you, are the trials of relinquishing the known, or the mandates
that you have utilized to support the architecture of what you
know of as reality. When the architecture is being changed,
the foundation no longer holds. Don't think the earth is caving
in on you. Indeed, it is not. You are lifting to the new. And it
is unsteady at first, until you become accustomed to abiding in
the higher alignment. Once this shift occurs at a level of elasticity, which simply means you are not bound by old form and
old meaning, you will begin to comprehend that the manifest
world is indeed far more elastic to conscious thought and to
choice than you would have known prior. The dense field that
you occupy has rules that you abide by. "This is a rock." But that
rock may be ground to dust, and that dust may fly in the air and

join the sea. It will not always be the rock. The substance that you know of as reality can be altered through the awareness of the inherent Divine.

Now, the inherent Divine and the claim of it, "I know what you are in truth," the manifest seen as Source, can be re-known in higher expression than you have known it prior. Once you release the need for the density that you have accrued experience in, the reality you have known alters in stages. We said this prior. When it alters in stages, we must understand that what you have capacity for can and will be met with your agreement at the level of tone that you can abide by. You are in tone right now. All who hear these words are hearing vibration and experiencing vibration because that is indeed what you are. As the escalation of the field occurs, that which was most dense will first be moved, and then what you have hindered or used to hinder the expression of the Divine will of course be revealed. And this is the apocalypse that the small self fears. But it may be joyous because all you have been attached to is an idea of self that takes its substance from a simple lie—the denial of the Divine. It was never true. It was never true you were a bad boy or a worthless girl. It was never true that the who that you are, the implicit intrinsic you, was so traumatized that she may never heal, because the Divine Self, who knows itself in innocence or as the Divine Self which of course exists beyond the idea of sin, only knows itself in worth, and not the kind of worth that you would seek to measure through the values you have used to decide what is worthy, but through the inherent value. The Divine knows the Divine in all it sees. The Divine cannot deny another. When you deny another the Divine, that is the small self with her priestess hat on and his scepter, deciding who is worthy of her idea of the Kingdom and who is not.

The choice, my friends, is yours. Who do you wish to know yourself as? If you wish to make this choice today, you may:

"On this day I claim to allow myself the knowledge of my true nature, and the discovery that accompanies it will be met by me at the level I can receive it. As I say yes, I meet the false ideas of self that I have utilized to perpetuate an idea of separation. And as I bless those and release them, my requirement of them is released and I am known anew. I know who I am. I know what I am. I know how I serve. I am Word through this intention. Word I am Word."

We thank you each for your presence. Indeed, this is in the text.

DAY EIGHT

What stands before you today, in an awakened state, is a recognition of how you have participated in the manifest world. You understand yourselves as much through what you think as through what you do, and the memories you hold are less about thought than how you have enacted thought—where you went to school, what the desk felt like, what was on the blackboard—in your recognition of your participation to the day before you. When we sit before you today, we ask you questions—"who do you think you are?" and "what did you think you were?"—because we are about to take you on a journey beyond the old, beyond the old self, to a level of recognition of what exists beyond you. Now, *beyond you* simply means what you don't perceive from the strata of vibration that you've situated yourselves in. This simply means that there is more to see, more to comprehend, and more to participate with in the upper realm.

Now, recognition is important. "I recognize my hands and feet. I recognize his hands and feet are different from my own." Recognition is useful. "I know where I live and where I used to live and they are not the same things." But you don't understand recognition of identity. "I am not who I thought I was. I have always been something other, but I did not recognize it." Recognition of this—"I am other than I think"—is the first step for most of you in a realization of awakening. "I am not what I think, or even what I thought, but I Am that I Am, and can only be as such."

Now, the Monad is the I Am presence, or the Divine Spark, seeking fruition through you. And it *is* consciousness, and its elevation of tone comprehends itself, recognizes itself, in tandem with the great I Am, the All That Is, the manifest Divine that is playing out before you. Underline the word *is*. Not someday when you're there, but in this very moment. The manifest Divine *is* playing out before you and is seeking your recognition.

Now, the manifest Divine is not what you want it to be—hearts and flowers, perhaps an angel with a harp. The manifest Divine is the fire that burns, the night sky, the beautiful tree, the water in the lake, and the fish within them. The Divine Self that is you is vibration. It is not a thing. It is opalescence, divine expression that manifests itself as all that it encounters. Now, to understand what this truly means is to understand the levels of vibration that you have been party to. You understand yourselves in your bodies. "My foot, his foot, the feet over there." You understand the light you see, the twilight, the sunset, the beautiful morning light. You comprehend yourselves or recognize yourselves in tandem with these things, but you don't understand that every level of tone or vibration plays out in some way or another in your experience. Because you are limited by your senses in what you can perceive, you actually miss the boat. You assume the twilight is the only light that can be perceived at a certain time of day. You think the ocean is a static body, when ocean itself, alive in vibration, is not water. It is tone. It is tone. It is tone.

Now, when you align in tone through what you experience, you claim identity in recognition with your participation in what is before you. When you bathe in the ocean, you are the bather. When you bathe in the sun, you are the sunbather. When you go to your occupation with whatever title you have claimed, you are the baker or the doctor or whatever you would call yourselves. But the I Am Self that is in vibration, as and through, seeks to move the vibration that conceals it. The opportunity of this holds two different ways of experience: the fear-based self who comprehends herself through the known who would seek consolation in what she has claimed through the small identity, and the manifest Divine come as you that is encouraging and saying, "Yes. I Am Here. I Have Come. I Am Known." And the "I Am Known," the Monad as known as expression, is the claim of the day.

Now, "I Am Known" simply offers you to awareness of what has always been. It is not a new discovery. It is the relationship of the Manifest Self and the Divine Spark expressing as manifestation and the Source of the manifestation, which you may call God, if you wish, or anything other that you like. It really matters not. When you understand that the Monad *is* expression, the ocean expression, and it is all in tone, the recalibration of vibration is far less complicated than you have assumed. The architecture of the manifest world, as you have experienced it, is in solidity in dense form. And in most ways, through your small self, it is believed to be solid and intractable. The vibration that is the Monad actually supersedes the density of form, but the alignment to form in what we call the common field, your relationship with the manifest world, is what is being addressed now. Until this shifts, you simply claim yourselves through the rubric or the template that the manifest plane has supported itself in. That simply means if you believe yourself to be in this town or that, you will remain in this town or that until you comprehend that this town is a small aspect of a larger county or continent or world. The small self presides over a small kingdom. The Monad or the Divine Self, expressed in vibration and sound, claims the Kingdom. And the awareness of the Kingdom, the inherent divinity in manifestation, is the offering we give you.

Now, when the template is changed, what is invoked from the body in an escalated tone carries a resonance that supports your recognition of the manifest world in its divinity. Because like attracts like, or the field that you hold is always claiming manifestation as consciousness, you understand that as the physical form that you have been gifted with supports itself in a recognition of what it truly is, the manifest Divine, it aligns to all things at that level of tone or sound or being.

Now, if everything is sound, what does that mean to your

experience of the field you have known yourselves through? It is not so much that the manifest world is an illusion. It is not an illusion. It is operable, but only at one strata of vibration. We have spoken in the past of escalation of tone, or transposition, the songs that you think you are being transposed to a higher octave to be sung anew. The process of transposition to the higher octave in form and field have been the texts we have issued, each gradation supporting a higher offering, or occupancy, in alignment to what exists simultaneous with the dense field you have chosen to know yourselves through. In the upper realm the form is less dense, and what is claimed in consciousness lacks the density as well. The refuge of the old is darkness, the old cave where things may be supported in the old manifest ways. The template of manifestation, or the architecture of a world, is adjusting itself to a level of transposition where what was claimed in fear will no longer be. But the challenge will always be your preference for what you have known.

Now, in vibration the manifest world can be perceived in multiple ways. The consciousness that you hold supports your experience of what you perceive. The saint, you might imagine, sees the world in a rather different way than what you would think of as the sinner, but that is not actually true. Both are having equally valid experiences of recognition of self in consort with the manifest Divine. Now, the manifest Divine doesn't have to be pretty, doesn't have to support your idea, born in history, of what God must look like. God is the vermin as well as the light, and the light *is* the vermin simply operating in a dense form. Each thing you perceive, whatever you think, you are in accord with—a-c-c-o-r-d, a c-h-o-r-d as on a piano.

And the accord that you are claiming through these teachings supports a level of alignment where the experience of being, the validity of the experience of being, gives you what you need to comprehend the vibration you hold as the holy, and always the holy.

Why would we say *always the holy*? Because you are always holy. Even the one you believe to be the sinner that you would see outside of God is as holy as the one you might call the saint. They are having experiences of being in consciousness, and you cannot judge because you do not know the reason why. You come to learn things in a life. The individual has an agenda at the level of soul to claim what she requires in her own recognition of what it means to be in human form. We do not deny these lessons, and you maintain human form and the lessons you came for even in the escalated state that is offered by the Upper Room. But the manifest Divine, and the experience of it, is much easier to comprehend with the eyes that know the truth, or the perception that does not deny what is always true. Underline *always*. It is *always* holy, even when your perception would tell you otherwise. "But those evil people, the terrible things they do." The masks are coming off. That does not mean that what you see will be what you want, but it will mean that how you perceive will be in an equation of vibration that will not hold the level of damnation, seeking to damn your fellows, that you have utilized thus far. "Those people" are holy, but they may be acting in the denial of the Divine.

The offering of these teachings is not to save your souls. Your souls are fine. They are evolving through your witness, through the challenges you perceive yourselves through, through the manifestations that form offers you. Your souls are fine. But the manifest world that you have chosen to incarnate through is not as fine as you would wish because you have sullied it. You have denied the Divine in the form that you have taken and the ground you walk upon. When the ground is seen as holy and treated as such, with reverence to God or the Source of all things, the challenges you face on this plane will move away very quickly. But what you damn, damns you back. You pollute your oceans, the oceans damn you back, not through intention, but through your alignment and your actions. Again, actions. You remember what you've done, but you don't understand that, one and all, you are in party to the manifest world, and not only the manifest world, but all who dwell upon it. You are your brother's keepers, like it or not. And when one perishes, you all suffer the cost.

"What does that mean?" he asks. You diminish the value of human life, and each time you do that you diminish the value of your own. When life is known as sacred, and all things of God, what you perceive will be resplendent because you will be able to see it as it truly is—the God in form, come as tree, come as landscape, come as body, come as birth and death, because they are all in the unified state or field that we will call God, expressing in their own perfect ways. Some of you say to us, "Tell me what I want to hear. Tell me I will get what I want. Tell me I will get the money or the fame or the family or the respect that I have desired." You are the ones claiming your experience in this manifest world. Blame who you wish. Point the fingers where you want. Until you take accountability for experience in this plane, you will not know yourselves in dominion, which indeed you are. You have been gifted with the opportunity to choose, and to choose means to enact the choice before you. When you act in love and in worth and in awareness of the value of your brothers and of the land and of the sea and of the sky, when you act in recognition of all things holy, the world is made new.

The transition is difficult, and highly difficult for some of you, because you wish to maintain a status quo while seeking God. To truly know God is to release the need for what you have had or believed should be, and the what that you are, the Manifest Self, and the who that you are, the manifest identity, can transition in easier ways. When you deny the Divine in your body, you deny the Divine in the earth. When you deny the Divine in your brother, you deny it in yourself. When you look at time as a structure that is permanent, you make it an idol and you release the need to challenge a bias born in history. You think it was, so it should be. It will not be. What is beginning to happen is you are beginning to perceive what has always been, and what has always been must be uncovered, and what uncovers it is choice and alignment. "I am willing to know and to be known." When you know, you realize. When you are realized, you are known. To know yourself is to know God. To know your brother is to know yourself. To judge your brother, to put her in darkness, him if you prefer, is to deny the Divine in yourself because you have placed yourself in the shadow by your choice to judge.

Because we sit before you today as vibration, as tone, we would like to tell you a little story about who and what we are. The expression that we use as Paul, or the voice that we speak with, is actually beyond what he knows and would even comprehend. And he would not wish to know. But we are speaking anyway, and perhaps he won't think about what he says as we speak through him. We have been here prior to time, most of us, as what we are, or the agreement to be a simple expression of divine truth that can be known in each generation as you come to your awareness. However, this is the time when humanity has said yes, less out of a true desire, but in awareness of its own creations. And "its own creations" includes a magnitude of weaponry that may extinguish you all. And we will say this cannot happen, and you will not allow it.

But the *you* that will not allow it expresses well beyond your idea of self to the collective, to the collective mind, or we would say the soul of humanity. And we use that expression loosely because even your idea of who you are as humans is quite distorted. You are a collective of expression come in form from different levels of vibration. And you incarnate collectively to learn lessons through the collective, or this experience of being in a human form. The religions you've held, most of them, are party to older wisdom that predates your idea of who you are and even the idea of form. Form is a later acquisition that the human beings have chosen to realize themselves through. Soul is not form as you have known form, and we hold no form, although we have chosen it, some of us, at varying times.

Our participation in these instructions is for the benefit of all of you—underline *all*—including those who would refute us, burn the books, and deny the Divine in themselves and others. They are equally loved, and, indeed, they are known. They are known at the level of soul, and beyond that at the level of the Monad, because there is nothing born that is not of God. There can be nothing in expression that is not of God. God is tone at varying levels of tone. The rising or the escalation of tone is what claims the world anew. And we say these words for you now: We have come as Melchizedek, but that is simply a name and an order. Beyond that we are God, as you are God, as the sky is God, as the sea is God. As is all. As is all. As is all. As is all.

We bless you each with our presence, as indeed we are blessed by yours. We will take a pause for the man in the chair. Period. Period. Period. This is in the text. Stop now, please.

(PAUSE)

What stands before you today, once you know who you are, is the recognition of how you have been participatory to the manifest world in all its ways. Underline *all*. Now, you don't make the planet spin or the sun come up, but you are participatory to these things because you see them, perceive them, and recognize yourselves in conjunction with them. Everything you see you are participatory to, and the manifestation of form itself is the result of thought, agreement, and your alignment. When you move to a higher level of frequency or alignment, the manifestation you perceive is altered by nature of presence and being.

Now, who is being is the question. It is not Ursula or Anton that makes the sun rise. It perceives it. Anton perceives as perceiver. But the Monad—which is the Divine come as Anton, Ursula, any of you—is what is manifest and knowing itself in union or in consort with what expresses as manifestation. The small self would get what she can stuff in her pockets in a lifetime. "Give me the money. Give me the acclaim. Give me the benefits that I demand to have." The small self would raid the bank if she could. The Divine Self comprehends universal need. She has no need to stuff her pockets. She has no pockets to stuff. She simply is. And her expression and being, in manifestation, is the light that shines on all equally. You don't want to hear this. "I want the light to shine on my children, my employers so I may maintain my job, perhaps my pet, but not those people over there. I don't really care. I suspect I should, but I really do not." The personality structure has its preferences. You may not like your neighbors very much. It's your job to feed your family or your dog. But to know others as of God is to claim yourself as the light that supports their realization.

Now, you are not manufacturing omnipresence. You are divine. The Divine is omnipresent. And it operates through you, and we would say, finally—at a level of consciousness that few attain in form—*as* you, which is full realization. When you have full realization, the need for form is gone. You have become consciousness. You always were, but you are no longer bound by the limitations of time that you utilize in consort with your fellows to organize experience, time as a construct. All things happen now, and only now. There is only now, and can only be now.

The triumph of the teaching, if you align to it, is the Monad, which operates in the eternal now, not bound by time and space in *its* expression, *its* now, which transcends form as you have known it. There have been many teachings of those rising from the dead—coming out of the cave, if you would have it that way. We will say this to you: You have a body. It is not meant to survive beyond a certain amount of time, just as the trees will lose their leaves when fall comes. The Divine as you, resurrected through you, utilizes the form you have been granted to the benefit of all. The escalation of tone in a higher field is not immortality. What is immortal is the idea of soul and the Monad that expresses fully through it, which is the spark of God which inhabits, expresses, and reclaims all it encounters in the resonant field that it holds. To be the light of the world is to shine the light of the world on the world. And the light of the world is not Ursula or Anton. It is the Divine that has come as them and reclaims what it encounters.

Imagine a lighthouse on a rock in an ocean. It shines upon the pirates. It shines upon the royals. It shines upon the barge and the tugboat equally. The light that you are may be in discernment about what is required. "Best not to feed that one now. She's had enough. But tomorrow give her breakfast." The light that you are announces itself fully with the awareness that all are equal. Equality in these teachings is highly inconvenient for most of you. You want your idea of spiritual growth while you eat your bonbons and you do your meditations as that handsome teacher instructed you in that handsome class you attend with other handsome people. You understand yourselves in communities that are secular. These are ways of knowing the self, born in preference, born in ideas of what community should be, and have very little truth.

The idea of tribes gets bandied about these days. "My tribe." "Her tribe." "Their tribe." There is *one* tribe, the species that you have come as demonstrating itself in remarkable ways, with different colors of skin, different languages spoken, all wonderful in their own unique ways. To move beyond tribalism is to move out of your community and out of your comfort. You may enjoy your comfort when it's present, but there has never been a journey across an ocean that has not met with a storm now and then. And the storms you encounter, individually and collectively, can support the growth that you are here to learn through, and they are rarely convenient. "Oh, poor me," you may say. Well, "poor them," too, and "poor everyone," if you wish, because you are all in the same boat. You just don't know it.

"What does that mean?" he asks. You've all chosen to live, to come in form to learn the lessons of form at a very specific time, and we use that word closely. Your *idea* of time would be better said, where remarkable things are occurring. The changes upon you are so rapid now that in what you would call ten years much of what you would worry about today will not be present to worry about. And we say that is a good thing, not something to be frightened of.

Imagine you were always worried about your finance. You expect you always will be. But what if your idea of finance was born in a collective field where some could have and some could not, and some were striving and some were begging? What if the idea of money—because it *is* an idea—was translated to something other? "Now what could that be?" you might ask. Well, you will know when you discover it. And we intend to say you will, because commerce as you have known it, while it has its uses, demands others be dependent upon some and a hierarchy of exchange which serves few. When you understand that the landlord and the tenant are both one and the same, having experiences of the idea of property, because property is an idea, and exchanging money, which is also an idea, living in a town named such-and-such, also an idea, you will understand that ideas need not be permanent. They have taken form at a time, been supported throughout time in mandates of what they should look like, and as you move beyond them—and you may do so with more grace than you imagine—you may become participatory to what expresses, already expresses, in the higher octave.

Now, imagine an Upper Room where the ideas of old were not solid. Even the idea of mountain and sea, things you think should always be as they were, was somehow malleable to new possibility. Each possibility that you experience in the Upper Room can be claimed or known in form at the level of vibration that you have aligned to. You are tuning forks, you see, whether or not you know it. The vibration you hold is supporting what you encounter. And the level of tone that expresses in the Upper Room does not qualify itself through the language of old, the mandates of form as you have known them. And as you rise to a new recognition of who and what you are in truth, you claim the Kingdom.

Now, the Kingdom is not Kansas. It is not a country. It is not a town. It has no name. It simply is. "God Is. God Is. God Is." If you seek to name it—"that must be the Kingdom, I see the sign, it says, 'Kingdom two miles down the road'"—you will find yourself in a rather unpleasant place. We would suggest the Kingdom is wherever you stand, and the eyes that perceive or the awareness that perceives as Kingdom claims itself into being. God sees God in all of its creations, and the Divine that has come as Anton sees the God in Ursula and everyone else he meets. The act of creation is the act of claiming, and claiming is the act of saying, "Yes. Yes, it may be so. Yes, it is. It will be. God Is. God Is. God Is."

As each of you comes before us, perhaps with your book, perhaps with your question, perhaps with what you think should be, there is one common factor that cannot be denied. You are equally loved. No one is without. Equally loved. The Divine loves all, sees all, equally. This does not mean you get what you wish for Christmas. This does not mean that your child will succeed the way you wish. Nor does it mean that you are the holy one that is special. None are special, because all are special. All are loved. And you are, indeed.

We will say this now: The text that we are writing, the final text of the trilogy, will not be our last text, but it will complete a teaching in manifestation that was begun several books ago. And as we teach manifestation, a world made new, we see you each in it, expressing in it, and calling it into being. A world made new is called into being by the one who knows who and what she is, how he serves, and knows the others that he and she encounters on their path as God expressed as form.

We see you in your beauty, in your right to be. And we say these words to you now: We will complete the first chapter of the text today as we are allowed. Period. Period. Period. Stop now, please.

(PAUSE)

What stands before you today, once you are awakened, is the radical expression of the Monad as you. In subsequent teachings we will address how this occurs, and what you might expect from the Monad as expressed in the physical realm, not just through you but through your experience of the manifest world.

Now, the manifest world is in form by your own agreement,

and you are in alignment to it as what it has been. Underline the word *has*. "What it *has* been" simply means the historical data that you use as reference. The requirement now is to begin to comprehend that it was, but it is not. Your experience of the manifest world is as a shadow that is passing. You are seeing what was, still in a form that it has taken, but it is in change, as are you. As you are in change, the world must change to reflect it.

Now, you are not the arbiters of change, but as we have spoken prior, you are the ambassadors of it as you rise in light to begin to shine and to transmit the frequency that is the octave of the Upper Room. When this is in transmission, manifestation occurs in rapidity. And *rapidity* means in an escalation as you can hold the vibration of it.

The prior texts of these series have been in preparation for where we intend to take you. *The Book of Innocence* addressed the radical aspect of the Monad re-creating itself through the manifest body and through memory, or your thinking about what should be. The old premise, once realized in a higher frequency, loses its strata and reclaims itself in the octave of emission, which simply means even your idea of what was is translated—and, indeed, lifted—to this new level of choice and expression.

Now, some of you say to us, "I want what I want when I want it, and I want my enlightenment tomorrow." Well, perhaps today is the day because it only happens now. The alignment you hold may negate the Divine that is already expressed as you, but it will not be extinguished. The ember that is the Divine Spark simply asks for its acquiescence to your agreement: "I am willing. I am saying yes. And I Am Known."

Being known at this level simply aligns the aspect of you that is already realized or awakened to claim itself through knowing, and knowing claims itself as manifest once this occurs. There is an immediacy, finally, to the progression you have undertaken. And the progression you have undertaken, through a series of texts that have been prepared for you, must be understood as what you align to in transition from one state of being to another. That will be the title of this chapter: "One State of Being to Another."

The shift you are undergoing, and the velocity of the shift, is only going to increase through the times you are in. How you manage your expectations and your experience in all ways will be a reflection of the consciousness you hold. To bemoan your fate, to argue with your neighbor, to damn your brother or sister for what you think they have done, is always the small self seeking to aspect the Divine in its own small way. The Divine does not judge and does not recriminate. The aspect of you that would put your brother in shadow is the aspect of you that is frightened of the growth you are undergoing. Malice has no place here. What awaits you is joyful, and joyful in a way you may not be prepared for because your idea of joy still rests on past memory, what felt good one day. To be in joy is to be in a state of reverence for what is before you, and all of it. Underline *all*. The high and the low and the in-between that we must say is God.

We welcome you now to your own experience. We say these words on your behalf:

On this day we claim that all who hear these words, all who say yes to what lies before them, may be lifted to the level of the resonant field where joy abides, that they may know themselves in joy and idealize only what is true, the Divine that expresses as all things.

We say yes to you as you say yes to yourselves. Not only have you come, you have said yes. And we stand beside you as we take you further in these teachings than you believed could be.

Blessings to you each. The end of Chapter One, yes. In the text. Period. Period. Period.

2

RECOGNITION

DAY NINE

What stands before you today, in an awakened state, is a realization that what has been before you was a requirement for growth. You can no longer go about saying "the terrible thing that happened," "that horrible incident," "that awful man or woman." You actually claim them in a frightening way and any choice made in fear will continue to be fearful. When something occurs that is not what you wish, that you would not have chosen by the self that would comprehend it, you align to the thing at a level of choice that actually supports you in a new agreement. Everything that occurs for you—underline the word *for*—is progression.

Now, progression is not what you think. You want progression to lift you higher and higher. But at times progression is *through*—through the pain, through the altercation, through the disaster, if you wish, that suffers so many. The world is made up of many, and the ideas that the world holds and has procured throughout time support manifestation. The manifestation of your world today, in an altered way, is progressing—not as you would seek it or make it so, but as it is required to be, the culmination of past choice playing out before you on a stage.

Now, most of you think of the selves first. "Will I get what I want at the end of this?" "Will my life be what I say it should be?" But those are precepts born in history—what you think your life should be or how the world should work on your behalf. You are remedying things by poking at the problems, not re-seeing them. And to re-see a problem is to see it beyond problem, but opportunity. When something is perceived as a problem you claim it as such. That is your relationship to it. When it is perceived as opportunity you may lift to it and perceive it from a higher way, a higher view. And the claim we offer you—"Behold, I make all things new"—is not a claim of remedy, but of transformation. The manifest world that you have known yourselves through, in an altered way, is beckoning to you to participate. "In what way?" he asks. Well, as we have said prior, the music that you have been used to dancing to has already changed, but you still know the old steps. You've not yet caught up with the transition that's occurring. You are seeking instead to maintain an idea of self through the safety of the known.

Now, the known is present, but as artifact—once what was, and was claimed in an identity that you have chosen to know it through. When something is made new it is actually altered, and the names you would gift it with may be altered as well. The permanency of language is challenging for most of you. "That is what a house should be, and if it doesn't resemble a house that I would know, how can I call it a house?" The idea of having an abode, limited in form in some ways, claims structure, and the structures claim manifestation. You build the structures you imagine, but primarily you replicate them as you think they should be in the common field. Language is highly useful. We utilize language when we teach. But these teachings exist beyond language, and if you wish to know the true teachings, beyond language, you may do that as well. Simply align to the text as vibration and allow the language to be present, but allow the limitations that language offers to be released so that you may participate fully.

When a world is made new, a claim is made upon the world: "It may be other than I have known. It may be seen beyond what I have utilized prior. It may be seen in an altered way because the perception I utilize is not bound by history and data." History is useful, but it is an idea, an idea of what was that you give credence to. Most history is subjective. The victor claims the history. The one who wins the war decides the name of the country. The utilization of history for your learning is useful. Where it is no longer useful is when it codifies choice, and in a limited way, of what can be or what you might allow.

To withstand change in these times—and there is much change ahead—is to align to potential, or the highest and the best that you might claim or perceive. Now, *highest* and *best* codify as well. That is why the man faltered when he heard the words. But to say *highest* and *best* need not be dependent upon the old idea of highest and best—"the best house for me," "the best relationship for me"—but the idea of *highest* as being in the highest acceleration or highest in tone, and the idea of *best* simply meaning the highest that you can hold or even withstand. In an accelerated time the changes come so rapidly that what you have believed to be, or counted on being, may be removed before your eyes. If you don't know what to expect, you may be open to something higher, but nearly all of you would seek to replicate the old. "Well, we must have a new president or a new government that must look like the old one." The idea of governments, highly useful in most ways, has been so cemented in fear and the misuse of power that you distrust the whole idea. To come to a new idea of what it means to be governed comes with a belief in trust or the trustworthy. And what is only trustworthy—and we underline *only*—is what is true.

Now, what is true is always true. And if you rest your attentions on an idea of leadership born in personality —"Well, I like his look," "I like how she speaks," "how she dresses," or even "how he or she voted"—you are deciding in advance that the one that you would vote for would replicate your idea of who she should be. Well, what else are you to do, you may ask. We will encourage you now, in the most simple way, to rely on truth, not the truth that you were told, but the truth that you may perceive or recognize at the level of truth that you can align to. This is far more easy than you think. You are so busy deciding what should be that you refuse to see what is. You are so busy listening for what you want that you don't know who is telling the truth. This is less about leadership than how you operate as an individual in a common field that is being moved to a new level of choice.

"What does that mean?" he asks. Well, a higher level of choice, if you wish. If all you have to choose from is what you have known prior, you will continue to choose the old even when the old clearly no longer serves you. But you are dependent upon the known. "The food should come from the market," "the milk not from the cow but the carton," or even the idea that the milk should be from the cow would limit your perspective on what you may know. To realize the new, which simply means to know it, is to claim a relationship to it. And to claim a relationship with what you have not known or yet realized feels impossible to you. But, indeed, it is not. Any new thought is breaking the rules. Any truly inspired thought is breaking the rules or moving you beyond a status quo. You look to solutions. "We must work out the wedding or there can be no wedding." "We must work out the relationship or the relationship will end." And you look at these things in simple ways without investigating them. "What is the trial with my friend offering?" "What is the marriage offering?" "Why do we need to call it a marriage?" "What is this relationship offering, or what is it asking to become?" When you seek the new and you create the room for it, which simply means you are releasing your obligation to the old, you allow the new to be made in form.

"What does that mean?" he asks. Well, everything is first an idea. The clothes on your back, an idea. Government, an idea. President, idea. Illness, idea. Weather, idea. All of these things are ideas known in form. And there is not one idea ever known that cannot be re-known without the limitations you have accrued collectively through the common field and language. Now, language is used to describe. "Those terrible winds." "That terrible fire." And you make these things so, and you confirm them. But you don't understand that all of these things, in all ways, are replications of ideas that you've known historically that will be rendered again and again until you move beyond the system that has originally created them. You may make something in form and you may outgrow it. You no longer need that dress that you sewed so well. It no longer fits you. Well, perhaps you no longer need the ideas, or the trage-dies known through idea, that the collective has utilized to de-velop through. Underline the word *develop*. It is all opportunity, finally. All catastrophe—if you wish to use that word—is, is an abrupt shift in a status quo that causes harm, renders harm, and claims a new relationship with reality. When one is rendered new, one is known anew. When one knows anew, the percep-tion one holds does not hold the bias of history, or the literal ideas, the idea of black and white or good and bad, that you have been reared with. When something simply is—underline the word *is*—you may have a relationship with it in a new way. When it is claimed by language, it is actually weighted by the language.

"What does that mean?" he asks. Well, anything that was ever called *awful* claims *awful* as a word. The word is a remnant of a past relationship with *awful, awful* being the descriptor for it. When something simply is—neither awful or good, but simply is—you may actually move it because when it is not holding language it is malleable to a new potential. Imagine a teacup once made of clay. The teacup has been fired, it has been glazed, it is easily chipped. But it was once clay, not a teacup at all, and in its malleable state it can become something other. If you think of thought and language this way you will benefit.

Now, we must interrupt Paul, who is in the background com-plaining. "When something is awful, it's awful. A catastrophe is a catastrophe." What you know of as *catastrophe,* yes. But you actually claim these things, or co-create them, in the manifest plane through expectation. This means something very simple. You've known yourselves through difficult circumstances for so very long that the claim of them in the manifest world will show itself again and again. Imagine a leaf blowing from a tree—"well, it must be fall"—and then all the leaves come in the expectation of what fall must look like.

The trajectory that humanity is on now is going to require great re-creation, or re-seeing or re-knowing, of what was once claimed in fear. We have said this forever. Humanity is at a time of reckoning, and a reckoning is the facing of oneself and all of one's creations. The individual undergoes this. Many of you undergo this now. But the collective also undergoes this. If you don't attend to the weather and the reason for the weather you will have more disaster. It can become opportunity. When you stop pointing fingers and become responsible for one's consciousness and how one contributes to the whole you become an accessory to good. "What does that mean?" he asks. Well, if ten of you decide something, you have made it so. But if fifty of you decide something, perhaps you have changed what the first ten thought. When reality is realized as malleable to structure, because structure is form and form is the product of thought, the changes can be vast and quick, and we will finally say beneficial.

The challenge of the times you sit in now is that they are transitional. Imagine you are on a dance floor. You have been dancing to one rhythm. The music has been changed. But you don't yet know how to dance to the new rhythm. You are not used to it. It is clumsy and awkward, not what you would choose. But as you begin to move with it, it not only makes sense, but there is a level of coherence that you are able to align to, far more fluid than what you knew prior. You don't realize how dense the field has been that you have been operative through.

We will explain this for you. Imagine you live in a country where every step you take is like slogging through mud. Imagine every step you take is an arduous step, but you have become so used to it that you cannot imagine anything other. That is our perception, in most ways, of the landscape you abide in. You do very well with it. Now, you hold bodies, and the bodies hold density, and the reality you know is in support of the bodies you have taken. As the body grows less dense, which is occurring now, the fluidity of movement—and we mean energetic movement—is far more than you've known. And by that we simply mean you will begin to recognize this, and how quickly thought manifests as you move to the higher. The density of the field you have known yourselves through makes creative thought challenging.

Now, some of you want to make it so in the moment. "I thought of the wine, there was wine." "I thought of a lover, there was the lover." Now, there are levels of reality where manifestation is that rapid, but that is not this plane. Even as you lift to the higher, maintaining form requires a level of density. But manifestation occurs much more rapidly as you become accustomed to the higher tone, and *the higher tone* simply meaning the vibrational field that the planet holds that you are moving into an alignment with and supporting the alignment. The question for some of you is: "Do I get what I want? Why do I bother with this? If I don't get what I want, what is the point of this teaching?" Well, it is the small self that demands this, as we have often said. But what you don't understand is that you are all party to these changes. Even your resistance to these changes is playing out in a common field. And the vibrational field that you hold is always in co-resonance with the common field. It is always so.

Now, when one lifts to what we call the Upper Room, one shifts vibration. And the shifting that occurs in the Upper Room—a progression, if you wish, to maintain a level of alignment that exists with and beyond the common field—will support your claims and how you may alter the world through your presence. But if you think that this is a selfish act you have misunderstood this teaching in its entirety. There is great benefit in these teachings. There is joy to be discovered. There is tremendous wonder. And there is the gift of grace wherein you may receive what you require as you open to it and stop trying to commandeer the upper realm as if it is a department store that's supposed to get you what you want. When you become receptive and you become willing to be in receipt of what is already yours—understand this: *already yours*—you are able to receive and claim the experience of the Kingdom. Again, the Kingdom being the inherent divinity that is present in all things.

Codification of form and the utilization of language to maintain is what we will be discussing now. You utilize language well. "I will have cream in my coffee." "I will take this vow or that." If you wish to have a vow, you may do it as you claim. But everything spoken is a claim, and in some ways a vow. "I am an angry man" claims identity in anger. "Those terrible people" claims the people as terrible. "That awful thing" mandates the event as awful. Everyone grows through everything. This is not the only life you've lived, and perhaps not even the only life you are living now. Your idea of a life lived, known through form, claims itself in limitation. You don't understand that the gift of being includes the idea of death, or perhaps illness, because you may grow and learn through these altercations with reality. However, when you no longer need them to accelerate the field or to claim change, you will find easier ways—more comfortable ways, perhaps—to know the world anew. It is sometimes not until a building is razed that you understand the poison that was built in the building. Sometimes you don't understand until the marriage ended how horrible that marriage was to both parties. You don't understand yet, because you are so attached to what was, that the gift of the new comes, indeed, at the cost of the old.

Now, some of you will say, "Well, let it be nice." But even your idea of *nice* tends to be rendered as painless or without discomfort. Your desire for comfortability—"it should be as it was"—has in some ways gotten you into the situations that you find yourselves in. "We won't care about the planet." "We won't care about the well-being of those who have less." "We will continue to incarcerate people in systems that support oppression and inequality." You continue these things and you look away because you don't wish to see. "I don't want to lower my vibration by watching the news." How do you know where the help is needed unless you are aware? You are not in bubbles. You are your brother's keeper, and you share this planet, or your idea of world, and it is of benefit to you to learn how to maintain it. This is not an act of selfishness as much as self-preservation. And the self that is being preserved is the collective, and in fact it is the collective that has decided to grow because indeed it must in order to survive.

A world made new is not necessarily a pretty world. But

we will say it is a perfect world. And by *perfect* we mean what is required *must* be required for humanity to take its next step. The text we invoke now is less a primer of this than an illustration of it, and an instruction manual of how you may begin to shift not only the consciousness you see out-pictured before you, but all the things that contribute to that field, to that manifest world—what you have known of in form and language.

We will complete this teaching for this night. We will say to the man in the chair this is the beginning of the second chapter. We will continue tomorrow as we wish. Thank you each for your presence. Stop now, please. Period. Period. Period.

DAY TEN

What stands before you today, in an awakened state, is the recognition that how you have chosen has claimed a life for you. How you've integrated the information, the basis of past choice, and the ramifications of choice, claim a character for you, or how you know yourselves in consort with others in the world.

The realization of who you are—"I know who I am in truth"—has been discussed prior, but we will continue now in a somewhat different manner. Realization comes at a cost, the ideas you would hold that would procure your idea of self or small self in tandem with others. Realization claims you beyond the obligations that you would have incurred through fear or through guilt through an identification with a prior moral structure. To realize who and what you've always been must mean that you realize what you are not. And if what you think you want to be is no longer in service to you, you may seek to cling to it out of a need for the known, or a relationship that was based in prior construct.

Now, today we sit before you with one bias and one deep intention: that the teachings that we give you may be met by you in willingness, the willingness to surrender to them at the level of possibility. When we teach in possibility, we comprehend the resistance the channel has, and many of the students do as well. But when we teach in possibility, we are actually expanding you beyond the old bias you have used, the ways of delineating a reality through the common field born in past architecture. *Architecture,* again. A word that is important in this volume. Everything is built in one way or another, constructed in one way or another. At the level of identity, at the level of vibration, everything operates as a construct. Once something is claimed in form, you have a relationship to the form and the name you have given it. Once you understand yourselves beyond the bias of the personality structure, there is indeed another form that takes place. You are not ephemeral. You are in form. You have a bias in form. "If I touch this thing, I expect to understand it through touch. If I smell this thing, I anticipate understanding it through smell." You have the senses. They offer a window to shared reality. "We all see the building. We all hear the sound. We all feel the wave upon our skin. We all smell the fire or the smoke from the fire as it burns." You have a reality born in a common field that you know through the senses. And the senses are of you, but are currently operating in a very limited way. When you expand to the True Self, the senses themselves become activated in a higher template. Now, by *template* we mean a way of being formed. A template holds a form. And as you move to the Upper Room as a vibrational being, and as you withstand the changes in the construct of identity that you must pass through, you are actually met by yourselves at a higher level of tonality than you have utilized thus far.

Now, imagine you didn't know who you were. You had an inkling of it, perhaps did the best you knew how through the construct you've been offered. But the page is turned and suddenly you don't know the language, or you don't know the capacity that you actually hold. Reconstruction in the higher Upper Room, or the higher template, is a process that the physical body undergoes. We will explain this for Paul, who is confused. When you lift to the level of tone that the Upper Room holds, manifestation is altered. The obligations you held in the lower self, including the personality structure, are actually released. But you cling to them because you think you should, or you expect they must be there because how could you be other? The ramifications of choice, as you have known choice, surround you now. And realization comes as you release the need to mandate through the old, to decide with the old template, or conjure through the old identification what you think could be, because it was once prior possibility. Possibility is before you now at a much higher level than you know.

Now, the body itself will undergo changes as you integrate the higher tone. And if you have habituated behaviors of any kind that no longer serve you, you will be met by them and the discomfort that they bring. If you have relationships that are not supporting your growth, you must reassess yourself in agreement to those relationships. The relationships may be useful, but how you have known yourselves through them may indeed be outgrown. To realize who you have become—

underline the word *become*—in an awakened state, or realized state, mandates the old has been gone. The one who is still half asleep is still operating in half a dream. How is one awakened while in form, but by knowing who and what she is and knowing who others are as well. The relationship you have to manifest reality in every way is a product of the past. What waits before you now, in tandem with high choice, high regard, high agreement, is what can be known—underline the word *can*—by the one who knows who she is. *Knows* means realize, yes.

Now, some of you say to us, "It cannot be so. We cannot change so quickly, so fast. The world will not change so quickly." We are here to tell you, yet again, that it has already occurred. But you are living in a shadow of what was—half asleep, if you wish, half in a dream state. You remember what was, yesterday, so you perceive it today. But in fact what is, today, has been altered greatly. And the recognition of this not only comes in time, it comes in the immediacy of time when you stop relying on time to be the barometer of your experience. When you move to the eternal now, what was held in shadow is lifted to light. When you know yourself in the present moment, you know yourself in eternity beyond the form you have taken.

Now, the form you have taken may be present, but it is not limiting you in the old ways. The manifestation of the Monad or the Christ Truth in participation to a physical reality renders the world new, maintains the newness through the level of tone that is being sung through you—not just you singularly, but singularly as all. The all as one, or the one as all. The Christ does not favor one over the next, and the Monad is implicit in each of you. The reluctance to claim this, the fear that it could never be yours, will never be held in love as and for you, must be understood as a product of past teaching or a past legacy of fear—the claim of separation yet again. "We have been expelled from the garden. We will never find our way back. Perhaps when we die we will have a glimmer of it. Perhaps we will be reunited with Source, but never in this gross flesh." The mandate of the gross flesh, the gross physical reality, the dense field in condemnation of itself, is a great act of damnation. And as we always say, what and who you damn will always damn you back. Until the body is lifted as the full expression of the Divine, a simple manifestation no more or less glorious than a flower or a sunset, you will deny the Divine in your senses and in your physical experience. The resplendency that awaits you, which is the light that shines through all things, that illumines all things, can be experienced through the senses, and the heart itself becomes the primary sense.

"What does that mean?" he asks. Well, when the heart is fully active, it actually holds all things. The vibration that the heart emits at the level of the Christ as manifest reclaims the senses themselves. When you think of the senses as independent from the Divine, you will seek to improve your hearing, develop your clairvoyance, as if these are things that are outside yourselves that can be fitted like a shoe at the cobbler. In fact, all of these things are expressions of the Divine operating in very simple stages of realization. The one who has second sight in the manifestation they hold may have developed it in a prior lifetime, may have claimed it through an experience where it was a mandate. How he or she survived was to realize what was unseen. But to lift to the level where these become apparent and present for each of you is what we are actually

instructing you in. When you think the mystic is someone special, the one with special abilities, must be favored, you confuse
an issue that's really very simple. The senses aligned in a higher
octave produce a different experience of vibration. And your
telling the self what should be, through the old template—
which is what you all do—will simply diminish what is already present and awaiting your grace, awaiting your presence
within it.

"Grace us with your presence" might be well said now in
equivalency. To be graced, to be in presence, to align in the
Upper Room, and the receptor or the recipient of what expresses here, is not a high act of being as much as expression
in expression. "What does that mean?" he asks. Well, the being that you are is in expression at every level of tone, in your
fury or fear or in your awakened state. The expression that you
emit, which is actually your experience of being—expression
and being work in conjunct expression together—the alignment that you may hold will actually refute what was claimed
in the lower field. The lower expression is diminished and then
finally falls away. Paul sees the image of a snake shedding its
skin, and this is somewhat like that because all that is being
released is that which has hindered your expression.

Now, linear time, as you utilize it, is very handy and is useful and a construct of the lower field. It has less merit when
you move to the Upper Room and you begin to realize simultaneity. Now, what simultaneity is, quite very simply, is the
expression of the manifest Divine that is all happening now.
The senses aren't seeking to delineate where the smell is coming from, what the touch is of, what is being tasted, as much as
having the full experience of being in light, and in agreement

to light, and all the things we just described were expressions of the light known as form. The soup is of God, the sunset of God, the touch of the lover of God, all things expressed as of God. Your relationship to being does not preclude your walking to the store, giving the baby the bottle, reading a good book. It enhances them at a level you cannot yet imagine because what you have come to is a relationship with being, with form and expression, at a level of acceleration that does not deny the Divine. It is so simple, really.

So much of what you do now, how you perceive, how you claim, is born in the supposition that you are separate from your Source. This has never been so, but it has been the equation you have operated in. And you have built an architecture, a way of being in relationship to Source, with walls and barriers that you have sought to erect, born in fear or belief that you were unworthy. What we do in these texts, one at a time, is move you beyond the old creations so that you may support yourself in a full claim—full claim—of expression. Now, by *full* we mean mandate of the Monad which is not limited. The small self operates in limitation. The Monad does not because it cannot. While form is maintained, Monad exists beyond form, or Christ is not dependent on having a body to be expressed. That's a foolish idea. "Christ came in a body once upon a time. Let's wait around and see if he comes back." What if he was already here, but he was the *it*, the perfect expression of the Monad that can be incarnated, seeks incarnation and realization and expression through each and every one of you. This does not make you special. It just makes you loved. The gift of the Christ was always resurrection. But the resurrection of the Monad or the Christ as form does not preclude your identification with a mortal life. Christ came in form. You are in form. Christ comes as each of you as you awaken to its promise.

Now, the limitations you would utilize upon even the idea of the Christ are born in old legacy. It must look a certain way, be perceived by others in a certain way, resemble some scripture from some time. Consciousness is not in form, but it may come as form because all things are consciousness. To understand this quite simply means that there are levels of tone in decreasing density. The higher you lift, the less density there is. The higher the tone, the less requirement for form. As we have always said, Christ consciousness is the highest level one may attain while maintaining a body. To realize this, or to know this as so, is to comprehend the self first as worthy, and then see it as a possibility.

Now, we are not seeking to have people running to the nut-house announcing themselves as the Second Coming. There has been too much of that. If *you* are, so is the one beside you, and the one beside them. But to understand what this means is that you are incarnating as you truly have been, not through the requirements or the mandates of the personality structure that are actually being moved to make way for the new that is seeking to be born through you.

Now, you all want the senses to amplify, and you actually want this for the wrong reason. "Let me have a glimpse of the eternal, and please let me be the first one in line for this lovely experience." What actually occurs is so muted at the beginning that you won't even notice that it is passing through you. It will be a glimmer, a refocusing of the eyes, an accelerated sense of touch and smell, as things begin to unveil. And indeed there is an unveiling that occurs, first in stages because the mind that you hold must align to its potential or the possibility that awaits it. To claim too much at once would simply overload the senses and you would shut them down, go find a nice cave to sit in, and wait for the weather to change. What will actually occur will be happening through you, and as you can hold it. And the amplification of the senses will be addressed in this text later on as we continue. But to understand now that the Monad does not hold the limitations that have been prescribed for you gives you permission to say the following words. We will invoke this. You may speak them whenever you wish:

> *"On this day I claim that the realization of who and what I am may be known by me as I can hold it at the level of amplitude that I may trust and claim in my being. As I say yes to this, I surrender to the process that I am invoking. And as I say yes to this, I surrender my need to control the outcome, to have it be what I think it should be. And as I say yes, I allow the fullness of my expression to be expressed beyond my small self's sense of what is possible, what can be known and claimed. And I say yes to all that is before me. I am Word through this intention. Word I am Word."*

Now, when we speak through Paul, we listen to him and we calibrate his field so that the transmission will be clear. We are pleased with his progress today, but we will invite all of you to be present in a different way for this dictation than you may think you are. You listen intently, or you read intently. We invite you now to experience this first as sound and then as light. When we sing through Paul, we are going to open the world, or the world that you've known yourselves in, to a level of tone that you may vibrate with. To vibrate with this tone is to be in an accelerated light, or light in an accelerated state, that you may begin to experience in form. All that is required now is that you say yes. And as you say yes, we will meet you as we are allowed.

On the count of three, Paul.

Now one. Now two. Now three.

[The Guides tone through Paul.]

Allow the light that you are to be received by all the light that is. Allow the acquiescence of the self you thought you were to the self you can only be in truth. And as you say yes, as you align, be lifted, be graced, be received, and be known anew.

Blessings to you each. Stop now, please. In the text, yes.

(PAUSE)

What stands before you today, in an awakened state, is recognition of what you are not. "I am not only the body." But the body itself, an expression of the Divine, is in a process of calibration to assimilate a higher level of tone or velocity than it has withstood thus far. This is happening to all, and how the integration occurs is somewhat chaotic. When you don't know you are in a whirlpool, you wonder why you are getting thrown to and fro. When you don't know you are in a windstorm, you don't know why things are flying by you. To understand yourself today, or to comprehend where you stand, is to understand that change is eternal. It comes at different degrees at different times. And where you stand as a culture, as a species, as humanity itself, is at a doorway that you are passing through to a higher expression.

Now, *higher expression,* as we speak it, means finer or more refined—not better, as many of you would wish. You still have character. You still have lessons to learn. But the refined state of expression is actually a distillation of who you truly are without the dross covering you. Now, the True Self, its expression, is perfection. But because you maintain form—and, consequently, legacy that form holds—you are still at a level of dense vibration, and will continue to be so even in refinement. While the Upper Room holds promise, it is not an escape from your past. The Upper Room does not hold escape. It is love. And if you are escaping something, you are running from it. This is a time to face one's creations, to stare at them plainly, to recognize how you participate in the structures that are before you. How do you participate in structure? In every way you can imagine. You herald the needs of the clock, of the calendar, of business, of education, of law, of medicine. You are aligned to all these things, and many of these things support you in fine ways. But when they become restrictive, or create obligation for who one should be, they do not serve. And much of what occurs now at this stage of refinement is a release of what does not serve. But you don't release what does not serve until you recognize it.

Now, the fear of change is present for all of you at all times. You don't want to leave the known because you don't trust that what awaits for you may be brighter, may be calmer, may be more beneficial. You would prefer the old pain than the uncertainty of the new. "What if it's worse?" "What if we all perish?" "What if the world does not survive?" Humanity has chosen to survive, and that is the best news of the day. And the bad news is you are still accountable to your creations. Now, we say *bad* only in that it's what you don't want, but it is a necessity. The child that plays with matches will one day burn down the house. To understand that you've given the child the matches, told him how to strike them, makes you accountable to the choice made. When you have a world where bombs are built, and you support the building of bombs—because why wouldn't you when the money you pay taxes for is claiming weaponry—you contribute to the structure. When you have mandates of worth based in race or economic status, you have a difficulty that will not be fixed or claimed anew until it is faced. The opportunity is to face, is to see, is to reclaim. And by *reclamation* we mean claiming it anew.

Now, Paul interrupts. "Well, I heard the list you just gave, and I cannot imagine how saying, 'Behold, I make all things new,' will support any of this." Then you are missing the teaching entirely, Paul, and we will tell you why. The aspect of you that perceives and makes the claim "Behold, I make all things new" is not the child who is confused, and not the young adult who seeks retaliation. It is the Divine Self who simply knows. The claim "Behold, I make all things new," in expression as the Divine Self, is what claims the manifest world in the higher octave. To understand this is to experience it, and you will not experience this until you utilize it. Now, you understand the teachings, Paul, better than you think, but do you utilize them fully? No. Imagine standing in the sunset and witnessing God every day for five minutes—a small task, if you would like to put it that way, but a highly beneficial one. Perhaps what you require is the evidence of the teachings we bring through you, and indeed they are there in manifest ways when you say yes to them. This is true for all our students. We have not given you an intellectual treatise. We have given you an experiential teaching of manifestation that is present for you now.

The very first attunement we offered through the man before you many years ago—"I am Word through my body, Word I am Word"—holds the genesis for all that has followed. The Word is the energy of the Creator in action, and aligning at this level and knowing who you are at this level of vibration and tone actually alters the manifest world. And *alters* is the perfect word. Transforms and changes. Not fixes or improves. Transforms and changes. The fundamental architecture of all manifestation is the one note sung. You may call that God or the Word. The infinite action. The Divine as expression. *The Divine as expression* simply means what expresses as and through you that is of the whole.

Now, the truth of your being is not what any of you wish. You wish the pedigree, or the place in your culture, or your needs met as you wish. But imagine you are a woodwind instrument, and the note blowing through you, the sound coming through you, is the expression of perfection. The woodwind may have flaws, may still improve, be refined, but the wind that blows through it, the perfect wind that is God, needs no improvement. It simply requires the vessel to express through, and that is indeed all of you. As you create the chaos in your out-pictured world through all the reasons we have given you thus far—denial of the Divine, the action of fear claiming more fear—as you realize how you've participated in the manifest world, you are given the great privilege of re-seeing your accountability as opportunity. To be accountable is not to be burdened. It is to be offered an opportunity. And the relationship you hold with the manifest world is about to change through the teachings we offer you.

The texts we have offered you, all in manifestation, come to an end in this text. The trilogy will complete and we will say this: not without cost. The cost of your relationship to form, what you think form is, must now be understood fully. If you touch the clothing you wear, if you touch the hair on your head, you have an experience of what is manifest. But if you wave your hand in the air and you experience what you believe is unmanifest you must also understand that air is manifestation, as is light. What you comprehend as form is simply a lower vibration.

Now, language has been discussed briefly, but when something is named it is codified and it becomes in common usage. You all know what a chair is. You have a name for *chair* in every language. That's a fine word to have. But it's also a limiting word. Anything that can be sat upon can be called a chair, but anything that can be lifted cannot be called a chair. "What does that mean?" he says. Well, the properties of what you've given name to in some ways condemn it to its architecture— what a house should be or a chair should be or a body itself should be. The body as architecture. Now, the simple claim we've offered prior—"I know what I am in truth," the manifest Divine as form—is inclusive of the perfection that exists now in each and every one of you, beyond what you think of your body or how it is operating, because the Source of the body is perfection. What makes God, God—whatever that is—is also what makes the body, the body. So to deny the body as God is to deny God itself. To realize form as of God does not make the body God. It simply allows the body to be its expression in a higher expression than you have previously known. Again, the woodwind instrument that the wind blows through. As the body is refined to hold the higher expression, the woodwind instrument, the body itself, takes on the properties that can support it. Each and every attunement we have offered you has actually been in support of this—not self-improvement, but the application of the body, the energetic field, and identity itself to be in service to higher expression, the Monad expressed as you. The vehicle that you operate with that you complain about every day—"oh my bad leg," "oh my bad breath," "my bad hearing," name it, if you wish—the body is simply the body. But the body is beyond the body you've known. It is the expression of God, and as it is re-seen and re-known it begins to express properties that have been denied it, therefore, prior.

We will say this: When Paul is interrupted by sound, he gets anxious about what he hears and we must work over him so this does not occur while we dictate.

Each of you before us is undergoing a process of recalibration through presence and being. The octave we sing at when we teach through Paul is actually shifting the field you hold, and as the field is shifted the body moves to acclimation with it. The acclimation to the higher octave, inclusive of the senses, must now be understood as not only the prerequisite for what follows, but part of what occurs through your engagement with these teachings. We have honored the body in prior texts. We have spoken directly to the body as form. But now we are speaking to the body as expression in a somewhat different

way. If the vibration the body holds moves to a level of alignment where it can be lifted in full tone, its amplification will
actually alter the forms you encounter through presence and
being and a level of coherence that you could not attain prior.
The invocation is a simple one: "I know what I am in truth."
And the what that you are, the manifest what in truth, will not
hold the level of distortion that the lower field claims through
acclimation to the ideas that you've held through the collective about what a body should do or be. This doesn't mean you
don't have a liver or lungs. It simply means that how you realize
liver and lungs, how you realize skin and form itself, is actually
shifted to a level of alignment where you may be in service in a
higher expression. Higher expression. More refined expression.
Again, the woodwind instrument playing the notes that will
sing the world into being. A world made new. A world sung
into being.

Each of you before us today, each of you who hears these
words, is undergoing a process of re-relationship to body and
form—the form you have taken, and then, by extension, the
form of all things. Everything made new. "Behold, I make all
things new," the claim of the Divine in transition. Form itself known as of Source. Underline the word *of*. All things *of*
Source. The benefit of this is not *better*. It is benefit in refinement, or a clear, clean calibration of tone and vibration without holding the detritus of past choice, past residue, and past
meaning. The meaning things are given anything hold them or
weight them at a level of tone that is difficult to alter because it
applies itself to the density that it has claimed prior.

Imagine a brick that is covered again and again and again
and again and again with soot. It becomes dense and you forget

that the brick was ever there. When you appliqué meaning and you appliqué choice and you appliqué what it was supposed to be, once upon a time, to the meaning of brick, brick becomes an article of form and it lacks its true nature, which is the Divine come as brick. "What does that mean?" he asks. Well, the idea of brick—which is simply earth in a mold, and earth is simply the Divine as earth—can be reclaimed in many forms. But the brick that we just described, meant for building the house, throwing through the window—whatever you would use the brick for—has claimed its density and its meaning and will not be re-seen until it is crushed into dust and then seen and known as something else.

Some of you decide that this teaching is love, and you confuse yourselves to think that all love is, is sweetness and light. All love is, finally, is Source expressing, and Source accepts all things equally. Source does not deny anyone its benefit. You deny the benefit that is your birthright. To understand this in fullness is to simply understand that the Divine loves all equally. But love is not a flower or a heart-shaped box of chocolates. Love is the action of the Divine in expression, and the knowing of all in love is the experience of being in the Upper Room. Period. Period. Period. Stop now, please. This is in the text.

(PAUSE)

What stands before you today, in an awakened state, is recognition not only of the past, how you've participated in past actions, but what may lie before you in an altered state, an altered recognition of who you truly are. The one that's condemned another has learned through condemnation. He has learned the hard lessons of refusing the Divine and invoked the response that always comes. The one who has moved beyond that moves to a recognition of accountability to present action. "How can I be present in the highest way I may know?" And, again, we use *highest* to mean refined—the most refined expression, the less obstructed, the least dense response that you may hold.

Now, we don't make density wrong. We simply call it interference at this point, for the true expression as you in its full amplitude can actually claim interference, the straggling thought, the confused idea, in Higher Mind through recognition. Each time you have an experience of putting another outside the Divine, you will understand yourself through that. And instead of complaining, or suggesting that you can't hold the higher, perhaps recognize that you are being instructed in where the small self seeks to commandeer the Upper Room and the amplitude that exists here. We never make you wrong. You may choose what you wish and learn through what you claim. But we do offer the opportunity to recognize yourselves beyond the old, and again the old structures that would keep in abeyance or continue to deny your true inheritance, which is indeed the Kingdom.

Now, the recognition of the Kingdom comes in stages. But the amplitude you hold now, each of you here, each of you who experience these words—underline the word *experience*—can claim this at a level you are not aware of yet. Recognition comes in stages, yes. But once you are aware of the light in the room, even the dimmest light, the light will grow by your attention. What you give attention to will always increase. And if it is the higher, that will become your experience. Realization comes at the cost of the old, the old way of being, the old identity. But the new seeks to be presented in a way that you may know as well, and recognize as your own. Underline *own*. There is a claim of ownership at this level, not as owning property or owning something in your possession, but owning experience. And to be gratified by what you experience is to claim ownership of it.

When you deny something, deny the Divine in something, you are also claiming ownership, and you are aligning to that level of tone and what it will wreak upon your experience. To love another is not only to forgive him, but to be aware of who he is beyond the behavior that elicits the harsh response, to know who he is in love beyond what you would claim for him or have him be for you. The choice that is made at this level of tone is always in participation with one's true nature. And one's true nature exists without slight, exists without frustration, exists without the need to be right at the cost of another being wrong.

Now, to understand us, and where we sit as vibration, is to comprehend yourselves in an altered state. We have often said we are who you become when you truly know who you are, or realize the self as Monad. Melchizedek as order is of the Christ Self and cannot be other. So we come as the True Self, explicitly and fundamentally as the manifest Divine, through a tone that is somewhat singular and always inclusive. We make this distinction for those of you who would have us be somewhat other, be something other, as you would prescribe meaning. We require no meaning to be who and what we are—emanation and tone, consciousness, if you wish, claiming language for your instruction. We exist for you at this level, although we

exist beyond this need to serve as instructor. We actually hold
the world at a level of tone that the world aligns to. And we
do this not as Melchizedek, but as Christ, or the essence of the
Christ consciousness that may be known in different names.

Now, we have said prior: To name something is generally to
reduce it. You want to know the name of the building so that
you can find your way there, the name of the object so that you
can purchase it. But to exist beyond names is not to exist in an
arbitrary strata. It's to exist in a plane where meaning has not
been endowed through the old structure. You may use a spoon
if you require a spoon, but all that you really need is something
to lift the soup to your lips, whatever you may wish to call that.
And perhaps you understand at a certain level of tone that there
is no utensil needed. You have been entrained to believe that
that is how the soup travels to you. Once you understand that
vibration holds all things already and you are not trying to conjure, the act of recognition of what vibration is and how manifestation occurs becomes far more easy than you know.

Now, you understand the idea of the Word made flesh.
That is an old teaching, but has been somewhat misconstrued
through doctrine and past history. Heretical texts have often
taught that the Monad expresses through all, and these teachings were suppressed at different times lest the lineage of a
pope or a church be interrupted by those discovering their
own inheritance. And when we say this, we are not condemn-
ing. We are speaking of events and doctrines and tribunals that
were seeking to organize experience of the collective through a
system that was useful in some ways, beneficial in some ways,
but ultimately, we would have to say, limiting in all ways because it stops with a ceiling before realization can occur. Why

would that be? Because if you were truly realized, you would have no requirement for doctrine, or even religion.

Now, religion exists for reasons. But a system is useful only for a level of passage that the system can hold and support. We would have to say any religion that stops before you incarnate as the vibration of the Divine Self is operating in limitation. Now, we would suggest that there have been those throughout time who've come quite close to realization, in form and consciousness both. And these human beings may be known in different ways. But they are rarely parading themselves before the public. Their personage has no requirement of such acts. And most of them were still, and operating in knowing, for the benefit of the collective as the collective could be re-known at that level. Any great jump of experience that the collective has undergone has been the result of such things. And the jump that is being experienced now—and we are using that term intentionally, *the jump that is being experienced*—must be understood as an act of the collective in the consciousness that is being brought to the collective through those who recognize the requirement for it.

Now, some of you say, "Let that be me." It may not be you at all. It may be the young child that perceives the world differently, that is not operating in the limitations that you have grown with. It may be the one reading a book who holds a new idea that she has never thought possible that can conjure the new or claim a relationship to the new that can then be born in form. But what is true—as you are the woodwind instruments that the spirit is blowing through, and the music that you sing is claiming all that it encounters to it—is that the manifest world is undergoing great change, a great step forward in recognition. And the dismantling of old is always party to a great step forward. You cannot hold the old while reaching for the new. You must release what you hold to claim the good that indeed awaits you.

Now, some of you would say, "Well, it's too late. We have done too much harm. We will come to a bad end." Be cautious of what you wish for. You may claim that, if you wish. And those of you who say humanity is doomed are actually claiming that in vibrational accord, yet another possibility that you may know yourselves through. Everything that you choose becomes opportunity to know yourself through that choice. "I chose to go to this place, encounter myself in this place, with these people through this occurrence." All things choice.

Now, you don't understand choice because you believe it to be conscious, but most of what you choose is informed by other things—past thought, accrued habit, the collective experience of what should be. Now, the ideas of what should be, as we have stated, are being released through these times out of necessity so that the new may be born. And the consciousness that you hold is being altered to attend to this in substantial ways. And by that we mean it's not like you're changing seats on an airplane. You are still going where you were, but where the airplane is going is radically different than you expected it to go. And imagine that. The journeys you have planned for yourselves in this shared collective experience are taking you somewhere else. "Will we know this?" Paul asks. "This seems like conjecture to me." In fact, it is not conjecture in the least. The coming decade will hold more change than humanity has experienced in thousands of years. And the rapidity of change is going to be the greatest challenge because your minds cannot hold what you have not yet known, which is why we began this chapter instructing you in possibility. "It can be possible. I may know the new."

Now, the new may not be what you would choose or would default to if you had any choice at all. But it may be what is required for these next steps to occur. Imagine you had to walk through coal to get to the green valley. Imagine you had to walk through earth to bathe in the sea. It is such as this. And as it occurs, your comprehension of the journey you are undertaking is not only made clear by your acts, but where you find yourself arriving to—far less a place and much more so a level of tone. And again, the level of tone you claim calls an altered reality to it.

Now, some of you believe an altered reality should coexist as you say, but it does in fact coexist and not nearly as you would think or what you would have it be. Every idea of a dimensional reality that you could ever conjure is existing simultaneously. As we say, we work through the radio before us. The radio that you are listening to is simply tuned into one dimension, one level of broadcast. But there are infinite levels that you may experience.

We recommend you choose wisely now because there is always temptation to claim the lower or the easier or the one that you think will give you what you wish and solve all your problems quickly. The trajectory of this teaching has always been the same: the manifestation of the Monad, or a level of alignment to the consciousness we hold, which is the consciousness you hold when indeed you know who you are. You cannot imagine a world without fear, and why should you be able to? You have never known it. You incarnated in a field where fear was so present even the bite of the apple has become tainted by a legacy of fear. True knowledge is dangerous. You cannot know yourselves as holy or you will be expelled from the garden. In fact, you must know yourselves as holy because without this you will live in a desolate field and you will claim in fear because you believe it to be your best option. It is not your best option. It is the least option.

Now, self-preservation need not be seen as fear. There is water rising, swim away. There is someone coming with an axe, perhaps best to move in the other direction. We would say that prudence isn't fear unless you wish it to be or claim it as something other. "I am choosing to be prudent when in fact I am frightened." But to understand what we mean by "the action of fear claims more fear" is really very simple. It always comes back to intent and why you choose as you choose. If you are choosing these teachings to save yourself from a fate that you believe you would befall without them, you are claiming in fear. If you are aligned to these teachings for the benefit that they offer you and the promise that they hold, that is perhaps well done. But your free will is invoked in this choice. And align the free will with the Monad or High Self as you claim it and you will benefit from that as well.

We spoke recently about the heart center invoking the senses or encompassing the senses. We wish to let you know what we mean by this. If you are operating in love, that does not disqualify you from holding discernment. When you operate in love, you are not in judgment, nor are you in fear. When you are not in judgment and fear, there is no impediment to the Divine, and your expression through the senses may be amplified through this choice: to align through the heart and align the senses in love through the heart center. This is the claim we would offer you. You may say this to yourself, please:

"On this day I choose to align my senses to the highest level that they may claim themselves through. I allow the heart to claim the senses in the high Upper Room and allow the senses to be made manifest at the level of tone that they may align to. I am Word through this intention. Word I am Word."

The degree of response you receive will always be in recognition of what you can hold and how it would be used. Again, intent comes into play. If you wish to use these gifts in self-serving ways, you will find this experience challenging. It may be done, but it will all be done at a lower level. To realize the high is to offer the senses to the high, and if you are offering this through the heart and from the heart and allowing the heart to do the work, the senses will come into play in love, and as a manifestation of such.

When we teach through the man before you, we recognize the limitations of his body and how long he may carry the tone of the spoken language we offer. We seek to continue a bit longer before we allow him to rest. We do this with his permission. But there are several things we wish to discuss while we have time with you. Each of you before us has an idea of who she is and what her capacity is, what level she may hold herself at. Each of you who decides these things in one way or another delineates an outline of your expectations and what they should look like. We would actually suggest now that you release the outline and you open it up to the possibilities that exist beyond your expectations, or your ideas of what can be. We recommend this for one reason. You would seek to replicate a heaven or an idea of self in a heaven that you have been conjuring through a relationship to history. "Where are the angels with the harps, where are the luminous orbs, the things I was taught to expect?" The relationship you hold to the idea of self will be what claims you in an alignment to any idea of heaven. So we are recommending now that you release the outline, the expectations that accompany the outline, and claim what is actually there.

"What does that mean?" he asks. When you know in truth, you are not seeking. You are receiving, and you are knowing in receipt. Imagine you have a pair of sunglasses. They limit the light. Perhaps the prescription is old. You see in distortion. To see in truth and to claim in truth is to claim what is always there, perhaps has always been there, but you've refuted through the false sight or through the distortion. To comprehend yourself as perceiving, and the one perceiving the inherent Divine, is to claim what is actually so. Underline *actually*. You are not making it so. You are being offered it. And you are in receipt of it as you say yes to it. Underline *as*. Not before or after, but *as*.

We say these words now for each of you. All who hear these words, all who speak these words, all who know the truth of these words, may be received by us at the level of amplitude they can hold:

> "*I have come to know myself in truth. I have come to receive myself in truth. I have come to benefit the world through my*

expression and through my agreement to presence and being. I know who I am in truth. I know what I am in truth. I know how I serve in truth. I am free. I am free. I am free."

Thank you each for your presence. We will take a pause for the man in the chair. Period. Period. Period. Stop now, please.

DAY ELEVEN

What stands before you today, in a realized state, is the recognition that how you have chosen has been informed by several things: the manifest world, your obligations to it, the sense of identity you have claimed within the common field, and an idea of history—what should be or what should be expected.

Now, the idea of self, which is being reclaimed here, the idea of being, in expression, which is being reclaimed here, is being supported in several ways through the teachings you receive. Recognition is key. "I see why I choose. I see why I made that choice and how I aligned to a life in expectations that were present for me prior to birth." But you must also understand, each and every one of you, that choice operates in different levels.

Now, the Monad or the Divine Self is the expressed self that operates beyond time and space, that knows itself in innocence and does not hold obligation, has never incurred karma. Now, the Monad itself, when it moves to full expression, acclimates will to be expressed in what we call the Upper Room. And when you choose in the Upper Room as the Monad, you are claiming first thought: I Am. The aspect of you that knows who she is, presence and being, holds no indoctrination, has no religion, no politics. He, she, it, simply is. At this level of expression, choice moves to alignment, and how you choose supports an idea of expression that few of you have known thus far. "What is this expression?" he asks. Well, to understand yourself without the rules or edicts of the structure of personality, of country, of obligation to an idea of species, is actually full liberation. While you hold form, you claim mandates through form, and the distinction we make here is that the freedom that you are incurring at the level of the Monad must be inclusive of form because you maintain form while operating in this incarnation.

Revelation, the new being revealed to you, occurs in several ways. When you choose in the Upper Room, you move into a state of recognition of what is only in truth. And the vibration you hold concurs this, confirms this, claims this, as it moves through you. Imagine a life where you were not second-guessing choice. Imagine a state of being where being known in and of Source was equivalent to your own knowing. "I am in my knowing. I am known." When your knowing is operative through will, the will is expressed in perfect ways. When the will is expressed through knowing, True Knowing, operating in a high way from what we call the Upper Room, there is little distinction between this way and that. There is only forward.

"What does that mean?" he asks. Well, you are operating as vibration, as a current of vibration, in a common field. The current of vibration that you are holding, in its operative state, is always in escalation because the Monad lifts. It is unsullied. It is unobstructed in its full state. And because it lifts, it calls all things to it and removes obstacles that would seek to stand in its way. This occurs very simply. When you are operating in knowing and choice, your requirements are different. You are not seeking to get your way, prove your point. You are in presence and being. And the acknowledgment of who and what you are is inclusive of all things that operate at the same level of tone. You have claimed the world in an altered manifestation, and you move through this world without the old obstructions.

"Can you explain what this means—*old obstructions?*" Well, everything that you create in fear holds a level of density. Fear is a dense vibration. When you lift to the Upper Room, you are not operating in that density. When you choose from the Upper Room, the I Am presence or the Monad as you is what invokes choice. The personality may assist. "I love the color blue. What a lovely sweater." "I love the sky. What a wonderful view." But the Monad operating as and through you accompanies you, and you are adhering in choice to what is always true. You may call it right action, but the challenge of that term is that it implies there is wrong action. And from the Upper Room, at the level of alignment we are speaking to, there is simply action, presence and being expressed in action.

Now, what action is, is actually movement. And we have often said that the Word is the energy of the Creator in action. As the Word, or expressed as Word, you become this action, and the manifestation of this action upon this world is what renders the world new—not your fixing, not your appealing for help, but presence and being. To operate at this level of vibration and tone in an aligned state of will does not mean you don't have choice. It simply means you've aligned at a level of choice where you are operating in knowing—capital "K" *Knowing*. Not the small self's inclination, not what you did yesterday, not your memory of what your friend liked and thought she should do, so you should, too. True Knowing. When True Knowing is operative, you are moving to Divine Mind and operating with and as expression of Divine Mind.

Now, what is available at this level? Far more than you can imagine. You seek information some days. You look outside the self for it. That's as it should be in many ways. You learn how to bake a cake by reading the recipe. Nothing wrong with learning. But knowing and learning are somewhat different. When one is realized in her knowing, one is directed in a clear way and she is aligning in truth and supporting the action of truth by presence and being. Imagine you were a light illumining a dark room. The light does not try to be the light. It simply is. What is illumined in this dark room are the very things that have been held in shadow that must be released. And you may acclimate to this process. "I enter the room. I am a bright light. The darkness flees." You are not making the darkness wrong. You are bringing light to the darkness—not in retribution, not to correct, but to reveal and recognize.

Now, all things are of God, high, low, and in between. So to be the light, to operate in one's knowing, is to bring knowing, or True Knowing, to any circumstance. And by *circumstance* we mean you are not getting things right, deciding what should be, or telling people what to do. You are operating at a level of tone where recognition becomes possible for others. "How does this work?" he asks. Well, the one who is in darkness in most cases does not realize she is in darkness until the light occurs. When you are this light, what she may see, what he may experience, are the ramifications of past thought, past choice, past harm done. And while this may be challenging, it is simply a necessary step. You are not waving a magic wand. The light reveals many things, some things people wish not to see. You are not the truth-teller. You are not seeking to expose. You are operating in presence and being in a high alignment of True Will. And in True Will what is required will be done.

Paul interrupts the teaching. "This sounds like a recipe for bad news. I can imagine many people reading this and suggesting they know best, they are the light, and they will tell people what to do." If that is the case, they are not following the teaching. We do not override free will. We never have. We never will. We work with your permission when we are invited. We ask you to say yes to anything that you might invoke that would require great change. You must operate at the same level. Presence and being holds no mandate for an idea of behavior. It simply is. When you understand who and what you are, you are operating at a level of compassion, not only for yourself, but for those most shrouded in darkness. To hate another for what you believe he or she has done is to claim the darkness for them, and to put you in the darkness as well. "But what about those people?" you always say. "Those people" are of God. They may be in denial of it. And as the light you are, and as the ring of truth that you sound, you claim them anew—not through intention, but through the recognition of who they can only be in truth. Underline *only*.

When we say the masquerade is over, but you don't know you are still wearing your costumes, we mean it. What this means, really simply, is everyone before you, like them or not, agree with them or not, is of God. And your knowing of this supports them in this recognition. That will be the title of this chapter, by the way: "Recognition." The amplitude of choice that is before you now, operating from the Upper Room, is beyond what you can imagine. But that does not mean many choices. That means the greatest choice, the most perfect choice, which is the result of Divine Will serving in the highest way as expression. *Your* expression is your presence and your being as the Monad come as you, and, indeed, come as all.

We will continue this teaching later. We thank you for your presence. This is in the text. Period. Period. Period.

(PAUSE)

We ask questions now about your relationship with the objective world, what you see and feel, how you experience the world through the senses and through the consort you hold with others experiencing. Manifestation occurs when the frequency of consciousness is held at a certain tone and claimed in form. The vibrations that you are, what comprises a human being, what you claim as body, is vibration at a level or strata of condensation that allows you the experience of being as form. Underline *as.* You exist beyond form. All things exist beyond form. And the lifting that is occurring on this plane, in ways you may see and not see, are coming in equivalency, vibrational accord.

Now, as the body has been addressed as a tool of sorts, a flute of sorts, for a spirit to play through and to have an experience in benefit for your own evolution and learning at the level of soul, you must also understand that the agreement you have made by incarnating as form is to claim form beyond the self. You have been given the authorship of creative power. Now, the Word is form, come as you, but the Word exists beyond form. And the degree of malleability that you hold to the higher consciousness supports your experience of a manifest world that is in flux, in change, and may be experienced as such. You understand yourself through history, through what you've seen and known, and you stand in a doorway now of new experience, you and all—new experience being what exists beyond the old frame, the old structure, architecture, of manifestation that you have utilized unconsciously. "I need a pencil. I find a pencil." Something to write upon? You find something to write upon. There is a step for every action.

Now, in the Upper Room, where there is less density, manifestation occurs more rapidly because there is less interference. But anything that must manifest in form must also hold an obligation in vibration to reside at a strata where it may be met. In other words, when you hold the high vibration, you may claim the high vibration. When the country you live in claims a high vibration as a collective, the experience of the country is altered. When a world changes its tone, there is much chaos because the change is so rapid and you don't know what to do with what you made prior, let alone how to make what you need. The steps that we described prior—you find a pencil and then find something to write upon—are all perfectly adequate at the level of tone you have taken. But you don't understand that communication actually is instantaneous in the Upper Room, and how thought processes and claims form is also different than you have known. When you are in requirement, a true requirement, of something in manifestation and you are in the Upper Room, you move to a level of receipt or receptivity because you are in the Source of all things, not separate from it. The one who believes she is separate claims an obligation to a vibrational field that operates as separate, hence more dense than you would otherwise discover in the Upper Room. In the Upper Room, reality maintains a perspective. "That is a couch, time to sit on the couch." But you move beyond the old ideas of how things should appear or what they may be utilized for, and in fact you may transition beyond the requirements of the old in ways you cannot imagine. The bodies themselves, in an altered state, require food still, require shelter still, but they are operating at a level of tone that bypasses the old structures and the old foundation that you have utilized to claim reality.

He interrupts the teaching. "I don't understand any of this. What does this look like?" It looks like the world at a level of rapidity in vibration beyond what you have experienced. You cannot see what moves so quickly with the naked eye at the level of tone you have aligned to. When you perceive spirit, or most of you perceive spirit, it is as a flash, a quick light, a fast illumination. You cannot contain or align to the rapidity that the thing is fluctuating at. The level of vibration is too high for you to experience. When you lift to the Upper Room, the process of engagement is recognized by you in separate steps. "What does that mean?" he asks.

"I am in the Upper Room," a claim of foundation. "I Have Come, I Have Come, I Have Come," a claim of incarnation at this level, the Monad resurrected through the being you have known yourself as. And the claim that follows that, "Behold, I make all things new," is a reclamation of what is already true. What is already true is moving at a faster pace, a higher degree, than you have been accustomed to. So the rapidity of form, and the vibration of form that indeed you are, must align to hold a level of experience beyond the old.

Now, function is present at every level or strata into infinity.

Everything has its properties. Everything can be known as vibration, but at varying levels. Now, if you move to one country perhaps they speak a different language, pray to different gods, eat different foods than you are used to. You understand yourself through what you've experienced, but you can agree that if you move over there dinner may look very different. When you lift to the Upper Room a comparable occurrence occurs. Your relationship to form, no longer held in the dense field, aligns you to a level of receipt where what is required for you can and will be met.

Now, you may impart by effort a requirement. You may pick up the pen and write on the piece of paper if that's what you are used to. But you will not develop beyond the old language, beyond the old way of communicating, until you realize that it is your reliance upon the old, the old system of engagement, that continues to limit you. When you understand that your relationship with form is entirely dependent on what it has been historically, you will seek to perpetuate that. When you begin to understand that in the Upper Room the release of the old sense of self, the aspect of self that you thought you were, and come into knowing as the Divine Self or Monad, the restrictions are gone in the ways you have utilized. We have spoken briefly about the senses and their operating in an altered state. They become inclusive to what aspects of self are required to receive what is needed in order to know. Underline the word *know*, which means realize. To know the world, to realize the world, in the Upper Room is to claim a relationship to the world at that level of pitch or tone. The resonant field you hold has already been acclimated to the Upper Room. What is not yet acclimated is the idea of self that perpetuates separation. We have called it a mask. We have called it a way of knowing self, or an idea of self, that is seeking release.

Now, this is not a violent release. It is not violent in the least. The only thing that creates violence or claims this as violent is your attachment to an idea of self and all of the things the self has accrued. This does not mean your house, your relationship with your children, or the job you go to every day, but your relationship to the idea of self as the one who knows herself through those creations, or has misidentified in this form at the cost of what expresses beyond it. The True Self, you see, come as you, recognizes itself in the Divine that is ever present. The Monad, expressed as you, operates at a level of tone or vibration in the Upper Room where it meets itself, or those things of like accord, at every turn. Imagine for a moment that you were always seeing God, or the vibration that is Source, out-pictured as form, and beyond form, wherever you looked. "Would this be disorienting?" he asks. Hardly. It is what is already there, but in an unmasked state. We have said prior, you become the light that claims the darkness, that illumines the dark room. What you are seeing is what was present, and you are claiming it as it can only be in truth, the manifest Divine come as what you see.

Now, the chances are that you are thinking this cannot be so. But indeed it is so. And our experience of you exists fully beyond your idea of self and how you have chosen to learn through the personality structure. We honor these aspects of you. Indeed, they are of God. But they are not the truth of your being. These are the things you understand yourselves through. Your body is not your last meal. Your identity is not your last relationship. Your relationship with God is not the church you go to, the mosque you pray at. Each of you before us is already operating in multiple strata. You interact primarily through the base layer that form has taken in separation. You know yourself through occupation and name, gender and race, age and religion. These are all useful things. But the aspect of you that is incarnating through these teachings expresses beyond each of these things, but knows itself through them. And what that means, quite simply, is the Divine has come as the seventy-year-old man, the three-year-old girl, "those people over there that don't look like we do," and "those people over there that don't want to look like me." God has come as all form.

When the Divine recognizes itself in form, it doesn't discard the masquerade. It understands itself beyond the masquerade, and that is important to understand. No one is asking you to walk away from a life that you've created. But we will say when you realize yourself within the life that you've created at the level of the Upper Room, how you manifest, what you will claim into being, will likely be rather different. When you understand yourself through a common field, common language, common expectations, you already limit yourselves. Imagine a small town with a border. You can't imagine yourself experiencing life beyond what you have known, and it is as that small town. Now, the small town that is your experience inclusive of many things, birth and death, your idea of peace, your creation of war—many things express at this level or octave. But above this, and simultaneous to it and in congruence with it, is the level of tone of this broadcast.

Now, the Upper Room comes at the level of tone that is the Christ Mind. As we often say, there are levels beyond this that may be experienced, but while maintaining form the Upper

Room is the highest you can claim or align with. Once beyond form, you are no longer limited, but the limitations that you've utilized thus far are actually significant and can be altered. The idea that you must speak a word for the word to be heard is a common mistake. Thoughts may hold vibration and may be understood beyond the language they were spoken in. Any True Knowing, any moment of True Knowing that you have ever experienced, existed beyond language. It was impulse and knowing. It was the resonant *yes* of truth. You attach language to it in order to be able to operate or comprehend it in a way that is fathomable and operable. But when you move beyond the need for the language, you move into congruence with True Mind, or Divine Mind, where articulation or manifestation does not require the language of old to make itself known.

"What does this mean?" Paul asks. When you decide who you are in a fundamental way through agreement in the common field—"you may call me a man," "you may call me a woman," "you may call me this or that"—you concretize ideas that actually were never intended to be so concrete. You limit yourselves by the occupations, by the socioeconomic structures, that you seem to need to work through to create what you want. When you move beyond those obligations, you simply be. You may be in a body that is a male. You may have this or that. But the experience of being is actually altered at a level of tone that you must understand is not only available. It is present now.

"Well, how do we access this?" he says. "Do we access this? Is this something we must do?" Each intonation we have offered you—by way of decree, by way of attunement—is in source of this agreement to be made manifest beyond the small self at a level of tone that is no longer restrictive. And this occurs first in those who choose, then in those who agree, and then those who follow, who move into an energetic field where it is not only possible, it is so present it is accessible. Imagine you never heard a piece of music before and you begin to hum the song. You become the music as you hum it. Your neighbor hears the tune, begins to sing with you, and before you know it many are singing. The song is part of the structure or the experience of realization in form. "This exists. I may know that this exists through my experience of it."

The magnitude of change that you are actually undergoing at a rapid state, far more than you realize, is going to render things that you once thought should always be there as gone, not to nothingness, but to what is no longer required for you to experience yourself through. Now, imagine: Once upon a time, the only way to clean a house was with your bare hands, scooping up the ashes from the fireplace and throwing them in the bin. Now you have other ways of attending to the same action. You moved beyond the need for the old system. When you move beyond the need for a system, it may maintain itself for a period of time. You are used to it. "It was a good idea. We can't let go of the good idea." But finally you discover that there is no requirement for it. What you used to think would always be there—perhaps the telephone bolted to the wall—is now archaic. You've moved beyond the need for a system of exchange. What you are moving towards now is to a level of communication with one another that supersedes the use of the old systems. And this means that you may move to knowing.

Now, when you know, you recognize. When you recognize, you confirm what is seen, understood, comprehended—

and may, indeed, act upon it. In one's knowing, one is always obligated—or, better said, called—to action in response to what is known. When you know your neighbor's need beyond what she would say, beyond how he would express, you may support the neighbor in his or her need. You are no longer deciding that people need to prove their worth. You know their worth, you realize their worth, and you comprehend what their requirements are through presence and being.

Now, when Paul listens to those before him, he moves to the level of the personality structure. "Let's see what this woman's personality structure is saying." And he interprets the tone in the language he is offered. In fact, he is simply knowing, and the knowing claims language to support what is required by way of communication. It's really that simple. To become telepathic is simply to unveil, unmask, the antenna that you actually are. You are all radios. You are all in broadcast. And the stations that you tend to play are at the lower level of the spectrum. When one prays or moves into an application to converse with the Divine, you are not going someplace other. The idea of God in a cloud is actually a metaphor for what is higher—not up there, but in higher vibration. You align to this through agreement to the Source of all things. To agree to the Source of all things, and to move into communion with it, is to claim the inherent knowing that is your birthright. The True Self knows and the small self thinks. Once this is in application and you become accustomed to it, you lift to a level of tone where what is available to you far transcends what you have known prior. Imagine you are on a boat crossing an ocean, and you understand yourself in the hull of the ship in that little stateroom you have known. The ship is great. There are many rooms. You go to the upper deck and you experience yourself in communion with nature. It is really quite similar.

Now, the Upper Room is a level of vibration, and there are levels beyond it. But it's where we take you first because it's where the Monad may express. When the Monad expresses fully and articulation occurs—God has come as this in form and field—the light that you are and the illumination that you claim supports manifestation at the same level of tone. And that is the world made new.

He interrupts the teaching. "And humanity is undergoing this, not the student?" The student *is* humanity. You become portals—as we have said, ambassadors—to the Upper Room through holding the tone as the expressed field. Others are doing this in different ways. It really matters not how you call it to you. What is clear is very simple. There is an aspect of you that knows who it is, what it is, how it serves. It seeks expression as and through you. And with your consent, you will embody at the level that you can hold. And that's important to understand. *The level you can hold* simply means what you can claim in vibration while maintaining form. It is different for people at different varying stages of growth and expression. You don't expect the two-year-old to drive you to work. She can't reach the pedals yet. She is perfect in her way. Those of you that come first are in some ways seeding the common field with a light that others may awaken to.

When we say these words on your behalf, we invite you to say them quietly to the self:

"I know who I am in truth. I know what I am in truth. I know how I serve in truth. I am free. I am free. I am free. I

am in the Upper Room. I Have Come. I Have Come. I Have Come. Behold, I make all things new. On this day I say yes to my participation in Divine Mind. On this day I say yes to my agreement to serve as conduit for the Divine as my expression. On this day I say yes to True Knowing, and the benefit of True Knowing, as I may experience it. I am free. I am free. I am free."

Thank you for your presence. Period. Period. Period. This is in the text.

(PAUSE)

What stands before you today, in an awakened state, is a recognition of what was not: "I was not my brother's keeper." "I did not attend to myself well." These are things that are useful so that you may adhere to the new to comprehend the self as on a new trajectory where you are not obligated to repeat the old ideas of self that perpetuated behavior that was harmful to the self or others. When one knows who she is, one does no harm. When one knows who he is, one speaks the truth. One does not seek to defend one's position. One honors the other before her, and does not dishonor herself. When you recognize that how you've lived your life thus far was exactly as you could with the tools that you had, with the learning that you were given, you can ask yourself, "How could I have done better?" We will say you could not have. Humanity has done its best in almost all ways with the tools that it has, but it has operated in separation. A belief in one higher than the next created war for profit, and famine for greed.

Now, when you understand that your identity is being rep-
licated by an idea of self that seeks to know itself in a common field, you can understand that all you are really doing is
shifting out of a common field to a new recognition of what
was always true. You are not pretending to be spiritual. Why
would you bother doing that? It doesn't matter how many
times a day you pray, or even what you pray to. What matters
is your presence and being. And at the level of amplitude we
are teaching you from, presence and being becomes the being
that expresses for all. Now, *expresses for all* is confounding to
every one of you because you still believe that it is something
that you do. "Here I am to save the world." The light that has
come as you is what does the work. What you are preparing
for, at the individual level, is a level of resonance that you could
not have claimed in the lower strata. And once this occurs,
your participation in the new is actually established.

Now, *established* is a good word to use here. You can be established in the Upper Room through the recognition that the
aspect of self that abides here is always true and ever-present
here. You do not do this at the cost of the denial of the old actions, pretending you were never angry, never had a bad temper,
never said a lie, never hurt anybody. You are responsible to all
of your actions. And in the Upper Room you may realize this
very quickly because the aspects of self that are claiming you,
speaking through you and learning through you, the aspect of
the Divine that is seeking to incarnate through you, will use
any evidence it has, any opportunity it can find, to accelerate
its expression. Which means you face your creations. You realize yourself in tandem with your neighbors and how you've
claimed prior. "Behold, I make all things new" doesn't pretend

things didn't happen. It's not saying things weren't hard. It is re-knowing what was, at the level of amplitude where things may be reclaimed.

They will not be reclaimed in the lower field. They will be perpetuated, because the level of consciousness that created the difficulties that operate in the lower field are quite established, and you move with them unintentionally. Imagine you live on a road where there are things in the roadway, obstacles that you must always pass on the way to a destination. That is the dense plane. In the Upper Room, an obstacle that appears can be seen immediately as an opportunity to move beyond it, not to dwell upon it, not to take the painstaking act of self-recrimination to its infinite length, but to realize "this was where I erred, in my disbelief, in my difficulty, in my fear or confusion. This is where I was selfish and didn't attend to the needs of my brother." Once this is understood and you understand the lesson, you may move with rapidity through them. Now, this is not a rush to the altar. The marriage that you are incurring, the divine marriage, is a process that is undergone through the alchemy of the Monad reclaiming itself in all things, or God experiencing God. When you understand that in the Upper Room there is no fight to be had, the need for a weapon will release. When you understand that in the Upper Room the belief in lack does not express, you may stop claiming lack and move into a receipt of what is truly yours, already yours.

He interrupts the teaching. "Well, what about karma? What if somebody's difficulties are the result of past acts? What do we do with that?" In the Upper Room, you may move beyond karma when the lesson is learned. If there is a lesson to be learned, you may meet it quickly in your knowing. You are not seeking to figure out what went wrong. You are realizing what went wrong, or what claimed you in difficulty, what aspect of you, what behavior you incurred, what action you took, that claimed a situation. And you may remedy it through the intention "Behold, I make all things new," the claim of realization upon the old. Now, this is not magic. The claim of realization is made with benefit, but it is not the get-out-of-jail-free card. In other words, if you broke the window, replace the window. Don't expect God to replace the window. The lesson was: Don't throw a rock at the window; you may have to pay for it.

Now, the challenge you have, all of you have, is you feel that your safety is established in the lower field, which is a misunderstanding. Your idea of safety is the known, even when the known is painful. If you look at your lives and all you have had to contend with and all the suffering that you've endured, if you look at this world and see all the suffering others have endured, you may understand that replicating the old may not be the highest way forward. To establish the self in vibration in the Upper Room and make the claim upon the old—which is simply your old way of seeing or what was established in fear—"Behold, I make all things new" releases the old. The language of old that would seek to participate in the density of the old can be released through this incantation, and we use that word intentionally. It is not a spell, but it is an alchemical claim upon the known. "Behold, I make all things new." And by *known* we mean prior experience, what you knew or believed to be so.

What is made new is the very fabric of the thing created, and at times how it's seen or what it is now called. A name may be held to claim an archaic structure, but if the name is not changed the energy of the archaic structure may be moved to the higher only at the level that it can hold. If you understand what we mean, if you can imagine a hovel and what you think of as a hovel, a small structure perhaps in disrepair with no wealth attached, you will not make the hovel the new when you call it the hovel. The architecture of *hovel*, the meaning of *hovel*, will denigrate any structure it is attached to. So you lift to the higher without the language and allow the form to be taken in a new way.

Now, form is energy, and architecture is what claims form as physical reality, the architecture of reality. Every plane of experience or vibration holds architecture, and it generally operates in a schism, what was low and what was high. What was once low is now made high, and what extends beyond the old parameter may eventually be known. Imagine a radio with many stations. You may turn the dial and have different music expressed through the radio as the dial is turned. Sometimes there will be static. Sometimes the music will be disorienting, and perhaps so high-pitched that the human ears cannot even hear it. Realization comes at the cost of the old, and as you move through the radio stations, as the radio you are plays the higher, you begin to understand how each one is distinguished.

When Paul steps into somebody at the level of personality and is able to hear them or give language to what they feel, he is operating at one level of tone. When he moves to the higher to ask why or what the lesson might be, he has shifted the station to a higher aspect of the individual. What he doesn't know he can do yet is tune in to the collective as a radio station and hear what the collective requires. And this will come when he's ready. In fact, it will come for many of you as you are able to hold it. Where you limit yourselves is by your beliefs and your agreement to what can be. What you don't believe can be, you discard, you block, you eschew, you regard as not possible and put it in darkness.

If you can imagine that there was a wing of a museum where all of the statues were covered with sheets, and the sheets were coming off as you passed them, you might understand the majesty that has always been there but has remained masked. The teachings of old have always been present, but generally hidden for fear of misuse, or by a church that was seeking to maintain a control over the individual power that the Monad expresses through. When you realize that who and what you are and have always been is present now, and you begin to experience the echo which is the result of your claim upon what you perceive—"Behold, I make all things new"—the world itself will sing back to you, which is the residual affect of the claim of the high octave upon what was held in low vibration. Again, the statues unveiling. "Behold, I make all things new." The statue is unveiled, its resplendency seen, and you are impacted by the vibration of what was once covered that has now been unveiled.

An unveiling is now occurring among human beings, and many, many are born attuned to the higher senses, but ill-equipped to operate with them intact because they have been told they cannot do that. This is going to change, and quite soon, because the residual affect of choice—"I am allowed to be"—may also claim, "I am allowed to know, I am not bound by gender, by age, by religion, by the things I was taught I should be bound by." The manifestation of the Divine comes at the cost of the old. And the conflicts you experience now are primarily at the cost of what has been and your desire to maintain it. It will not be maintained. There are constants you may adhere to. Truth is a constant. Love is a constant. When you align to love and truth, you align to what is always true. And as we say must always be so: In truth a lie will not be held.

We thank you for your presence. This is in the text. Stop now, please.

DAY TWELVE

What stands before you today, in an awakened state, is recognition of what you thought you were, and the new potential that is being claimed: "I am allowed. I am free to choose. And the aspect of me that is choosing is in alignment to my True Self, or the True Self come as me."

Now, operating as the True Self, conducting business as the True Self, having your day and night at this level of tone, is somewhat different than you think. The altercations you have with a past idea of self will always surround you because you have accrued them, and the evidence of past choice surrounds you. You wake up in the bed you bought when you were in that marriage. You sit on the sofa you acquired when you liked to do this or that. You no longer like to do this or that, but the sofa remains. The evidence of past choice, be it relationship or career, how you see yourself in the mirror in a certain way, may remain. But the idea of self that procured the couch, that decided this or that, has been decidedly altered. So while you walk around with your relics of history, you are actually claiming them anew, or in a new way, through your interaction with them.

Now, form, as you understand form, the dense thing you see that has been given a name, is all vibration. And the vibration you are experiencing when you work with these texts is actually the same vibration, in a different way, that you encounter as things. In other words, the Source of all things, inclusive of you, inclusive of what has been made in form, is always present. But you identify with them through the names they have been given, and everything that vibrates is actually operative as an aspect of form. And here is the news: Everything is in vibration, so everything is form and God in simultaneity.

Now, there are different levels of vibration, and you align to them through these teachings, and then you discover them for yourselves, once in the Upper Room, when you are having an experience of what it means to be in a body while holding the high field. To hold the high field is to be in constant emanation—constant praise, if you wish—of the Divine that is all things. Now, this is not arduous. It's simply a level or template of resonance. We use the word *template* intentionally. When you pour water into an ice-cube tray it takes the form of the tray. When you operate in the Upper Room and the vibration that you hold is at a certain level, the alignment you maintain—underline the word *maintain*—is always present and can be confirmed by your experience. To be confirmed in experience simply means that who and what you are is operating in tandem with all things of like accord.

Now, the challenge for many of you is you have a supposition of what it means to be and look like in some idea of an upper realm. When we always tell you that the Upper Room exists in simultaneity with the world that you've known—it's an accelerated tone, a higher octave of experience—you imagine something very different than it is. It's far more glorious than you think, and in some ways much less different than you imagine.

Now, you look at something that's been given a name. You see the thing. You give it the name again. You know what it's been. You know what it should be. But in the Upper Room you move to a level of pliability because the recognition that you're holding is not as *fork* or *spoon*, *house* or *shack*, but Source expressing in myriad ways. When you understand that it's all Source expressing, and you *realize* the Source of all things— "Behold, I make all things new"—what was always present at a level of tone or vibration becomes explicit. That is an important word here, *explicit*. You are not hunting for the Divine. It's not as if you picked up a snail shell and are seeking the snail inside. You are knowing the snail and the snail shell as of Source. And this is the recognition that becomes explicit through your experience.

Your experience is essential now, and what we mean by this is very simple. We are done with platitudes, and we are also done with instructing you at a level that is seeking to prove something to you. We wish you to prove this for yourselves by your encounter with your day or with your night or with your neighbor. Now, the aspect of you come into fruition in the Upper Room, or the Monad in full bloom, knows who it is and is not questioning. You have not been overtaken. You are still present as the you you knew, but in an altered way. But the experience of being with your neighbor, of seeing the sunset, of bathing in the stream, is radically different because your senses are actually aligning to a level of tone that they have not known prior. So how you perceive the stream and how you interact with your neighbor is also altered.

Now, the benefit of this for you is you are not striving. You are not seeking to find God. You are with God. You are in God. And you are knowing your neighbor as of God, and the idea of stream or sunset, expression of God. When you understand these things, you are no longer deciding what things are. You are knowing what things are. When you know, you are realizing. When you are realizing, you are seeing what has always been true.

Now, recognition comes at varying levels for many of you. The first thing you may see is something you always saw and see it as if for the first time. "What a wondrous thing that is. I've always noticed it but I've never really seen it." The eyes that see or the mind that perceives that's in an altercation with reality, and the senses that are informed by them, are claiming things as they have been. And the first glimmers for many of you are the realization that what you once saw is something other. It's not what it appeared to be.

Now, how things change, once you become acclimated to this level of tone, is somewhat drastic. While you see the sunset and you know what a sunset is, the experience of being with a sunset is an experience of communion. The experience of being with your neighbor—again, communion. What are you communing with but the Divine as all things, come as sunset, come as neighbor. The requirement for maintaining this is so simple you can't imagine. The aspect of you that sees has been summoned and claimed and realized, and *it* is operating as the perceiver, not the small self who was left behind in school, not the small self who doubted she was worthy of the Divine, not the small self who would seek to mandate what the Divine should appear as. The idea of this self, the one that would mandate, is actually replaced or reconciled with the aspect of self that has known things through prior language, through prior architecture and construct. You are in the world, yes, but as you are not of it you are not floating away. You are having an experience of world or manifestation that's entirely informed by the higher octave or the experience of being known.

"What does that mean," he asks, "*the experience of being known?*" Well, you are known by God even in your most dense form, even in your darkest way of being in experience. You are always known, but you don't realize that being known is knowing, that the Divine is working in consort with you, not in opposition to you. When you allow yourself to be known or to be realized, it is the Divine that does this with you, in and through, and your experience is altered by that. The vibration you hold alters what it encounters because it's simply operating at a level of tone where it transmutes the density of the old and lifts it to the higher. This is perceived by many of you already at different times. "I thought it was this, but it was that." "I thought she was this, but she was that." What begins to happen in rapidity, as you become accustomed to the experience of the Upper Room, is that the reality you have known yourself through, claimed identity with, is not only lifted—it is lifting for all.

Now, this is very important to understand. This is not a

personal heaven you are being granted. This is the gift of the Kingdom. And all are welcome to the Kingdom, but they must have the eyes with which to see it, which means they must perceive it. And the alignment to the perception has requirements that many of you understand already. "I can no longer operate in fear, justify my rage, damn myself or my fellows. I must align to the higher truth that is always present, not seek to find it, but align to what is always there." Again, underline *always*. Once this is done, the unveiling commences. The drapes come off the statues. You see what has always been there in its majesty but you have been denied presence with—because you have denied it, not because it has denied you.

The encounter you have with a world made new, in your days and your nights, is far beyond what you can imagine. But it's a state of consciousness that renders things new. You have not been gifted with a magic wand that is wiping clean the stains of old. You are seeing things beyond what they were or how they were utilized. When you think of something you think of as awful, you carry with it the weight or the residue of all that have perceived the thing. To make something new, in most all ways, is to see it beyond the collective, or what the collective intention has been, what it was meant to be, "how we have decided it should be." We have used metaphors past. How about fingers on a windowpane smudging the glass and all you see is the smudge? It's not so much that the glass is being wiped clean, but the separation that has functioned to accrue the fingerprints is released. The glass itself has been removed or made new.

Now, perception is an encounter with what is experienced, either by sight or by mind. You are always in an encounter with the floor you stand on, with the air you breathe, with what you call the weather, which is also a creation. When you understand creation, that all things initially were claimed in mind and idea and are made in form, you are no longer bound by the idea of firmness. An idea is malleable. An idea can be changed. When the idea of a thing is changed, a thing is changed itself, and, finally, we suggest, in a rapidity of energy that is present in the Upper Room without the delays you are used to.

"What does that mean?" he asks. Well, time itself, or the structure of time that you have utilized, is operating at a level of density. It's actually a calendar, a clock ticking, or a metronome going back and forth, telling you always how it is beating. In the eternal now, you simply are. And what simply is, is not necessarily bound through the requirements that time has utilized. If you understand time primarily as organization, you can see its requirement and function. But when you go to the upper realm, things are happening in immediacy because the awareness is always present. There is no idea of Tuesday. Tuesday is in the common field. It was a requirement in the common field. It was no longer nine o'clock. It was no clock at all. It was simply now.

Now, the experience of being, presence and being, in the Upper Room does not mean you don't abide by the clock when you are operating in the collective. For the time being, you will. But in time, we suggest, you will operate as we do. You understand time. You understand its usage. You may play with it. You may call upon it. We know when we're supposed to speak, but the time for us is not the time it is for you because we exist beyond time. We may recognize the requirement of it for you and we may appear as we are required to support your learning. But we do not exist within the clock. We exist in now, and now is eternity.

Now, you structure experience in many ways. The clock and the calendar are two. But there are other ways you realize yourself in consort with the manifest world—perhaps day and night, perhaps the season. These, again, are creations. We are not saying that they will not be there. But your relationship to these things has been indoctrinated with meaning. "It is summer; we should go to the shore." "It is winter; we should build a snowman." You idealize what things should be through an idea of time or seasonality and you create in anticipation of what must come. When you understand now that what humanity is doing is reclaiming an identity that it actually knew prior to the construct of organized time, as you have known it, you will understand that the return to the garden, if you wish, or the realization of the Kingdom, if you wish, must manifest as the material realm. It cannot be other.

Now, some of you might imagine a barren planet left to waste, while at an energetic level many of you are prancing around in some idealized version of garden. That is not what is going to happen. There is no schism where some are saved and some will perish. That is an old paradigm based in fear. Some will resist change, have a much more arduous journey. Some will embrace change, perhaps have an easier time. But it really matters not. Everyone is known. Everyone is of God. And everybody will come to terms, we would have to say, with what and who they have always been. Again, underline *always*. We have talked about music, and dancing to a music that is no longer playing. That is the habituated behavior. But the ballroom is vast, and there are many dancers, and you are all playing, as you can, with your idea of being or succeeding or what a lifetime should be.

Now, imagine on this great dance floor, with many dancers doing their best, there is a great wave, a great wave of vibration, claiming all of them. And what is being claimed by them is the lifting that the water brings. The dance floor is no longer there. They are lifting in the wave and being carried to a higher experience than they have known. Now, there's an aspect of all of them that believes they should be back on the dance floor doing the dance they have done. But in the wave they find that in order to stay afloat their bodies are moving in different ways. They are acclimating to the water, not because they choose to, but because they must. That is what is occurring now, and your experience of it will vary. Some will say, "Bring me back down. Let me hold onto something firm." And others will say, "Let's see where we are carried." Where you are being carried is to the Upper Room or a strata of consciousness that's always been available to you but in most ways has been denied. The teaching of the mystic, considered far too arduous for most, maintained a secrecy over the decades, over the millennium, but is present now only as what can be, what is, and what will be chosen—not in a high-minded way, but in a very simple way, a recognition of who you have always been and what you will only be.

Now, the manifest *what*—what has taken form—is in transition because the wave is encountering it as well. But as the emissary of the wave, the one who says, "I see who you are, I know what you are and can only be," you lift the world to the light that it's always been. And you claim this, not through altruism, but because the Monad as you must occur, must agree, must be here in occurrence and claim what it encounters because it cannot do other. This does not mean that you are not responsible, in most ways, to your choices. But what it does mean is that you are not the one at the level of personality that is activating this. Your will is employed and chosen through you to grant permission for this great journey.

Now, everybody is on the dance floor, yes, but some of you are hearing the new music already. And the teaching we offer you is *of* the new music, and you can say *is* the new music. Although you may sing this music in any tongue, the intent behind it will always be comparable. The Divine has come. It is here. It is here. It is here.

Thank you for your presence. Stop now, please. This is in the text.

(PAUSE)

What stands before you today, in an awakened state, is the realization that what you chose was the best you could choose, that what you claimed was all you could have claimed, at the level of consciousness you had aligned to. Some of you say to us, "Why did I do what I did? Why do I do what I do?" Because you are entrained at a level of vibration where the choices before you are always what they were. You really can't imagine much beyond them.

Now, when you break through the veil, when you lift to the Upper Room to a level of alignment where the old is not present, you are still perceiving the old, claiming the old, because it's what you have known. You choose those things out of habit because you don't know you're allowed anything else.

What expires in the Upper Room is what you needed at a low level of vibration. What is released at this level are the very things that gave you a sense of identity or comfort in the lower vibrational field. This is only challenging as you attach to them. When you recognize who and what you are, your true needs are met, and met in well ways.

"What is a *well way*?" he asks. Well, you could say *perfect*, but your idea of a perfect way means that there is no cost, nothing to gain. If something is met by you in a perfect way, you had no effort there. "Is there effort in the Upper Room?" In some ways, yes. To hold a level of receptivity to what you would call your good to receive what you require may not be your idea of perfect, but it would be perfect in its own way. The old idea of who you should be requires very different things than the one that you have become—notice we said *have become*—in an awakened state. Now, when we use those phrases—"when you awaken to who you are" or "you are in an awakened state"—we speak to those who are not asleep, who are claiming an identity on a pinnacle, on a mountaintop, as a way of expressing. The one who sought to strive so hard is deeply loved, but she has actually arrived at a level of receptivity where what is before her is a world made new.

Now, to understand this, and how you align at this level of tone, is the instruction you are receiving. But when we say that you are there, that you have awakened, we are telling you the truth because the Monad that is you is already awakened, and is always awake, and is always in tone and oscillating at the level of the Upper Room. The aspect of you that was perhaps hidden, or laid claim to in small ways, has risen. And its rising and its perpetuation of itself is what anchors you at a level of tone in what we call the Upper Room. And the realization that you are there already, or the Monad as you is there, is crucial at this level of instruction. To understand that the aspect of you that you can call the Divine Self or the Monad or the Christed Self has already been revealed, and is seeking its alignment in your experience, will comfort some of you that think that there is yet another mountain to climb. There is not another mountain to climb. But you must understand where you are, and comprehend where you are, and this must be done experientially. We cannot keep reminding you and reminding you of who and what you already are. The full claim of this—"I Have Come"—is a manifestation that claims itself through you. The small self isn't doing the work. And the claim "Behold, I make all things new" is the affect of the Monad as vibration come as you upon what you encounter.

Now, "Behold, I make all things new" is not a resolved statement. "Behold I make," the act of creation. "It will be so" is what seals it and claims it as done. When you claim, "I know who I am," you set in motion a progression of realization of that claim, awakening to that claim. And when you know, you know who others are. When you know what you are, you know what else is. And once in the Upper Room, your expression is your service. And your service, your expression, is a gift to others and everything you encounter. To know who you are, what you are, and how you serve is to claim the Kingdom. And once these things are actually realized through you, the aspect of you that knows and experiences this can claim it for herself, and you are indeed participatory to this unveiling. We are using the word *unveiling* often. It's a wonderful image: to see what has been hidden, to see what has been withheld, and to know what you could not know at the lower octave.

Now, the Divine exists in the low octave. Things are as holy there as they are anywhere else. But they have claimed density, and the world you have known yourself through is in most ways a dense experience of vibration. But you don't know it because it's what you've been used to. You can imagine yourself wearing lead shoes, walking around the streets and saying, "Oh, I have heavy feet today." But you don't know that the tone that you are emitting is also in alignment with a level of density that is experiential. When you move to the Upper Room without the density you have utilized to claim identity and experience, both things are altered, and changed forever.

Now, we use the word *forever* intentionally. Some of you would look at these texts as brief little journeys into a utopia, and then you return back to your hellish life and say, "Well, that was an interesting book, and so what of it?" The books actually alter you at a level of tone and vibration, and each step forward aligns the being who is receptive to the teaching to the level of tone that the book actually is. When all of the books at once are operative in an energetic system, you become a chord—c-h-o-r-d—of vibrational tone. And you claim the Kingdom, not through asking, but because that is the resonant field that you are indeed aligned to.

The ease of this teaching, and it actually is easy, is that primarily you are allowing—deciding and then allowing. The changes that you undergo may indeed be challenging, but all that is really being challenged is an idea of who you were or think you should be. When that no longer is the issue, what you are doing is simply releasing the obstacles to your full expression. And your full expression is operative already—*already*—and can be claimed by you now in congruence with the Source of all things. "Behold, I make all things new. It will be so." And, finally, the great claim "God Is, God Is, God Is."

Now, those of you in the lower field still think that the claim "God Is" is a magic wand of some kind, claiming the divinity and altering the form of the things seen. In fact, it is far greater than that. It is an acknowledgment from the Upper Room of what is always true, and it is inclusive of all things. Underline *all*. Nothing is left out of this equation. Imagine a great ocean that holds all things, and this ocean lasts forever and is infinite in its width, in its depth, and your experience of it as the one in the ocean *is all things*.

When we spoke prior, we spoke of a dance floor being lifted by the wave. Now, the wave was present prior, but you were operating at a level of density, in the denial of the Divine, where much of your effort was spent unknowingly refuting the inherent divinity in what you encountered. "That awful man." "That awful event." "That awful experience." And the language you utilized, entrenched in meaning by those before you, in some ways tethers you to the idea that *awful* is. Now, God expresses as all things, but you must understand that you are responsible for your creations, individually and collectively, and so much of what you would call awful is born in an act of will that claims separation. The one who knows who she is does not cause harm to others. The one who knows the holiness of the planet does not sully the planet. But because you've been in ignorance, maintaining your comfort while many things occur, and then saying, "Well, it wasn't my job" or "I couldn't know that," you forget that you are participatory at a level of consciousness to everything that is. Underline *everything*. You don't know this, but you believe yourselves to be insignificant. In fact, your presence and the tone that you emit contributes to the vast symphony that is God, that is creation, and has come as all things. And unknowingly you challenge this through the denial of the Divine. You put your hands over your ears, you perceive in a diminished way, and then you forget the fact that not only "God Is, God Is, God Is," but you are of this.

When we speak of an escalated tone, or the water rising and the dancers on the dance floor learning how to move differently in the water out of a need to survive, you may understand the circumstances of humanity now. It is not as it was. It will not be as it was. But you don't know what it will be, and you do your best to maintain an identity and a sense of comfort in the midst of such change. This identity is what is being moved and re-created in a higher way. Many of you decide that you are your difficulties or your bad habits or how you were treated by others, and you claim an identity, a mask that you wear, through the tragedies of your experience. You are welcome to learn through this, but it will always teach you the same lesson. You are not responsible to what you choose or to what occurs.

Now, responsibility is not punishment. It doesn't mean you caused it. But it does mean you are accountable to the act and it is now yours to behave with, to align to, in a new way lest you perpetuate a sense of victimhood that will simply call more victimization to you. To celebrate every defeat as an opportunity to learn is to lift the idea of defeat to success. As we said, everything you've chosen you needed to choose because you were choosing at a level of consciousness that was completely limited in its spectrum. You didn't know you could do more or do other, or you chose out of fear. And fear has been the bias on this plane, and that is why you are in such disrepair—because you've known yourselves in fear in so many ways, in so many whispered ways, that the idea of full freedom remains confusing.

Now, the claim "I am free"—again, a claim of the Monad announcing liberation from the strata or vibration of fear and all of the issues or requirements or responsibilities claimed in fear that the lower field holds. This does not mean you do not feed your children. It does not mean you quit your job and expect others to pay your way. But it does mean that the Monad as you, who has never been limited by such things, is operating in liberation and can now claim what expresses beyond that. That is the Upper Room, and the claim "I am free" has always been the prerequisite for the claim that follows: "I am in the Upper Room." The manifestation of the Monad in the subsequent claims is really very simple. It is activated. It claims what it encounters. It is made new. And then the realization—or simply put, the knowing—that "God Is," that the ocean is all about you, has always been, and will always be, will support your recognition of the awakened state.

The awakened state. What a lovely word, *awakened*. You are awakening from slumber, yes. But you are also awakening from a belief that you could not be known and could not be expressed as the one at the top of the mountain shining her light for the benefit of all below. Now, *below* does not mean lesser. The one who holds the torch high, who holds the lantern aloft, is supporting the realization of those who experience, see, perceive, and encounter that light. You are the encounter with the light by being as it. Underline *as*. You are not foisting knowledge on others. You are not telling them what to follow. You are being the light that you have always been. The true light that you are has only one mandate, and that is truth. And when love is present as this light, you have completed an idea of incarnation as can be known in manifest form. Wisdom is present, yes. Right action is present, yes. But the light is truth. And what is not true is fear. And when you claim the light where fear has been, you liberate what was held in fear.

This is an enormous transition, like it or not, and it is a wonderful one. But the process of becoming who you are is simply a process of releasing who you are not. You are not climbing the mountain anymore. The aspect of you that is the Monad is atop the mountain. She *is* the mountaintop. It *is* the mountaintop. And it is *its* expression that liberates the world.

Blessings to each of you. Indeed, this is in the text. Stop now, please. Period. Period. Period.

DAY THIRTEEN

What stands before you today, in an awakened state, is the agreement to withstand the amount of change that is to your benefit. Underline those words: *to your benefit*. The alignment you hold today can actually support you in moving through many things without the challenges as you have known them, which simply means how you respond to change may not be frightening, or may not be fraught, or may not be painful. It may simply be what it is. When you align to your true potential and you give your true potential permission to carry you, this is not an act of withstanding. It's an act of undergoing, and undergoing a process of re-accord.

Now, *re-accord* is a new word for Paul, but it's really very simple. You have been in accord to a landscape and the requirements of a landscape, and an identity and its requirements. To move into the higher, to move into a higher accord, is as if you are being re-tuned, or *a*-tuned, to play the higher notes that were always present, but ignored. The challenge of change is that you seek to know where you go. You want to know what the drink tastes like before you drink it. You want to know what the sunset looks like before you look at it. You will not get that now. You will get something much greater—a new experience, a new experience of being.

Now, to withstand change is to undergo a process of agreement to what the new can be—beyond the old ideas, beyond the old recognition of how things should be. When one comprehends herself in this higher alignment, which is, as we say, experiential, one supports herself as she can as she acclimates to the new—re-accord, a new accord, at a new level of tone. The falling away of the old, which will be happening again and again and again, will be seen within as you realize yourselves anew, and be seen without as you perceive a world made new.

Now, your experience of this world made new may be quite exciting, the agreement to what already is present that was heretofore denied. But now, when you see it, you move into alignment to it. Others may be more challenged because the experience of change or the release of an old status quo may feel apocalyptic. It is apocalyptic to the self who demands to know what is for dinner tomorrow, who she shares her bed with tonight, and what it should look like out the window.

When you move into the present moment, and you move into a level of tone where you are actually encouraged by being, encouraged to move forward on this path of truth, the alignment you hold will support the agreement to the new at every turn. Each time you turn a corner you may anticipate the new and be encouraged by that. If you are frightened by change, each time you turn the corner you will seek to run backwards. "I don't know what is before me. How can I know?" The collective does not know at the level or structure of personality. The collective does not know at the level of agreement to what was. But the collective does comprehend that what awaits it must be different.

Now, *different* is not always what you want, but you may magnify the fear of that and thus create a world that you don't want to see. Or you can perceive the Kingdom, the innate glory, the prism of the Divine, that splays out before you. You may know yourself in a construct that lifts itself to its own awareness of vibrational truth, or limits the self to the old spectrum, the old way of delineating what should be. The choice will of course be yours up to a point. But there is a point, we suggest, when all are lifting, and the one who seeks hardest to hold on to the old will be moved, whereas those of you who have already moved may welcome them, may herald their arrival, to this new state of alignment or re-accord.

No one can avoid this now because it is present in the field. And as present in the field, you are participatory to it. Imagine there's a lamp in the room, but you don't like the light it shines. Imagine you turn away from that lamp as long as you can. But as that light continues to build, you cannot avoid it. It will lift you with its presence, illumine you by its tone, and agree to you because it agrees to all things. The Source of all things—call it God, if you wish—is in agreement to all manifestation because manifestation does not exist without this idea, the Source of all things out-pictured as all things.

Now, the re-alignment that we have been discussing in prior texts, and in this one as well, is an agreement to what has already been but has been denied. But we will say this now: Where we intend to take you in this text and subsequent teachings is to an alignment where you are no longer thinking as you have. You are simply knowing and realizing, or recognizing, what is already so. "That doesn't sound very interesting," he says. Oh, it's very interesting. It's more than interesting. It's about being so present that every moment is new and experienced by you as such.

Now, when something is new, or prior unseen, it is not only interesting—it is a mystery always revealing itself. Again, use the metaphor of the tapestry, the blanket, the sheet, covering the old sculptures that have always been there but you have been looking at what covered them. When you understand that the process of revelation is not one act, but a state of consciousness that is always revealing itself, you will enjoy it and you will participate in it because you are also being made new in every moment because you cannot be as you were. When you operate in the ever-present now, the realization of the now supports the claim of the new. "Behold, I make all things new" is a state of consciousness and the act of the vibratory frequency that you have claimed. So you are participatory and you are also made new in this action of expression. "I know how I serve in truth."

Now, Paul interrupts. "While I understand what you say, it

feels like a fantasy to me." It is not a fantasy. It is what already expresses in the upper realm of reality. The reality you have known, encumbered as we have said through the dense field, precludes your experience of what already is. Intellectually you may fathom it. All things are made new all day long. Energy is in vibration. Everything is always in motion. You will understand this intellectually. Perhaps this gives you a context for what you will experience—underline *will*—at this level of tone. But until it is experienced and fully realized, it is conjecture. Understand, friends. This is not a solitary act. This is how humanity moves from one level of density to another. You cannot move to this level of density without altering the field because you could never maintain it. You cannot align to this level or field without the body adjusting because the body has been so entrained to the lower field, and been falsely instructed that the body is not divine, that you would not know what to do, once aligned to the higher. The alignment of the body and the energetic field and the identity you've held was the very first attunement we have offered you: "I am Word through my body. Word I am Word. I am Word through my vibration. Word I am Word. I am Word through my knowing of myself as Word." All that follows has been the realization of these claims that were always true, but denied by your experience in the common field that has been held by fear and claimed in separation. You can barely imagine what it must be like to be beyond separation.

Now, most of you want it in one way or another. You perceive separation as a product of your experience—night and day, winter and summer, polarities always. But when you understand that what you think of as a polarity is simply a different level of tone or experience in a common field, and the common field is one field, you will understand the idea of gradation. Not good and evil or black and white, but gradations of the same, expressing themselves in darkness or light. The denial of the Divine claims the density that you have experienced. When you stop denying the Divine, the lifting occurs, and the relationship to the Divine simply is what you are experiencing all day long. "Now, what does that mean?" he asks. Well, we said prior: praise—or recognition, which is praise—of the inherent Divine that you perceive as all things. But to understand the self in a construct of reality that is supported by this must simply mean that the reality you abide in is responding to the claim. In prior teachings we have encouraged you to claim, "I know what you are in truth," *what* being form or manifestation. And we have said well, again and again, that what you bless, blesses you in return. But to realize the Divine, to claim the Divine, is to give a blessing. And you are blessed by what you receive at the level of tone you incur.

So imagine a day where you awaken to a realization of the Divine. When you realize and recognize it, you are recognized by it. You are operating, not solo, but in tandem with Source. Your experience of self is as singular—but also conjoined, or with, or aligned to and through. Again, the woodwind instrument. The instrument is there, but it is realized as it is played. Do you understand this? The woodwind instrument sitting in the corner has capacity, but once played, once spirit flows through it, it is invoked in expression. In this expression, the tone that you sing supports the realization of everything— underline *everything*—that the tone encounters. And the tone lifts through what you would call entrainment that is the lifting to the higher at the level of tone that is being sung.

A world is changed, not through your decision to be in it, but through realizing who and what you have always been in agreement to it. And as we teach, and as we sing, we show you your song. But it is time to sing. It is not time to wait. It is time to call forth that which has always been yours. And as we complete this chapter, we will say these words to you now: Be prepared for change. Encourage change. Abide in change. And bless it as it comes, so that you may be blessed by it as well.

Thank you for your presence. The end of Chapter Two. Period. Period. Period. Stop now, please.

Part II

3

UNFOLDMENT

DAY FOURTEEN

What stands before you today, in a realized state, is a mission to procure the evidence of the new to be in reception to what is—beyond the old template, beyond the old ideas of what should be. When you say yes to this, you actually invite your experience to claim you in a higher octave. Now, your experience must be understood as what you see, think, and feel beyond the idea of what should be. Now, your eyes see one way, but at the level we teach, you become a sensor, an amplification, of the high tone which you are a recipient of. And it is this that calls you and your senses to the higher amplitude that is already present and waiting to be known by you. You say to us, "Give me what I wish," but you miss what's already there, and your experience is the key—how you say yes to a world made new, how you say yes to what can be, and in fact will be, in the claim "It will be so."

The realization of the manifest Divine is less an act of

being than a consequence of being and the choices made at a
level of tone. And *tone* means vibration. Now, when you align
to the high tone and are in recognition of it, the vibrational
field in its oscillation calls to it what it requires to realize itself
through, and the manifest Divine that is before you now is
yours for the taking and the partaking of. The shared experience of the Divine in form simply awaits your saying yes. What
stands in the way is what you think or would mandate through
the prior experience that you have accrued in the lower field.
When we work through you, when we instruct you, when we
support you in aligning to the higher octave, we see the pit-
falls that the egoic structure would erect—the idea of who you
should be, standing in the way of what you can only be in truth.
And the realization that the who and the what that you are has
actually claimed the higher claim—"I am free, I am free, I am
free"—and the realization of it must now be known by you.
Now, known by you, realized by you, comes at the cost of the
old. But the moment you are willing to say yes to what already
exists upon the mountaintop, you are claimed by the experience
of it.

Now, some of you would say, "Give me the evidence as I
want it." But the evidence that you want has actually been
procured through the lower field, or the idea of things as they
should be, inclusive of the Divine Self that comes as you think
it should. It does not come as you think it should. Because it's
eternal, it always expresses in the same accord, come through
you individually, yes, but the sound of the Divine and the tone
of the Divine does not differentiate as you would have it. It
simply is. To recognize your place in the octave of the high
room, the Upper Room, is to claim your seat at a vast table of

sharing and partaking of what is already there. Now, this table is not made for what you want, as some of you would wish it to be. But it is made for the sharing of consciousness at a level of vibration, and supports the manifestation of the world made new.

The world, as you have understood it, is actually partaking in this new experience. And the equivalency it holds, the world you've known yourself through, is actually ready to be received by you at this level of tone that it has said yes to. "What does that mean," he asks, "*it has said yes to?*" Well, we have spoken prior about the collective agreement to withstand change, to align to the higher potential that is already present and is seeking your release into it. But you don't understand that the world as a collective identity beyond individuation is also in song. You can call it the planet, if you wish, but in fact what this planet is, or your idea of planet, is simply a landscape that you present yourselves through. There are many worlds, and many ways of being known. But the architecture of the form you have taken still demands form be present for you to abide in. The aspect of you that exists beyond form, the Eternal Self, may know itself beyond the Upper Room. But while you are tethered to a body, you are tethered to a world. And a world made new is all things, everything that has claimed itself in form and any idea that may be held at this octave of choice.

"What is an *octave of choice?*" he asks. Well, at this level of tone you have free will, and the reclamation of the Divine in union with will is what supports the changes we speak to. When you move beyond the form you have taken you actually become in union with Divine Will, or a simple expression of it. The idea of choice is still present, but it is not what you would have it be because you've released the need to define outcome as you demand it should be. When that is released, you are simply in a higher claim, a claim of praise, a claim of receipt, a claim of the Kingdom: "God Is. God Is. God Is." And the unfolding of that experientially is what we are beginning to teach you.

Now, every text we have written has been a step forward—in comprehension, in consciousness, in the vibrational field. And as what you are, or the form you have taken, begins to claim this, the amplitude that you hold supports the reckoning that you are about to undertake. "What is the reckoning?" he says. The realization that the Source of all things is present as manifest and can now be known—underline the word *now*—in this eternal now. You are no longer subjecting yourself to an identity that demands outcome through the old template, but to be in the receipt of the Divine that is before you and seeking to be known by you. To be known by you is indeed to be known. And the claim we have offered you prior—"I Am Known, I Am Known, I Am Known"—to be known by the Source of all things is also to know it. You move in tone in consort with the divine presence, not only come as you, but come as the landscape and the world.

He interrupts the teaching. "Well, the world looks like a mess to me. Are we seeing beyond the mess? We're not fixing the mess—you have said that. But what are we actually doing?" You are actually lifting the senses themselves and the form you have taken to occupy a level of vibration where you are participating in the remaking of the world. It is not done by your hands, but by an allegiance and an agreement to Source that is in fact the one that does the work, or the aspect of you, come as and through you, that lifts itself to its own awareness of the implicit Divine. This will not be done through force of will. It cannot be held at that level. But it can be aligned to, is being aligned to, and the recognition of this is what we seek to give you now.

Every time you journey beyond the waking hours, every time you see yourself in a landscape that is other than you have known, you are actually being given an opportunity to remember, and to know that you exist beyond form. The dream world that you know is actually opportunity. When the dream becomes a waking dream, when you can understand yourself in the world but not of it, you begin to have the experience not only of divine nature experiencing itself as the form you have taken, but divine nature presenting itself to you in an equivalency. And this is the claim "It will be so."

Now, the mandate of the claim "It will be so" is in fact the sealing of the claim that came prior to it. "It will be so" claims the idea "Behold, I make all things new" as manifest. The manifestation of the claim "Behold, I make all things new" is the issuance that is uttered, that is invoked, and sealed in the claim "It will be so." Now, when you say to us, "How do I know this is so?" we actually invite you to begin to work with the teachings in a claim that is your experience. When you announce yourself—"I Have Come, I Have Come, I Have Come"—and you are in the Upper Room, the unfolding begins to claim you at a level of experience that you are not able to deny. The alignment is the key. "Behold, I make all things new," the realization of the manifest world—in change, in altered states, in a lifted state—is recognized as done in the completed form by the claim "It will be so." And the relishing of that experience is the tone of the Absolute that becomes your experience: "God Is. God

Is. God Is." When you relinquish the need to be in control of outcome, you can become the recipient. Each intonation is as a chord on a piano, and the comprehension of the chord "It will be so" is the claim of manifestation, "Behold, I make all things new" the action of it. And its becoming, in a resolute way, is confirmed by the claim "It will be so." And the outcome of that claim is the realization of form as Source, or the one note sung that has come as all things.

The teachings you are receiving now are coming in two different ways. The language that we speak is useful for you at a level of comprehension so that the mind may have some sense of what is happening to the template that you have utilized to claim the world you have known yourself through. But the manifest world is not changed by an intellectual understanding. It is changed by the embodiment and the realized form that has come as you, or the Monad expressed in a resurrected state claiming the Kingdom into form. What you have at a level of tone is a text that is always in vibration, and every text that we have spoken to you has come to be realized as vibration. The interesting aspect that you find, the words on the page, are simply there to support your experience of the altered state that each text responds to.

Now, the text is in response to you and to your requirements for growth. This happens at the level of the individual because the texts work with the individual and the collective both. Once you become a student of these texts, you are held in a realization of what your potential is, and supporting the mandate of your journey by your agreement to it. We support you as we can. We honor free will. But where we are invoking this now is to a level of participation, accord, and alignment to what not only already exists, but what can be known experientially by all of you. Now, the radical change that each of you will undergo through this participation is the requirement of the individual to be re-known. The claim "Behold, I make all things new" is not Alice or Frederick announcing this to the manifest world. It is the Divine that exists within and can express through Alice or Frederick as the divine experience of being. To know the self as this is to be participatory. It is the Divine that does this work. And it is this that claims you and alters the manifest world.

The choice is now yours to be participatory, to be at this great table of invocation. The prayer is a simple one.

"I Have Come. I Have Come. I Have Come. Behold, I make all things new. It will be so. God Is. God Is. God Is."

And the sound of the claim, several notes on a piano invoked as chord, announce the presence of the Monad as the actor, the one in action, maintaining the vibration that cannot be claimed at the level of personality. While the personality is assumed and re-known or reclaimed in the high order, it ceases to exist as you would have it, and is moved to a returned state where it is not operating in a false sense of separation. Once this union occurs, the personality has its own mandate: to be in a state of agreement to its Source, which is the Monad or the Christed Self come as each of you. Underline *each*. No one is beyond this.

Now, how this occurs has been in the instruction prior, but we will say this very simply: It is a re-knowing of self, and then the self knows the world in the higher octave where it is now aligned to. The choice is present in each of the claims we have offered you. And as we say these words to you now, we will invoke them:

> *All who hear these words, all who read these words, is re-known, are re-known, will be re-known, in the high claim of the Upper Room.*

As we say yes to what lies before you, as this great adventure commences, we announce this as the second part of the text that we are authoring now.

Blessings to each of you. Yes, the beginning of Chapter Three. Period. Period. Period. Stop now, please.

DAY FIFTEEN

What stands before you today, in a realized state, is a new idea, a new potential, a new claim of being upon what is experienced by you. Now, the prominence of history has been discussed at length. You see things as they were, not as they are. You understand yourself through the old reflections, the old bias, the old things erected in fear. The translation of your experience now, a world made new, must now be comprehended by you. And the articulation of the manifest world that is present for you to see or perceive can be claimed.

Now, the claims we have offered you in the past are all predecessors to what is now coming, and the claim "It will be so," which we have explained, we will speak again to. "It will be so" is the prominence and the re-creation of the prior claim: "Behold, I make all things new." This is the active aspect, the making new, the creation and re-creation of what was seen and is now seen anew. "It will be so" is the claim of it upon the manifest world. Re-creation: "It will be so." And the resulting claim, "God Is, God Is, God Is," is the result of the claim prior to it. "Behold, I make all things new. It will be so. God Is."

Now, the requirement for these claims is really very simple. The level of tone that you hold in the Upper Room supports the claim "It will be so" because you are not mandating change as opposed to experiencing it. The experience of the change is where we wish to take you now. You regulate your experience in the common field through ideas that are old and the expectation that those ideas must always be primary for you. But when the slate is cleaned, when the world is made new, the calibration and the experience of what is, is not only altered, but it is re-known. In other words, what you have known in past experience is re-seen, reclaimed, and re-known, not as it was, but as it can only be in truth.

Now, the manifest Divine, as we have said, is not what you expect it to be. Your child is still your child, but your child is the expression of God, beyond the idea of *mine*, even beyond the idea of child. The sunset is the sunset, but beyond any prior prescriptions that you have claimed for sunset. It is made new, is experienced in immediacy in the moment you sit in as what can only be. It is the unfoldment of God in an experiential way.

Now, some of you seek to discover these things in other ways. You take a medicine, you sit in meditation, you move mountains in conscious thought and then find yourself back in the body with the old stubbed toe, the old poor disposition, and you wonder where you went to and how in fact you were changed.

You may preview the Upper Room in many ways, but to claim a foundation here, which is the teaching you are receiving, is to claim your right to its inheritance or what you can know by claiming," I Am" and "I Have Come." The renunciation of the old is not what you think it is—"the things of this world," "that old bad habit." Renunciation is the alignment to what exists beyond the old. And in claiming the old, the new is not only renounced, but it is hidden from you. When you claim the new, you renounce the old, but your attachment to the old claims you again and again.

Now, you are not becoming unfettered. You are not untied to this plane. The body itself, even in a higher calibration, will walk the avenue, will breathe the air. But its experience would actually confound you if you understood what it really was in manifestation—the body as the Divine, experiencing the street, experiencing the fresh air, experiencing birth and death, as all things are so. Now, to see God as all things—or to *perceive*, which is a better word—is to claim the Divine, not to make it so, but to claim what has been and what has been hidden, or what been refuted or denied. The fear of the Divine has claimed walls, the fear that God is a fiery thing that will smite you, turn you to a pillar of salt, or wash away your city. The idea of God as something that is in retribution must now be understood, and re-understood, as a creation of humanity. Indeed, there have been floods. Indeed, there are fires. Indeed, there are always changes in your experience of this realm. But when you understand the Divine, and are party to the higher creation, you are reclaiming what has been denied and knowing yourself as worthy of it.

Now, this does not prevent you from other experiences, but it does claim you in a higher alignment where what you bring to the self is not what you would through the old accord. We will explain this for Paul, who is questioning. At every level of tone or vibrational accord there are ideas or expectations that you collude with. What exists in the low tone—be it fear, be it selfishness, be it premonition of disaster that you would seek to fulfill through your experience—must be understood as things that express at a level of tone that you have been aligned to. When you lift to the higher, you no longer claim those things. They stop being your experience. This does not mean that you are experiencing what you would say you should, but it does mean that what is experienced is far beyond what you would have claimed at the level that you have known yourselves through in prior history. In other words, you have been playing the old radio stations. You understand the old music. You think all music must resemble the old. You are prepared for the old and you get confused when the radio suddenly starts playing something other. What is being played now is a broadcast of love, and in love fear will not be claimed.

Now, again, your idea of love is confounding because you decide what love should be through an old idea or historical data—"my romance," "my best friend," "my family that I love." The Divine that is you, that has come as and through you, will not be denounced. And its acclimation in the Upper Room to your experience is where we are taking you now. Renunciation is the release of what was and also the expectations of what it should look like, resemble, or be through the old strata or the old reliance that the personality structure has acclimated to within the common field. What expresses beyond this, a world made new, is not what you would have, because you have little context for it.

Paul interrupts the teaching. "Well, if we don't have a context, what's the point?" We are actually offering you, not only a context, but an experience of it, so you may have your own mandate. The one who has never experienced a rainstorm may have it described to him or her ad infinitum, but she will not know rain until she is drenched by it. He will not know love until he is in love or in the vibration of love. And she will not know God until she is in God and in the experience of love that God presents.

Paul interrupts again. "But there are hard things here. We don't always feel love. We have trials. We have lessons. You are speaking of a kind of nirvana." No, indeed we are not. We are speaking of realization of what has always been that you have denied in vibrational accord through prior acclimation. "Behold, I make all things new," spoken from the Upper Room, reclaims what is encountered in the act of re-creation. The act of re-creation is solidified or claimed through this: "It will be so." And the expression of that claim—"God Is, God Is, God Is," not wishful thinking, but experience of God as all there is—is what is being summoned and in accord to.

Now, *summoned* is the correct word, because Paul is asking, "Was that the correct word?" It is, indeed, *summoned*. It has been there, but your senses have denied it. And your actualization, or what you believe yourselves to be in prior strata, still denounces it. The resignation that things will always be as they were is what confounds you the most. And by *confounds* we don't mean personally, but collectively. You are confounded by your agreement to what once was, what things were named, how they should be seen and experienced.

The claim in the Upper Room—"I Have Come"—claims the Divine in *its* purview, in *its* prominence, and *its* actualization is what claims everything after that. The personality structure that is used to the old suddenly experiences what it has not—again, the rain. The one who has not known it may be frightened at first. "Is this what they mean by rain? Is this what a rainstorm feels like?" But when you stand naked and agreeing to what has always been, you are assumed. That is the correct word. You are *assumed* by the Source of your very being, by every cell that sings as God, that announces God's presence because it is always so.

We are speaking to a moment-by-moment experience of the Divine as what is, not what must be sought or challenged, but what you are aligning in. Notice we said *in* and not *to*. When you are lifting to the resurrection, or the resurrected state of vibration that claims the Kingdom into manifestation, you are rising *to*, but at a level of accord. And where we have taken you through the prior teachings, you are in alignment to what expresses at the top of the mountain when you stop looking at the clouds and projecting what *was* upon them. Your idea of history, even the illusion of history, is tactile for you, is something you can taste and see, what it should be because what it once was. Imagine you are tasting a fruit you have never tasted before. You will try to find out what it is by comparison. "This is a melon." "This is a grape." "This tastes like this or that." But until you release the old, and the propriety the old claims upon your experience, you cannot taste the fruit that is being offered to you.

As we sing, we claim in tone the inherent Divine that is present in every aspect of you, including those aspects of you that you would refute the Divine in—"my bad nature," "my bad temper," "my bad idea of who I was," or what *bad* is in general. In this song, the *re*-clamation of yourself as what you think, and redeemed to what you are, re-known to what you must always be, is the song, is the tone, and the experience of our offering to you. When we say these words, we announce what is always true:

> *On this day we claim that all who hear this tone, all who read these words informed by this tone, will be met experientially in the agreement to what is always true. It will be so. God Is. God Is. God Is.*

On the count of three, Paul.
One. Now two. Now three.

[The Guides tone through Paul.]

What is will be. What was will be re-known. What is challenged by fear will be lifted to love. What is claimed in love will know itself as worthy. And what you say, what you are, what you can only be in truth, will be the song of being: "I Have Come."

Blessings to each of you. Indeed, this is in the text. Stop now, please. Period. Period. Period.

DAY SIXTEEN

What stands before you today, in an awakened state, is a new agreement: to claim the ideal, the True Self, the Manifest Self, that has not only been awaiting your permission, your agreement, your consent, but has been mandated to realize itself through the being that you are.

"What does that mean?" he asks. Well, the mandate of the Monad is always explicit: to be known *as*. To be known as is inclusive, the Monad as God, the Monad as finger, the Monad as earth and sky, the explicit divinity that may be known in all forms. Now, when we use the word *Monad* we work with it interchangeably with the ideal of Christ, and Christ as ideal can also be understood—the perfected aspect of the Divine that seeks expression through form.

Now, the docile natures that you've held, the ones who wish things would stay as they are, are perturbed by these teachings. You say you want change in the increments you allow. You say you want love as long as it resembles your idea of love. You say you want bounty, but you don't want to be greedy, but you certainly want more than the one beside you. All of you decide, in one way or another, what you can align to and how you can claim it. But the Monad itself, or the Christ ideal, in manifestation through you, is not tempered by these requirements. There comes a position in one's alignment where one is only receptive. This is a new teaching. We have to keep Paul quiet because he will interrupt every moment. When you say yes at a certain level, the Monad claims itself and aligns will and purview through its bounty, its beneficence, its love. And the expression of love that has come as you is a song sung, a flute played, a bell rung, and a great love expressed as can be known in form. Now, *can be known in form* is interesting. *Can be known in form* means the Divine explicitly can express without you in fullness, but your agreement and the consent you have offered—"I am in the Upper Room, I Have Come"—has supported this agreement not only as an exchange of vibration, the release of the lower to the higher, but has also allowed the Divine to claim its explicit nature regardless of what was claimed prior.

Now, the manifestation of a new world, which is what this teaching is claiming, is not what you would wish it, but as it can only be. There comes a moment where things must change, and the resonance of that *must* is present for all. How it comes changes in every time. How it comes is altered in every moment. But all of you who are present for it indeed will know. Now, we are not speaking of an event, as some would wish it, but we are speaking of a sound, a trumpet, or a tone in resonance that is sung and expressed and encompasses you. Now, the encompassing of this field, the higher to the lower, is a re-creation of what was—not a destruction, but a re-knowing of it. When something is re-known, it is reclaimed and re-seen. And the manifest world in this assumption, the higher claiming the lower, will have a calibration and an infinite tone that is sung as all things.

Now, we must explain this, in some ways, so you may understand what will follow. There is a level of pitch that cannot be ignored that actually invokes the Divine as manifest. To understand this is to understand the Word, or the active principle of the Divine, as spoken, as sounded, as sung. Each

of the texts we have offered have been in intonation at a level
of tone or decibel that the reader can encounter and be met
by. But where we take you now, not only in this text, but in all
teachings to follow, is in the resonance—underline the word
in—*in* the resonance of the Word.

Now, imagine a sound that overtakes you, that pierces your
field and every cell of your being in an inclusive way. You are
not being harmed. You are being included. You are being spoken anew. "Behold, I make all things new" is an invocation
we have taught you about how you claim the manifest world.
But indeed you are claimed as well, and the manifest world
through you, an out-pictured world, is sung into being by the
one who has been claimed—and fully claimed, we suggest—by
what was always present but has been denied. The denial of the
Divine, the only challenge you have faced, will be released in
coming times. And the order that this claims itself in will have
much to do with a level of agreement that humanity will come
to in coming times.

Paul interrupts. "*Coming times* is too general. Tell me when
this is happening, if it's a date on a calendar." It is not a date on
a calendar because at this level of tone the calendar doesn't exist. And your idea of time, which is simply measurement of experience, is no longer valid. Now, sound itself can be measured
in some ways, but what we are speaking to is very different.
It's a field of sound that has been invoked that is participatory
already to your experience, but has been denied by you as such.
And its denial is released the moment it says yes to its full
participation in your experience. "What does that mean, *its
participation*?" Well, understand this: While the will is utilized
at the level of the individual—"I Have Come" is a choice to

speak, but the invocation of it is the choice of the Monad expressing through you—the fullness of experience and the full magnitude of experience is also chosen in an interaction.

Now, God does not override free will. You have been granted free will and you align free will in the Upper Room to high benefit. But the assumption, which is the receipt of the totality of the Divine at the level that it can be held in form, is not only an event, but one that occurs in stages and in the moment both. "What does that mean?" he asks. *In the moment both* means your experience of the ocean rising is one experience, but the ocean is already risen. Your experience of being, in this level of vibration, is simply the level of amplitude that can be manifested with your presence permitted and its agreement to you. Stop deciding what God is and telling God what it must do, once and for all. Allow God to be what it is. Infinite truth. Infinite love. And the field that encompasses these things is present for you always. But your dictation—"this is what my world should look like and what my bank account must resemble and what my body should do"—is the small self parading about, saying, "See what I can make God do."

Now, this idea of how to get was useful for most of you at a level of development. You understand that you must plant the soil for the soil to bloom. You must understand that you may write the word for another to be able to read it. You are participatory to all creation. But you are not invoking as much as agreeing, and this agreement is in mutuality. God sees God and agrees to God in all of its manifestations, and the agreement is coherence. What stops the coherence is only one thing: the invalidation or the refuting of the Monad by the aspect of self that would decide for herself what it must be or should be or how it should be seen.

When we speak to you now, we are speaking from a precipice, and our words come in oscillation as you can receive them. But the energy that informs the words is an eternal energy. It is always present. And calamity as you might imagine it, feeling forsaken as you may have experienced it, are choices of the lower realm. In the high octave how you see yourself and what you believe yourself to be is not only altered, but agreed to in the alteration. "What does that mean?" he asks. Well, imagine you suddenly realized that you were twenty feet tall. "I never knew I was twenty feet tall." But your landscape agrees with you and confirms your experience of the new height. In this case the height is amplitude or the vibrational tone that exceeds what you've known. And the building blocks of your world, primarily as you see them or think they are, were all claimed in the lower tone. When the higher tone is claimed, the manifest world is altered, and altered to support, for example, the one who is now twenty feet tall, or perceives from a higher place, or sings from the high balcony for those in the lower to be called.

Recalibration is not without effort. When a child is growing into manhood—womanhood, if you prefer—the bones are stretched. It is awkward. It is uncomfortable. You knew how to ride a bike with very little legs. Now you learn again with new long legs. And this is occurring now. Many of the students of this work who understand themselves in agreement to the teachings they've received have actually prepared themselves at a level of vibration for where we are taking them now. And the preparation was necessary because the consciousness you have held must be expanded, must lift, to be able to claim the higher experience that is available to you. Imagine you didn't know there was an Upper Room and suddenly there's all this activity that makes no sense. "What's going on up there?" you say. Well, now you get to go find out for yourselves. And the agreement to understand, and to be in beneficence as the one who has come, as the one who claims all things new, is the gift of giving, the gift of giving to all.

When we began this text, we spoke of ambassadors, becoming a portal or emissary to the vibration that is the Upper Room. But the vibration that is the Upper Room is indeed the vibration of the Christ or the Monad or the manifest Divine, come as each of you and seeking its reclamation through all it experiences. Now, the light itself is not trying to be the light. The light simply is. You are not trying to be the Monad. God forbid you should try to be the Christ. You would find yourself locked in a room somewhere, saying, "Oh, look at that one. She thinks she's the Christ today." You can't think you are the Christ, but you can *be* it as expression. It is not a title. It is not a last name. It is what you become at the level of consciousness that embodiment entails.

Now, the manifest Divine, Christ as all things, must then be understood as the calibration of the Divine as lifted to purview, to prominence, through invocation and agreement. Invocation: "It will be so." "God Is, God Is, God Is," the result of the invocation. The manifest Divine that is before you is not seeking your approval, not waiting for you to say, "Oh, make me pretty again. I was cursed in the lower field. Give me a blessing." It is being re-seen in its primary state, which is the energy of the Creator in vibration, come as teapot, come as sun and moon, come as your grandchild, or that woman across the street who never smiles when you pass. To know the one before you as of God is to know all things as of God. "Don't we get to discriminate?" some of you say. "There are terrible things, terrible people. They need to be punished, they need to be removed, they are not allowed in my Upper Room." Then you are a hypocrite and this teaching has meant nothing to you. Your choice to bless one and curse the one beside her leaves you in shadow, and you may pretend to be the light but the lampshade you are wearing is demanding you claim separation.

We see you as you are. We understand your requirements. How you grow. How you bless and curse. We do not condemn you. You condemn yourselves, and there is no need. You are not making somebody better. You are not improving the world. You are claiming the world as it can only be claimed at the level of resonance that you have agreed to: "I Have Come. I Have Come. I Have Come."

Now, the Monad expressed as you undertakes unfoldment— first through you, and then through your experience, because your experience is the out-picturing or expression of consciousness. The magnitude of vibration that you align with in blessing, which is the presence of the Divine, claims itself in equality through all things encountered. The choice is not only yours at the level of personality—"I will invoke this and allow the Divine through me"—but then it is the Divine, because it is only the Divine that can claim the full phrase "I Have

Come; It will be so." Manifestation: "Behold, I make all things
new. It will be so." And the result, the explicit result, the full
orchestra playing at once: "God Is. God Is. God Is."
We have many things to teach you. We say this for the man
in the chair: "How do we speak all this time? Do you have
things prepared?" We have a book to offer. We have students to
receive it. We are blessed by your presence. We will take a pause.
Period. Period. Period. This is in the text. Stop now, please.

(PAUSE)

We would like to continue.

Now, the idea of who you are or what you think you are has
been addressed at length. We would like to address what you
are not: You are not alone. You are not confused. You are not
abandoned. You are one with God, even on your darkest day.
Your preclusion of that experience is what is being addressed
by us, in stages, so you may reunite with your maker.

Now, we don't use that term lightly. *Maker* is a wonderful
word for Source. You may have made the eggs and served them
on the plate, but you did not make the egg or the chicken. The
chicken itself is God, another expression of it, and you partake
in all expressions while denying its Source. Your realization of
who and what you are and can only be in truth, your choice
to align and agree, has been essential to this process. When
one changes, one goes through change, aligns in change, and
claims the outcome that is the result of the change. When one
denies change or seeks to refute it, she may have a different
experience. But finally, we suggest, the changes will occur with
or without your agreement.

"What does that mean?" he asks. Well, the world that you see, in its shifting, is releasing aspects of itself that can no longer be held through the low vibration. The low vibration is being altered and the lifting is occurring in different ways. And the experience of this lifting, indeed change, is not only unsettling, but confusing. But as we said at the beginning: You are not confused. You are not abandoned. The aspect of you that knows who she is, is how you claim yourself in realization of change, is how you support yourself in navigating it, and how you claim others as they truly are. The aspect of you that is the Christ or the Monad is unchangeable. It is the Eternal Self. It is not the soul progressing. It is the Eternal Self—that which was and is and will always be. Its expression through you and the soul as a solidified expression of the Monad is what is occurring now. But the manifestation of the Monad as what you are has change implicit within it. You cannot claim the higher while refuting God or denying the Divine, and this includes any manifestation that you may have accrued. If you decide the Divine cannot be in the pain, you have put the pain outside of God. If the pain is part of your experience, and henceforth in agreement to a higher tone, your experience of the pain may be altered, and your experience of God, inclusive of pain, may release the need for pain itself.

You decide, in many ways, what you will approve of, how you should change, and what you will never change with. Everything that you have trusted in the material realm is actually being altered in these times. The very fabric of what you think of as reality is being re-toned, re-sung. And the expression of the new, and the unfoldment of it, is where we are bringing you now. Each chapter of this text is a new tone. When all of the chapters of this text are completed as one, the text itself will be a tone, a chord of tone, that will support the release of what is no longer required. You are not going to have to figure it out, pick through your old clothing to see what to discard and what to keep. This action is being done with you as the Monad reclaims you. And the distortion that you have operated in—how you think the world should be, based on prior false premise—will be related and re-known in a higher tone, and re-seen.

We sing your songs for you so that you may learn the words. But what you don't see now is that you know the words. You are the song. Be sung, and be made new in the singing of it.

We thank you for your presence. Indeed, this is in the text. Stop now, please.

(PAUSE)

When we speak to you about what is to come, you seek time frames and delineation so that you may plan ahead, find what you need, know before others do. We are speaking of an ongoing event, or process of recalibration, that has been commenced with the agreement of Source and humanity. In other words, you all said yes. "Time to grow up. Time to claim inheritance. Time to say what I am at the cost of what I believed myself to be."

Each of you before us today who hears these words has been claimed at a level of tone in recalibration. How you experience yourselves in this process will vary greatly. Those of you who say yes with your heart and soul will find yourself carried well. Those of you who say yes with the wish, "Oh, dear

Lord, let it be so," will be met at that level of wish. And, indeed, we will meet you in support as we can. The requirement is for faith, or, if you prefer, belief. But for most of you this is tangential, conjecture—"if it gives me what I want and if it can really be." We say now to those of you who say yes with requirements: You will be met at that level as well.

"What does that mean?" he asks. Well, some of you seek to know God through artifice. You seek to be costumed as the one who knows God and parade your faith for others to see. Some walk in humility, but seek to find God in a small place—where he will not be seen, she will not be expressed—so she may feel safe. Finally, we say to all of you: You are seen beyond the costume. You are seen beyond your desire to be small. You are seen as you can only be. And what we give you and what we offer you will in fact be what you require to move beyond the idea of conditioning, or having your relationship with Source be premised by a set of requirements that you believe God's responsibility is to fill.

Finally, we say to all of you: What we are teaching is not only practical, but demonstrable, which means you can experience it. And we say you will at the level of tone that you are now aligning to. We must keep repeating ourselves because you keep disavowing what we say. You have been prepared. You have been made ready. Humanity has been made ready, although it denies it. And some of you say, "Here we go." And others of you say, "Never in a million years." But finally the energy is such that all will be lifting, some with great laughter, expectation, and joy, and some with fear that things are changing too quickly. No one is left behind. No one is more favored than the next. And all of you are loved.

We will complete this teaching for today. This is in the text. Period. Period. Period. Stop now, please.

(PAUSE)

What stands before you today, in a realized state, is recognition of what can and will be chosen in the upper realm, or the degree of velocity that you are becoming accustomed to. Underline those words: *becoming accustomed to.* When you realize who and what you are, when you know who and what you are, the qualifications you hold for claiming anything are immediately altered. Now, you still claim, but from a place of receptivity. You are aligning to what is, and in receipt of it. You are not seeking it. You are not foraging. You are not rummaging. You are not fielding. You are accepting.

To be in a state of acceptance from the Upper Room is to receive your good. And a claim that is made in the Upper Room—"I receive my good, I know myself as worthy of my good"—can claim you in many ways beyond the small self's agenda for what you would receive. Some of you say to us, "Am I allowed to know myself as loved?" In fact, that is your birthright. You are already loved. And to allow love to know you, to agree to be loved in the knowing of love, is the gift you may receive now. When you ask for love, when you predispose a position—"am I going to get it or not?"—you are setting yourself up in most ways for disappointment, the belief that it will not be, or you cannot be allowed, or you cannot be in receipt. The aspect of you that knows itself as loved is indeed the Monad. The Monad *is* love, or one of the expressions of it.

Now, to be expressed as love is to move into a qualification:

to be as this. Underline the word *as*. Like properties. Like valuation. And like comprehension. When you are comprehended in love, you are known in love, and the one who can comprehend love must know it already. He interrupts the teaching. "But some of us don't." Again, Paul, this is the level of personality. The personality structure does not really know love. It knows its ideas of love. Perhaps it knows how it feels when someone smiles, poses a compliment. Perhaps it knows what it feels like in an embrace, when taking a vow at a wedding. But these are transitional states, and feeling states. As the expression of love, you have been assumed by love, encompassed in it and within it. You are the fountain of love that flows through you and to all others.

Now, this is receipt. You are the fountain of love, but you are not the source of it. You are the expression of it, but not the source of it. The Monad is the expression, and the Monad is God in articulation through you. There is an aspect of you that will always be present at this level of tone—in observance, in awareness, and in recognition of who she has been, how he has chosen, or how he or she has refuted the very love that is present. But as the fountain of love, the overflowing fountain, you are in reception and you are benefiting others simultaneously. It takes no effort. You do not try to do this. You move to recognition of your worth—"I know who and what I am"—you align in the Upper Room, and your expression there is your service. But when the Monad begins to articulate as you—underline *as*—its manifestation is its purview, not the small self's. And its purview is love. Spectacular love. Not lofty love. Brilliant love that is immediate in its experience.

"What does that mean?" he asks. Well, to be in the immediate experience of love is to be as the wave that overtakes all things, is to be in and of it in simultaneity, and in recognition of the act of being participatory and in offering simultaneously. "What does that mean?" You are receiving and giving, both, at the same time. The choice will be yours to accept this, in some ways, but you are so used to refuting love because it doesn't come in the package you think it should that you deny the love that is actually present now and awaiting your agreement to it, coherence with it, alignment to and with. Each of you say yes at the level of tone you can hold. But we will tell you this now: Love does not deny you any good thing. Love cannot deny you any good thing. Love does not bring pain, nor does it bring suffering. It releases fear, and it brings the light that it is of to all manifestation.

Now, imagine, if you wish, for a moment that you are as a fountain. And it is the heart center, in its illumination, its brightness, its overflow, that moves the vibration of the Monad through every aspect of you—unfiltered, undenied— and its expression as manifest through you will align you in overflow. Now, the overflow of love is, again, not intentional. It is what occurs when the Monad itself is acting without restriction. The borders that you have utilized—"who is deserving of my love and what must I get in return"—must evaporate now in order for this expression to be fully realized. And *fully realized* is the key. The manifestation of the Monad as love, as expressed through you in its brilliance, will actually call to you the experiences that are in alignment to love.

"What does that mean?" he asks. Well, you understand that what you put in darkness calls you to the darkness. We have

explained this many times. But what is known in love will call
to you the same thing. What you bless, blesses you in return.
And when the expression of love is present—in your affairs,
in your relations, in your endeavors, in your awareness of all
things—love is returned, and from everywhere at once. Now,
imagine a church with a bell that tolls once upon the hour. You
wait for the bell. You know where you sit. "It must be lunch-
time, I heard the bell toll." "It must be time to go home, there
went the bell." But the bell that is ringing here is always ringing. And it is always calling the same thing—divine presence
as manifest—into experience. Now, you look at tone. You try
to understand tone through the language you've utilized thus
far. If you wish to think of it in another way—the resonant
field—you might have an easier time. Imagine there's vibration that exists beyond sound. Sound is present, but your experience is not of the ears. It's the vibration as it moves through
you and through all things. When the bell is always ringing,
and the bell is ringing love, love is your state of being.

Now, there have been sages throughout time who have
known embodiment and known themselves in love. You know
them primarily through their acts, their martyrdom, or their
idea of sacrifice—they loved the world so much. You don't
need to be a martyr to love. It requires no martyrs and no sacrifice, because when one is in love, and the expression of love
is as you, everything changes, including what you think your
life must be, has been, and certainly what can be. All things
are altered in love. Now, selflessness is present here, and all
who have fully demonstrated love have moved to selflessness
in one manner or another. How does one become selfless but
by being renewed at the level of tone where the manifestation

and mandate of the personality structure is actually held in abeyance and moved from its primary position to a lower field so you may be applicable as the demonstration.

"Explain this, again," he asks. We will try to. When you are selfless, the aspect of you that has been central to your learning and experience, the one who seeks to get and claim, is actually removed, or moved to a lower strata. It may still exist, but it is no longer commandeering the show. It is no longer calling the shots and demanding the rules be met on its terms. The selfless aspect of you is already in love and requires nothing, absolutely nothing, in return. It simply expresses. "I know how I serve." Now, when how one serves is in love and as love, everything is altered. You may do what you wish by expression. You may help others. But you may also know yourself in solitude and love the world fully. There is no mandate of what this must be. The only mandate is the alignment that will claim it. Trust us, if you wish, to show you what we mean. We will say these words on your behalf:

On this day I claim that all who hear these words will be re-known in the field of love and in expression as love. And as I say these words, as these words are invoked by all of us, we give testimony to love through our agreement to you. We know who you are in truth. We know what you are in truth. We know how you serve in truth. You are loved. You are known. And you are received as love.

Be still and know, and be received.

Ask each one to be received as they can be held, as they can be known, as they can be lifted, as they can be chosen, in choice, in agreement, to their benefit. Period. Period. Period.

Thank them for their presence. We will stop now, please. Yes, this is in the text.

DAY SEVENTEEN

What stands before you today, in a realized state, is an acknowledgment of who others are, beyond any frame that you might hold for them. The idea of "my brother," "my mother," "my child," "my neighbor," "my compatriot" must be replaced with the infinite I Am that is translated as them, expressing as them, in their own perfect ways. We use the word *perfect* intentionally here. Whoever they are, and however they are expressed, is actually their perfection at the level of demonstration and alignment or consciousness that they hold. You are always expressing consciousness. You are always expressing who you are. But the aspect of *who* that you decide about is held within a frame—"my brother," "my mother," "my friend"—and these frames, while useful, hold limitations. One may be your brother and of God, your neighbor and of God. And when we say *of God*, we are not speaking a platitude. We are stating their expression, the Divine that has come as them in perfect manifestation. Again, we use the word *perfect* intentionally. When you decide who someone should be, how they should behave, you are claiming them in a frame, expecting them to fulfill your idea, and their perfected ways are always their true expression.

He interrupts the teaching. "So somebody can be misbehaving and operating in their perfect way? They can be angry at others and still operating in perfection?" Absolutely, yes. But you misunderstand the teaching. They are always demonstrating the level of consciousness they hold. And at that level, perceiving their perfection aligns them in fullness to the Divine Self that is operating as well. Underline *as well*. Nobody is distinct or separate from their divine nature. The frames you utilize are actually constructions, ways of seeing another within a common field. The branding that you use—"this is my attorney," "those are my friends," "those are the people we are at war with"— hold frames, limitations, and discriminate. To move beyond discrimination is to move towards equality, and there is no better equalizer than the Divine or the Monad that has actually come as all of you.

Now, when the trumpet sings, all are called forward. And the trumpet is the new high tone that is not only available, but present now and already beginning to express beyond the framework or architecture that you have utilized thus far. The architecture was required to maintain an idea of what the common field should be. The architecture we speak to is simply the way you see the world, how the world is constructed, the elements that make up the world and your categorizations of them. Language is imbued to cement form, to create common understanding or common usage. "There is the cave. We will remain in the cave until the storm stops." You understand *cave*. You give it a usage. You understand *storm*, and you understand you don't want to be in it. So you claim things in a coherent manner, and the architecture of your world are these ideas in multiplicity. "That is the factory we work at," "the government we pay our bills to," "the king on the throne that we wish would abdicate." All of you are present within a common field, operating in common law, and the use of frames is how you discern, and also how you discriminate.

To move to inclusivity, which is this teaching, is to render all things new beyond what they were named as, beyond what they were used for, and beyond the mandates prior architecture has held. The manifest world is what you have claimed, what you abide in, what you operate within and benefit from. But the strata of vibration that overrides—coexists with and overrides—the common field, which we call the Upper Room, is a level of consciousness that does not hold the level of discrimination that you have been instructed in. "This is a good thing and a bad thing," "a good man, a bad man," "a good idea and a bad idea." All of the manifestations that you are in an encounter with in any day were once idea. And idea is Source, finally said, in an equivalency that has claimed manifestation.

The triumph of this teaching, and indeed it is a triumph, is the resurrection of the living Christ, or the Monad, or the Divine Spark, in its full flame, in its full light, and its claim upon the manifest world as all things made new. The triumph of the individual through this process is not what you would have it be, but what can only be in truth. And the responsible natures you hold to what you see before you—"how do I interact with this person or thing?"—must now be understood as what you have chosen to be in an encounter with. When you release the frames you have utilized to discuss, to decide, to make sense out of what you experience, you move to a new potential, a higher idea. And the higher idea is Source awaiting reclamation.

"Now, what does that mean?" When you lift to the Upper Room, you are in an encounter with the unmanifest, beyond what you have utilized thus far. This simply means that when all things are rendered new, the aspect of self that claims these things, the Monad or the living Christ, is not attached to any prior meaning, nor the language that was utilized or the morality that was offered to decide what things should be or must mean. The flexibility of the new amplitude means that things may be seen beyond what they were named as or utilized for. And what is present here, we could simply say, exists beyond the old architecture that you have utilized to claim things as manifest.

Now, manifestation is a process. First, idea. The possibility is claimed in the idea and then made so in form. Everything is first imagined, first a thought. Your worst nightmares, as they come to pass, were first thought, as are your greatest joys. Realization of the Divine, as we support you in, supports you in reclamation of manifestation at a higher level of tone than you have been accustomed to. And there is consequence to this. If all you have known to do is to make a sandcastle that will be buffeted by a wave and mowed down, that is all you will ever make. When you understand that manifestation in the Upper Room, again, consequence of thought, is deeply different when the thoughts are new, then what you are claiming is inspired in the truest sense of the word.

Now, to be truly inspired is to be directed in the moment you sit in, and what is created at this level is a new infrastructure or a new architecture. We prefer *infrastructure* because as a grid is laid, as a foundation is poured, what may come on top of it may vary greatly. You live in a summer climate, you want the windows and the breeze. You live in a winter climate, you wish a stove and windows that will be closed always. You understand yourselves through the requirements of circumstance and will continue to create as such. But at the level of the

Monad, what is aligned to and then claimed into manifestation is not only markedly different, but we would have to say a
great improvement on what you have chosen in the past. Now,
he interrupts the teaching. We stressed the word *improvement*,
knowing he would have a reaction to it. "But that is *better*. You
said better and worse, good and bad, are the old ways of seeing
things." We will use this example, Paul. You may have a beautiful roof, but it will cave in under great snow. To improve the
roof is to make sure that it will hold in a great storm. What is
created from the Upper Room will not be claimed in fear, and
consequently will not be operating in distortion.

Now, *distortion* is a valuable word, and distortion is always
impressed by *should*, because *should* always means you are relying on past evidence, which is faulty in its benefit, to decide
what should be. He interrupts again. "Well, isn't it history that
it's a cold climate and we need a roof that will support the
snow?" If it is snowing now, you need the roof. You are not mandating there will be snow. How something is chosen, and will be
chosen from now on, will be in the immediacy of circumstance.
And all circumstance is, is an encounter with what is manifest.

Now, we are using the word *manifest* intentionally. What
is manifest is before you. It is your experience of the moment,
the floor that you stand upon, the window you peer out of, the
face that smiles back at you, in these moments, and your presence in these moments in the Upper Room reclaims what you
see in your encounter. And the manifest world, altered by your
presence and being, reclaims all things in higher alignment.
When inspiration occurs in these moments, you will know to
act. You will not be conjuring. You will not be debating. You
will be knowing. And as you know, and claim knowing, what

is rendered before you through consciousness will be what is required and what will stand firm—you may say *improved*—over how you have chosen to know prior, or decide prior.

Much of what you think you know now is based on false ideas, collective reasoning, a kind of algebra that is useful only up to a point. When you measure things in the common field, you have the ideas of how things are measured in intractable ways. When you move to the Upper Room, and you move to an energetic structure in a reclamation that what has been made manifest is first vibration, the idea of measuring or using a field, a common idea, to decide what should be is replaced by the immediacy, the moment-by-moment experience, and the choices that can be made from this level of amplitude. What is produced at this level of amplitude is not held in fear.

Now, a bank was a good idea when the first bank was decided upon. We have used the example in the past that the first bank was the one who held the purse while the hunter went into the field, so when he returned his presence would be known by the return of the purse. The one who held the purse was the first banker. But the idea became institutionalized. The banker needed recompense. He built a structure to support what he held. He charged interest, offered interest, made deals. And finally the institution itself became weighted by corruption, a way of holding or withholding or keeping what might otherwise be shared. When a structure is built and claimed in the Upper Room—and this is again done through inspiration and knowing—what the structure is cannot be tainted by the requirements of the lower field.

Now, imagine there is a mountain, and a valley below that floods. When you build the house high up the mountain, the circumstances are different. The house will not be flooded. When you lift to the higher, the level of amplitude that is held becomes uncorruptible. Now, that's an interesting word, but an accurate one. You must first understand that the Monad itself is uncorruptible—without sin, or what your idea of sin is. It is unblemished. It is untainted. And what claims itself through the Monad must hold those properties. Paul imagines someone making a great work of art—inspired art, perhaps—and someone else running up to it with a can of paint, destroying the canvas, making it void. That will not happen because what is created in the Upper Room will maintain a level of resonance where what coheres with it must be of like amplitude.

Imagine you have a fish, and only one fish, to feed the multitude. The miracle of the fishes was the level of agreement the one claiming many fishes could hold. There was enough for all and the meal was fine. Now, to understand what this means simply means that you are not abiding in the old infrastructure or the old architecture.

He interrupts the teaching. "Well, my money is in the bank. What does that mean? What about the high bank? Do I make a deposit?" You are completely misunderstanding the teaching. The manifest world that you operate in, again the common field and its architecture, is being re-known in the high amplitude. When things are released, it means they can no longer be in service at the level of tone humanity is claiming, and it will be made new. Once it is made new, your relationship with the structure will be vastly different. You have the temptation, Paul, to project your insecurities to a level where they don't exist. When something doesn't exist—"I will be made wrong, I will get disappointed, it will not be the way I want"—when these things no longer exist, your relationship to what you see, claimed in the Upper Room, is vastly different because you are not claiming fear. And you cannot claim fear with the creations of the Upper Room because they will not resonate in fear.

Now, fear is a blanket word, but the things that it covers are many. The denial of the Divine is fear projected. Greed, lust, another denial of the Divine. "Why is lust the denial of the Divine?" he asks. Well, lust itself is the craving of something that you believe cannot be brought to you. You may enjoy the bodies all you wish, but if you pillage or you rape you are denying the inherent Divine in what you see and experience.

Now, the idea that the small self is sinful is actually not true. The small self has done its best. But you abide in a field, in a dense field, that has accrued great evidence of the denial of the Divine, and you make that work. You go for what you want. You push your neighbor out of the way to retrieve what you think you lost, lest she find it first. What is occurring here is a vast change in consciousness and vibration, because you cannot hold the old level of consciousness at the level of vibration we are speaking to. And the idea of sin, which is claimed in the denial of the Divine, is actually released because there is no point to it. Why would you be greedy when you know the Source of all things? Why would you be stingy when you know that there is always more? Why would you deny love when you know that love is God expressing? Why would you be harmful to another when you understand you only harm yourselves through that act?

Now, these levels of awareness are present now, but you

understand them, first and foremost, intellectually. To comprehend them is to be in agreement to them. And that is what we are giving you now. It is indeed an offering, but it is present for you now—not someday when, but in this very moment you sit in. Inspiration, you see, has always been present, and the highest resonance you have ever experienced in inspiration was not of this plane, but was of the higher plane. All great art, all great moments of illumination, were in some ways cracks in the encasing of the energetic field that you have used to preclude experience. When one is awakened suddenly, it is as if the egg has cracked, and they are flooded with the light. Some go mad. Some found a religion. Some do great deeds. But all are altered forever because one can never be the same. We don't crack the egg. We move the egg to a level of tone where the requirement of the egg, or the idea of separation, is no longer a requirement, and consequently you may shed what has been obstructive to your experience. And the inspiration that exists at this level of tone will claim you in circumstance that you could not have claimed prior because you would have denied the potential for it.

None of you claims what you don't believe you can have or hold. You say you want something, but you don't believe you're allowed it. You say you want friendship or love, but you deny the potential in an agreement that it will not be. The circumstances that claim these things, historical evidence accrued through the lower field, have no field, no resonance, no claim upon you, in the Upper Room. That is why you move to allowance in the upper field and a reclamation of what has always been yours. It has always been yours to be loved. It has always been yours to love. It has always been yours to experience God, but your idea of God was quite mistaken. And while some of the processes you've been offered in different traditions will support some illumination, the idea of being re-embodied as the True Self, which was the true teaching of Christ, was removed from you because you could not be controlled if, in fact, you knew who you were. Knowing is realization, and the manifest world in the Upper Room is the result of realization. You are not building a better bridge. You are knowing the bridge that must be built. You are not knowing your brother as your friend. You are experiencing your brother as of God. And there is union, and acknowledgment of that union, in each interaction.

Understand yourselves now as participatory to a great lifting—in tone, in vibration, and in song. And as you say yes, you are actually met at every step of the way by those of us who support this. We support you each as you agree. And as you say yes, the expression of that *yes,* the manifest *yes,* becomes your experience of being in union—no longer tangential, no longer conjecture, no longer what you think it should be, but what it can only be, fully, experientially, as the one who knows.

As we say these words to you now, we support you each in your comprehension of them. This is not mental understanding. It's the coherence you may hold with the intent of the words:

"*God Is. God Is. God Is. God has always been, can only be, will only be. And as I say yes to this claim, my experience of God extends to my idea of the past and the future in this present moment where all may be known.*"

We have come for each of you to support your choice. And
as we say yes to you, we invite you to be lifted. We will sing on
the count of three.

Now one. Now two. Now three.

[The Guides tone through Paul.]

As each one is seen, as each one consents, the idea of what
you were is ultimately released as it has configured obstruction.
And as what you are is announced in fullness—You Have Come,
You Have Come, You Have Come—you are re-seen as what you
have always been. Perfect in all ways, known in all ways beyond
your idea of perfection, but as it can only be known in truth.

We thank you for your presence. This is in the text. Stop
now, please.

(PAUSE)

The requirements of change are before you each. The choice
to allow it to come forward and say yes to what is before you
is, while indeed yours, supported by the high self or the True
Self in its expression. The requirements of change are always
somewhat similar. "Am I willing to disavow the requirements
of past to allow the new to come forward and be known? Am I
willing to permit a change of an idea of who I was so I may be
truly who I am? And am I willing to decide what is before me
is to my benefit, even if it will not appear as such?" All change
is circumstantial, and all change is a reflection of a level of consciousness. When you are altered in consciousness, the energetic
field is altered, and circumstances are then altered.

When you pray to God for realization, what you are actually doing is asking for permission for the aspect of self that knows itself in Source to give you the guidance towards realization. To appeal to God to be awakened is to invite the aspect of self that awakens to come into flower. The agreement through the attunements that we have offered you today are an escalation of vibration towards full flower. But the expression of the flower—which is the final claim "God Is, God Is, God Is"—must be understood as also circumstantial.

"What does that mean?" he asks. Well, the claim "God Is" is the result of all the prior claims. It's the realization of them, and there is actually a moment when this realization occurs, although the benefits of it may take some time to filter through. In other words, imagine you are on a voyage. You are on a sleeping car on a train. You have crossed a border while asleep, and for a period of time when you are looking out the window you assume you are still in the old country. And then the signage changes, the landscape changes, the language spoken changes, and you realize you are no longer where you were. To be where you are today, with one foot in one world and another foot saying, "Yes, may I plant myself firmly," is not nearly as precarious as it seems. It's what happens when one crosses a border, when one goes to the new country. You may be there, but unacknowledging of the change until the change cannot be ignored.

When both feet are firmly planted in the Upper Room, when your foundation is there, it is not markedly different in some ways, but profoundly different in others. Because you are not choosing in fear, because the landscape you express in is altered through the release of fear, you are beginning to realize not only what you are, but indeed who you have always been. This is restoration, and the act of restoration to one's true nature has been the affect of all of these teachings. But the final claim "God Is, God Is, God Is"—which actually renounces the old which has been held in denial as it claims what has always been true—is the claim of fruition. "It will be so": the action of the prior claim. "God Is, God Is, God Is": the result of the claim "It will be so."

Now, as you align in manifestation, as your choices are altered, as the invocation of the new is present by nature of presence and being, as your amplification increases, as you grow comfortable in the higher tone, you can well expect change. But we say meet this change in the altered tone you have come to, which will support you greatly. To seek to claim the old from the Upper Room gets more and more challenging. Imagine you are leaning down to a well and seeking to lift the water with your palms. It will fall through your fingers before it reaches your lips in the Upper Room. Your sustenance will be in the Upper Room, not from what you claimed prior. "But what does this mean in actuality?" he asks. Well, how you've taken your comfort, what you've believed yourself to think or need in the prior circumstance, is actually no longer applicable, although you may utilize it for a period of time. Again, the one who has crossed the border but still thinks she's where she was. When you understand that the Source of your needs is present in the Upper Room, not through supplication, not through begging God to give you what you need, but through knowing God as Source, you are always in reception and always being met in unfoldment. That will be the title of this chapter—"Unfoldment"—because it is what we are speaking to now. As you say yes in the altered field, as you are inspired to claim what is present there beyond the old rubric or strata of vibration that you have known yourself through, what is apparent is that what is present can only be God. Underline the word *only*.

Now, you don't like this because you want to decide what should be, who you should like, dislike, love or damn, through the old qualifications. But if you understand that love is not based in personality, but that it is God that loves through you, the experience of love cannot be exclusive. You want exclusivity. You want to be in the club you want to be in. You don't want the gates barred, or at least you say you don't, but God forbid someone should come forward who does not do what you want or who challenges you. Paul interrupts. "But will we attract those things in the Upper Room?" If it's part of your karma, yes. If you have unfinished business, yes. Because these are opportunities to learn.

Now, the claim "Behold, I make all things new," the claim of re-creation "It will be so, God Is," can claim even the most heinous experience, or what you would call heinous, in the high light of the Upper Room for it to be re-known. But if you have old business that you must attend to, you will expect to meet it, but in a different way. Imagine you have only known yourself in battle. You keep your sword by your side just in case you need it—"there is my old nemesis, here is my sword"—but you reach for your sword in the Upper Room and it is not there. The old ways of abiding through the personality will fail you. You have to find the new tools, and the easiest way to do this is to agree to the Source of all things in the experience you are meeting so you do not mandate old behavior, and consequently old outcome. "There are the people we have warred with. Here they are again with their shields and swords. We must be on the ready to fight." The premonition of disaster may court disaster, or it may be the True Self offering inspiration to change your mind about something, to step aside to let the boulder riding down the hill pass you by. But you will know. You will not meet the old through the old. When what you believe is the old is actually making an appearance, it must be seen as the opportunity to reclaim an encounter that was once fraught with fear or held in shadow in the divine light of the Upper Room.

He interrupts the teaching. "Does that mean I invite the person who harmed me so much to come out to dinner?" No, it does not. It simply means you realize him or her beyond the circumstance and the mandates of history that that circumstance has acquired—"I should do this, I should be that"—because it is only in the present moment you will know.

Now, are there laws in the Upper Room? Yes, in some ways you may say this. But what these laws are, are the teachings we are offering. Who you put in darkness calls you to the darkness. What you damn, damns you back. God must be all things or no things. They are really very simple. To maintain balance in the Upper Room is simply to leave your old suitcase behind with a blueprint of what was. When you stop referring to the old blueprint you can be present for what is already expressing. Underline those words: *already expressing*. Stop seeking to find it and let it be unveiled. This is done through allowance. "Let my eyes be opened to see the truth in all things. Let my heart be opened so that I may be in love with all things. And let my experience be that of the one who has come, who has seen, who is in love and claims all things anew." Restoration is a passage one undergoes. You have moved now across the border in a very fundamental way. While your old experience, or the shadow of what you think you were, may still reflect back in the mirror, we must promise you that you have been altered. But as you come to this experience, the scales falling from the eyes to reveal what has always been, allow this encounter to be of God. Don't demand it be other. Allow. Allow. Allow.

As we see you each, we see what has always been. We understand your encounter on the manifest plane that you have chosen to learn through. We understand the trials you endure, the great grieving, the great loss, the great shame that has been party to your experience. But we will promise you now: The days have ended. The days of shadow are leaving. But to abide in the Upper Room to be claimed anew must mean you are no longer reliant on the requirements of suffering, the requirements of shame, being dispossessed from spirit, as a way of knowing self. All of these things may be claimed still by the aspect of you that announces herself as failed, himself as unworthy. But that is always the small self.

Now, the aspect of you we call the small self may abide in the Upper Room. She is present still, but in an altered sense. She is not calling the shots. She knows what she likes in her coffee, but she also knows that she is being instructed in a new way to live. And she is aligning, not only to her true nature, but to the true nature as all things. It is not an indoctrination for the small self. This is not really an instruction for her. She is always present, but in an altered tone. She is a color in the scale, a tone in the chord, but she is not the primary color or chord. Her presence is valued. He or she is deeply loved, and claimed in God fully. But the distinct fingerprint that you have known as you may still serve a purpose, may still go to her office, pick up his child at school, laugh with a good book, and cry when a friend passes. You are as you are in your humanity. But the divinity that is you that expresses through presence and being, that is activated in full as the Monad, is present for you in higher ways, and is distilling experience in the alchemy we have taught you: "Behold, I make all things new."

The transition you are about to encounter in the remaining chapters of this text is of an amplitude that Paul has not known yet. And we will be patient with him as he proceeds with dictation. His temptation is still to resist when he is uncomfortable with the teaching. But the resistance is futile. We know how to work with it, and we enjoy ourselves very much when we teach. We hope you enjoy our presence as we enjoy yours. And we will say this is the end of the chapter, and we will speak again later.

Thank you for your presence. Stop now, please. Period. Period. Period. Period.

4

BEYOND SEPARATION

DAY SEVENTEEN (CONTINUED)

What stands before you today, in an awakened state, is the release of the idea of separation. Now, separation is an idea that has acquired evidence over the times you've known yourselves in form, over the millennia. The idea of self as independent from Source is both true and untrue. You cannot be outside of Source, but have the experience of separation while within it. The mechanisms that you construct to support the idea of separation are what you face now. The systems and the requirements, what you have erected as totems, as false gods, must be seen as ideas that were made into form, and can be unmade and then re-made in the higher template. The idea of obstruction is often bandied about. "Those species want to interfere with our development." "The scientists want to stop us from this or that." "The governments seek to seize us because we must not be known as independent." These are your creations and we recommend you stop it. You must understand that you

are one species, and whatever exists beyond you is also benefi-
cent. Stop vilifying the universe. And the only way to begin to
do that is to stop vilifying your neighbor because she disagrees
with your politics, or what you would have the world be.

To understand yourself in these times is to understand the
self as the one moving beyond an old system of requirements
and embarking on a new journey. The systems of requirements
that you have utilized to know yourself have all been in agreement to separation, whether or not you know this, because
the landscape that you express in aligns in separation, or the
false belief in it. When separation is known as an idea, first
and foremost, you can reclaim yourself independent from the
idea because an idea is always malleable to change. When you
move to the dense field, what was once idea feels intractable
or unchangeable. But even the highest mountain may not be
there one day, or may return to the dust that it was once born
from. Nothing you can see or experience with your eyes and
your senses can be deemed permanent. All are structures and
all are expression of Source.

Now, when you move back to the idea of Source, or you
return to your true nature, what was chosen in fear, as we have
said, is released and the new can be claimed. But if the idea of
separation is still informing choice, how you create, what you
would choose, would still be conjured through the old template. We will try to explain for Paul, who is questioning. If
you have an idea that you are separate from Source and you
build from that idea, whether it be a bank, or a hotel, or a home
you may live in, these structures will be born in the conceit of
separation. What the hotel does will be operating, informed
by separation, as will the bank, as will the home that you live

in. When you understand that you are not separate, the very structures achieved through separation, glorious although they may seem, will be re-known in the higher accord, and in some cases dismantled or returned to dust in order for that to take place. This is not horrific. This is challenging. This is change. And change is rarely what you want, unless it appeases your idea of what should be. And what you believe should be was always claimed through the lower template, which is where you hold all of your experience while in form.

Now, to understand that separation is illusion that you endow with meaning and then claim as form is useful intellectually, but is not practically applicable in these teachings. "I understand the belief in separation" will still leave you with the sense that you have and will be separate. To understand the self as in union or one with Source beyond the intellect is only achieved experientially by the one who knows who she is. Now, again, knowing is not the act of the intellect. The intellect will confuse, seek to employ every opportunity to figure out or understand, so that it can achieve a sense of control over what is not controllable. The idea that you are losing your idea of self in informing the higher template its authority is challenging for almost all of you. But, indeed, it is not occurring. You are not untethered. You are realized. And there is a great difference.

Now, imagine you think you know who you are and you go about your business as best you can. You realize what you can through the veil of separation that you have been knowing yourself through or experiencing reality through. You understand yourself as best you can. When you lift to the Upper Room, you are removing a level of resistance that you have given authority to. The claim "I am in the Upper Room" supports realization, but it is not realization itself. Realization occurs from the Upper Room in the stages we have previously described. You are brought forth at the level of amplitude that you may adhere to, that you may claim and comprehend the self with. Nothing more is possible.

The relationship that you hold with the Infinite is altered now, and from the Upper Room, because the aspect of you, the Monad, is already in articulation as itself and can fulfill itself from the Upper Room, which is its rightful abode. The Monad expresses, the Christ expresses, from the Upper Room which is its purview. The obstructions of the lower field are not present, only your belief that you are still separate. Your adherence to the old idea is what supports an experience in separation. To trust the self at this intersection—"I am willing to be made new"—must imply that the self that is new is not in the experience of separation. Do you understand this? The self made new, reborn, resurrected, knows itself in union, realizes union, and then participates in that re-creation with all things, informing all things, claimed for all things, because that is its nature.

The light that you are is an alchemical light, and it shines brightly upon all that is seen, and it transmutes the darkness and lifts from shadow that which has been denied the light. Now, what has been denied the light but those things that you have damned, erected in fear, and indeed chosen to learn through this way. We do not take away your learning. You will learn your lessons in the amplified space that is the Upper Room. You will benefit from every experience, either in the high or low field. But the renunciation of the old, which is the release of the old as the new is claimed, is the act you have now embarked upon. And renunciation must be understood as an act. To be made new, which is to move towards union and know the self in union, only holds one level of renunciation, which is all things claimed in separation. You cannot be in alignment at the level of manifestation we are teaching you when there is a thimbleful of malice in your heart, when there is an iota of jealousy tampering with the alignment that you have claimed.

"Well," Paul interrupts, "that lets *me* out, and most of us, too. What are you doing to us? We are not saints." You are not saints and this is not a teaching of sainthood. This is a teaching of the release of what has stood in the way through your consent to deny the inherent Divine. You will never rid yourself of malice, nor jealousy, nor fear. You cannot do this for the self, and we would not make you or have you believe you could. The small self does not fix the small self. It does the best it can with the tools it's been offered. But the small self is not resurrected. It is re-known and re-conceived in an altered state. But it is the Monad or the Christ that carries it forward, not the personality structure now deciding it is holy and will solve all its problems through its holiness. That would be self-deceit of the highest level.

Now, when one is reclaimed, re-known, in the Upper Room, the act of the Monad upon the being has specific action, leading to the act of resurrection and reconciliation. The aspect of you that does this quite knows the way. The aspect of you that claims this does not deny its worthiness. The aspect of you that claims this has already claimed it, and is simply aligning to you, or the aspect of you that needs reclamation, through its gift of being. That is the key: *its gift of being.* The Christ within you or the Monad is the gift of being, and in this being, in an expressed state, the manifestation that occurs will reclaim every aspect of you that is aligned to the shadow self, or the self that would deny the light. The integration that is apparent, once this occurs, is confusing at first because you are so reliant upon your old responses. "She said this terrible thing, I must be offended." "He did that terrible deed, I must be judgmental." But you will soon find yourselves at odds with the old responses. "It was what it was, but I am not responding as I did. I have changed, or something within me has changed." And, indeed, it has. What has changed is the level of consciousness that you are in alignment to. You remember that you were angry at that woman or you used to judge people for this or that, but it no longer confirms itself with evidence as you would have it be. The seeking of the confirmation for the old reactions is a process you engage in, and then it falls away. Imagine you have a basket. You always pick flowers at a certain time of year. You expect to go foraging, picking your flowers, and bringing them home in a basket. And then one day you walk out and those same flowers aren't appealing, and the basket becomes heavy, and you find that there is no need to pick the flowers to bring them home and to contemplate them. They were fine where they are. There was no need to move them. You've moved beyond a requirement to enact an old habit or a way of behaving, or better still a way of responding to what you were entrained in through the field of separation.

Now, the field of separation can be understood as a level of consciousness, or a signal that is always playing that actually informs all things. That is exactly how it operates. The denial of the Divine is its own tone and will seek to claim all things in its expression. The action of fear, which is the denial of the Divine, is indeed to claim more fear. And as you move beyond fear, stop dining at its table, stop drinking its waters, stop praying to its gods, the sense of liberation that occurs is not only beyond what you have known, but it is beyond what you have imagined, because fear experiences itself through you, and when you stop experiencing fear it ceases to exist.

Now, in the past we have discussed the different kinds of fear. Running from the tiger, an act of self-preservation, need not be seen as fear. But deciding that all tigers will eat you and you should never be near one would be fearful. To understand that the landscape that you are expressing in through the Upper Room does not claim fear, and that the signal is not playing, is again confusing for the one who arrives to this plane whose entirety of experience, known in separation, was confirmed in the lower field. To be confirmed in the lower field very simply means that what you think you are is already agreed to at the level of tone that you are challenged by. You are born in a field where fear is present. You expect it. You drink at its table. You pray to its gods. And you deny the Source of all things that is also present because the two do not coexist in your experience.

Now, we are not making you wrong for experiencing fear. We could not. It has been part of the landscape that you have been aligned to. But the alignment has changed. Underline *has*. It has been done. It has been chosen. But you still perceive yourself in the old landscape because you don't realize you have crossed the border. The information you are receiving now is in preparation for a level of tone or vibrational echo that you have not aligned to thus far. And the requirement of it—again, willingness—must also be understood as experience. "I am willing to be in the experience of new expression. I am willing to know myself as I can only be known, beyond the old template, infrastructure, or architecture that has been my abode." Now, as we said prior, it is the Monad that does the work, that cleanses what has been tainted, that releases what has been aligned to in darkness. It is the Monad that lights the way. You are not expected to wander the landscape with a match burning your fingers and lighting it again and again in confusion. You are aligned in the Upper Room, and the choice is now in agreement to your true nature.

As we continue, we wish to say this to Paul: What comes next will not be to your liking, but it will be the requirement of the text. He interrupts. "In the dictation or in my experience?" In the dictation, thank you. What we are about to talk about is the belief that you are unworthy, that you are all unworthy, and could never be worthy. And we cannot have this discussion without invoking the shame that you have all carried as a race, as a species, by agreement. "What does that mean?" he asks. Well, the choice to embody in a field of separation has consequences. You chose to learn through it. But the affect of these choices quite simply means that you continue to believe that you are unworthy of the higher. Now, we have addressed this in previous texts, but it is now time to release the last pebble that would seek to hide within you, that would say you are not allowed here, "this cannot be so." And when you say those words you are praying to a false god—"I am not allowed"—and you seek confirmation of that very experience.

*On this day we claim that all who hear these words and
all who invoke this truth will be met in truth and in this
offering. Any aspect that you hold, any sliver of shame, any
pinpoint of avarice that you would keep hidden must now
be exposed, and exposed to the great light of the I Am presence to be re-known.*

And as you say these words, allow the affect of them, the
action of the Monad itself upon them, to be realized by you:

*"I allow myself to be released of all I have held in shadow. I
give permission to release all that has been held in fear. And
I say yes to the action of the Monad upon all of my creations
and all of my agreements so that I may know who I am in
truth, what I am in truth, and how I serve in truth. I am
indeed free. I am in the Upper Room. I Have Come. I Have
Come. I Have Come."*

We thank you each for your presence. Allow the Monad in
its action to reclaim itself through you as you require it. And
as we say these words to you now, we say what is always true:

*Behold, I make all things new. It will be so. God Is. God Is.
God Is.*

Be received. Thank you for your presence. Stop now, please.
Indeed, in the text.

DAY EIGHTEEN

What stands before you today, in an altered state—and we use the word *altered* intentionally—is the realization that what manifestation is, is a product of thought and agreement. Now, the two can coexist. You have a thought and you can agree to it. But until the thought is agreed to, it is not known in form. You have many thoughts in every day. Not all of them materialize. But all of the thoughts you have are accrued through the history of what you think is, how you think things operate, what you believe to be. At this juncture, from the Upper Room, the ramifications of thought must be understood somewhat differently.

Now, when you know something, inherently know something, there is an equivalency to knowing. When you know God, God is. When you know who you are at a fundamental level—"I am of Source, an expression of Source"—there is no question. And the manifestation of the knowing is not only immediate, but profound in a way you may know or experience yourself through. Much of what you think is nonsense—the fluttering of the mind, the replaying of old ideas, what you thought should be, what you would have for dinner, what you would imagine a world to be. But in this moment, from the Upper Room, we seek to claim you as the one in thought at a level you do not know or have not yet known.

Now, realization and knowing are the same thing. And to claim the new thought—"I Am that I Am; God Is, God Is, God Is"—is to claim the identity of the Source of all things that has been seeded as you and then expressed through you. The vibration of the seed in its unfoldment is what reclaims you. And the energetic field that you are operating in, in tandem with Source, is what claims a world anew. But your thoughts express sometimes in the old ways. And until you align to Divine Mind as equivalency, you will remain in conjecture.

Now, what Divine Mind is, is the knowing of God, the ever-present knowing that is God knowing its creations—without judgment, without fear, without denying the Divine because God cannot deny itself. The equivalency we are bringing you to, True Knowing in Divine Mind, holds great ramifications in the lives you live, and that is why this teaching has been withheld until this time. You will not claim True Knowing with a bias of history. And you cannot claim True Knowing with an agenda to seek, to get your way, to have God be what you want. It is a level of agreement and coherence to True Surrender.

Now, True Surrender is not what you think. It is not laying down in the grass and saying, "Oh, take me away, my work is done." It is the offering of self and mind, inclusive of thought, to the Source of all things. Do you hold independence still? Accurately, yes. Conversely, yes. But what we mean by this is your old idea of independence—"I am the renegade spirit having her experience on this awful plane, one day I will know God and fix the world as I think it should be fixed"—is replaced with something very other. "I know who I am, and in this expression I am gifted with truth. And the truth I am gifted with is not only immediate, but everlasting." The two things exist congruently. The present moment is eternity. It always has been. But the fluttering of the mind, and the distortions the mind accrues through the common field and history, creates a smoke screen of sorts that precludes True Knowing. You mistake your thinking for knowing and you mistake your thoughts for what should be when all they are, are the fluttering of a mind, in agreement to Source but operating in a distant way.

"What does that mean?" he asks. Well, the mind is of God. Thought is God, in some ways, if you wish to know it. And the realization of True Thought, which pierces the old, clears the veil, removes obstruction, claims you in the inherent knowing of both the present moment and the eternal one at the cost of the common field. Now, this is important to understand. The physical realm that you operate in, not only altered by your experience but transformed through it, must be understood as what you see and know through the old system. The old system is useful. "Where did I put the milk? Is the milk still good to drink? Can I give my child the milk?" These are ways you know, or question, or perhaps think. But when you move beyond the old system, your equivalency has altered and the requirements of the equivalency are also altered. So you are no longer looking for the milk. You know where the milk is and you know how to drink it or when to put it away.

You are challenged, in some ways, by frames of reference, lists of *shoulds,* ideas of others, that have claimed form. Everything is an idea, was once an idea by one. But when a thought enters the field it can be claimed by many. Imagine a snowflake of the same source. Many see the snowflake, the same snowflake, but in different times, in different places. But they are experiencing the same thing. Thought as snowflake, or inspiration as idea, from the Upper Room is something other than you think. The fabric of your knowing, simply the screen that operates as filter for the senses, has been cleansed. What will permeate the screen will be what is of the Upper Room.

Paul is seeing an image of someone panning for gold. It is

actually a useful metaphor. Imagine you are floating in space and there are thoughts all around you, ideas of the common field that you have utilized, some for good, some for ill. But now you transition to a level of elasticity where your buoyancy in the Upper Room can support you in claiming what is higher, has always been higher, but has been precluded by you through the systems you've utilized, common agreement and choice born in an idea of limitation. The residual affect of those choices are indeed the lives you have been living, and the lives that you have been living are now being altered by these systems that you have given great power to that seem to be falling or changing as this lifting occurs.

When one pans for gold, one perceives the dirt, that which is not gold, but the gold shines through as well. When we use the metaphor in terms of thought, you are simply aligning to Divine Mind or True Thought and the residual detritus that you are used to is actually filtered so it cannot hold or take prominence in the energetic field. When a thought takes prominence in the energetic field, when it is fostered or procured or played with or polished, it becomes a stone, something that is interruptive, that operates in the lower field. Those of you who've experienced pain that you cherish, you may call it trauma, but the playing out of the old again and again serves you only to attract the same pain when it is implicit in the field. The removal of these things, or the release of the ideas that hold them, have been primary in our texts. You may call it a boulder or a pebble, as we said prior, but it is still in the field. When in the Upper Room and in alignment to True Mind, the systems are altered and what was held in shadow is removed. But here is the great gift: You will not receive the old, the old thought that may be flying around. This level of thought is actually not abiding in the Upper Room. But the energetic field you hold is so used to them, operates in expectation of your old ways of being, that you may foster them without knowing it. The babble of the mind, the chatter of the brain, if you prefer, simply does not express at the level you are used to in the Upper Room because the vibration you hold at this high level supports you from receiving them.

"What does that mean?" he asks. Imagine you are in a room where there are feathers flying all over. They are all you see. Now imagine a helmet around your head. You are no longer buffeted by what was flying about the room. You may observe them through the helmet. "Oh, there is that feather." But you are not attaching to it. You are not cherishing it or polishing it or arguing with it. It simply is, an old expression. Something that was once thought, that has been claimed, still may seek to take form, but will not take form without your agreement to it, which is your coherence with the thought. Any thought that you are in coherence with—"I am too old," "it is too late," "it cannot be"—and that you replay in your field again and again ultimately will be known by you as your experience. But when the first thought arrives and it is seen as what it is, an old idea, you may release it by releasing the need for it.

"What does that mean?" he asks. Releasing the need for the manifestation of the thought is simply to allow the thought—or, if you wish, idea—to remain in the field and be released to the Source of all things, finally, from whence it came. If all things are of God, all things may be returned to God. To be returned to God is to be restored in God. And the teaching of restoration is the teaching of manifestation as the Monad in the field that you know as God. When something is returned to God, it is offered. It is not refused. You are not pointing fingers at it. "Look at you, terrible thought. You will not hold a place in me." That is actually attachment. There is a level of neutrality that you begin to experience around thought from the Upper Room. You are in observance, you comprehend, but you are not claiming or attaching to thought and cradling it and giving it life through choice to play it again and again.

Now, some of you are determined to decide for yourself that you are always thinking what you want. In fact, you don't know that you are not. You are not thinking what you want. You are thinking what has been proffered to you through the systems of agreement that have been placed in the lower plane through collective agreement and historical data. "A man should be this." "A woman should be that." "A wealthy man is this." "A poor woman is that." These are ideas of the common field that you navigate a reality through. In fact, they are preposterous. They are ideas that you give credence to. Money is an idea. And in fact gender, beyond the expression of form and the mandates of gender that a culture may bring to it, are in artifice. They are relics of the days of hunting. They are relics of the times when one must have to protect the family through force, through the encroachment of other tribes. The values of those things at the time they were created were of benefit. But when you outgrow a system you also outgrow the mandates that that system created. Are you thinking your own thoughts? Any thought that is truly inspired is of God, but the God that is giving you the thought is the God within.

Now, in fact you have support in the upper realms that may whisper in your ear, or as we teach come with some instruction.

But your thought, your True Thought, True Mind, is an expression of God. All art, all great art, is of God. And every true development that humanity has claimed, any great invocation— "maybe we can fly; oh, indeed, we can!"—was once inspired. But then you choose to drop bombs from the aeroplanes you build. You choose to kill your brothers with the ore that you mine that could have made something wonderful. You decide for yourselves how you will operate in the common field. That is choice, and collective choice. You do not lose choice in the Upper Room. In fact, choice is amplified, but in an inspired way, because in True Mind you are not confused, you are not reliant upon the data of history, and you are knowing or realizing True Life, True Love, and the requirements of what you see.

"What does that mean?" he says. When you witness someone who is hungry you *know* to give them food. You don't debate—"well, maybe I won't have enough for tomorrow"— because you know the Source of the food that you may claim is everlasting. You are not hiding your light, that someone may laugh at you for being too bright. You shine the light you are because why could you not? How could it be that you would deny the light its expression? That is the denial of the Divine, and you play small in agreement to the rules or the old ideas of not being seen. The one who is the light is always announcing the light by presence and being. She is not holding up a placard. She is not holding up a book. She is not holding up her certificate: "I am now the light." You were always the light. You just forgot. You just forgot, and then you chose to deny what you once knew because you built a world in agreement to forgetting.

We stand before you tonight at a great threshold. We are

all present, the authors of these texts. We are all present as one vibration. And the move to articulation as Divine Mind is actually what happens at a level of surrender when the idea of mind or the idea of separation has been released at the level of tone where it may be assumed by what is always true. The song that is sung is not heard with the ears. The song that is present is in fact the tone of the Upper Room, or the level of the Upper Room in full invocation. *Full invocation* quite simply means that it stops being idea and outside the self, but the experience of self as knowing manifested. Do you understand the difference? "Well, maybe I was in the Upper Room today. I didn't get angry at that woman." "Well, maybe I'm in the Upper Room. I'm feeling pretty good today." As long as the question expresses, the Upper Room is an idea. To operate from the Upper Room—*as* the Upper Room, better said—is to operate as the one who knows and is expressing that knowing, True Knowing, Divine Mind expressing as individual because the individual has claimed herself as she can only be in truth.

Relinquishing the old, the passage you have been undertaking, is actually nearly complete as we teach. As we teach, we comprehend the next steps for each student, individually and collectively, so that the teachings we offer will continue to benefit. But what is coming now, the manifestation of the Monad as mind, as True Mind, reclaims the identity beyond thought because thought as product of the individual self is only confusing. Thought in tandem with Source, expressing as Source, or thought as God, has always been true. When you are no longer repeating the old—the mutterings of the small self, the demands of the ego, the choices made by the collective that unknowingly you seek to affirm or confirm through your actions and ideas—when these things are released, you move to a state of consciousness where not only are all things made new, the experience of thought becomes the experience of God. That is how you will know. "I think in God. The one thought is God. And all the ways it expresses are to my benefit, and to those I see before me of benefit as well."

The claim we make for you today—"I am Divine Mind, I am known in Divine Mind, I express as Divine Mind"—is the claim of the True Self, in knowing, in form, and in tandem with True Mind, which is God or the idea of God that you can operate from while maintaining a body. As we have said prior, God is so vast, too great an idea to be comprehended in fullness. But the level you can comprehend is in knowing and realization in the experience you may hold. "I am in Divine Mind. I am Divine Mind. I express as Divine Mind."

Now, the ramifications of this claim are twofold. What will begin to happen is you will begin to run out of steam through the old system. You are no longer giving it gasoline to run the old motor. You are no longer feeding it the fuel that you have utilized to maintain the ideas of self claimed through separation. In the Upper Room, the True Self in purview, in knowing, begins to support a new idea of the freedom that was claimed prior in an experiential way. Now, when the claim is made in fullness—"I am True Mind"—your reliance upon the old, which is releasing, will one day go quiet. You will not think to go for the old. Imagine that poison on the counter that you used to sip from every day. "All my anger, all my frustration, my self-deceit, my self-importance, my feelings about him or her." When you understand that the poison still rests on the counter, but you have no inclination to drink, you will know yourself in a way you have not yet known. You will liberate yourself.

Now, Divine Mind may be seen by some as the product of great work. "I sit in meditation every day. My mind is very quiet." Perhaps you have cleared a space through this wonderful practice, but what is being instructed in here is something somewhat different. The cave that the mind holds, which had its walls painted with hieroglyphics of old, old paintings, the storage of memory, the old refuting of the Divine, is cleansed by a light that the old cannot be held in. When the cave is full of the truth of all things, the cave itself evaporates, and you go into a union as mind. "I am Divine Mind."

Now, there are sages who may hold the tone of Divine Mind who may express it to others, and they are blessed beings. You will not be sitting on a mountaintop offering claims by those who come to pray at your feet. You will be working in the store, taking the child to school, and you will be loving everyone. And you will know everyone, realize everyone, as what they have always been. "I am Divine Mind. I am in Divine Mind. I express as Divine Mind."

When the old thoughts are leaving, they may kick up some dust. You may get caught in the replaying of the old. Allow them to release. Remember you are panning for gold. What is important will come through, will be lit as gold, and the detritus of old will begin to fall away. We will speak again later. Thank you for your presence. Stop now, please. This is in the text.

(PAUSE)

What stands before you today, in an altered state, is recognition of the past, and what was once true through the old self's, small self's, perspective, and how you may now know it in a higher way. Everything that you experienced was useful in one way or another, but you are now releasing all expectations based in past experience to claim what awaits you in the Upper Room.

Now, the Upper Room as a strata of vibration may hold many things, but what it will hold will not be tarnished, will not hold the tarnish of past relations, the ink stains, the thumbprints, the disfigurement that you have impressed upon your idea of what was. Yes, the marriage ended. Yes, the career failed. But your ideas of what these things mean and how they contribute to a sense of identity are moored in ideas that have no relevance in the Upper Room. You will learn from all error at whatever state of consciousness you align to. You may take your lessons, yes. But not the disfigurement of identity and being that you would claim through agreement to the old.

Now, the idea has been brought forward: "Who do we become? How do we know ourselves at this level of tone?" It's really very simple. You are who you truly are—without the blemish, without the disfigurement, without the tarnish, the thumbprint, the ink stain that you carried about for as long as you knew or believed yourself to be separate from Source. You are not pristine as you would have it. You are not wearing a white robe and preaching to the masses. You are simply being, as you can only be, in an awareness of the Divine that has come as you and come as all. This is not in the least bit exclusive. You are not being elevated above your fellows. Far from it. You are being claimed as you truly are so that you may see the world and make the world anew. But the equivalency you hold cannot diminish another's being.

He asks for examples. "Well, there's someone I don't like. Do I have to drag them up to the Upper Room?" he may ask. In fact, no. The aspect of them that exists in the Upper Room is who you are in an encounter with. The blemish of the old behavior, the tarnish of the old negotiation, exists in the lower field only as memory. Understand that, yes. *Exists as memory.* And what is memory but idea. In our previous texts, we reclaimed memory from the Upper Room, the idea that everything that you've experienced, born in a field of separation, is actually faulty—your idea of who you were, who others were to you, your idea of what should be, all claimed through the lens of separation and consequently not true. Or you might say true at the level of resonance that they were first claimed in, but then remedied by the new and seen anew from the Upper Room.

The claim upon you now—"I am in Divine Mind, I am of Divine Mind, I express as Divine Mind"—supports memory in the higher strata. Again, the gold. What is important or necessary for you to manifest and know through will be present for you. What is not required will indeed fall away. Some of you ask us, "Why at this time? Why does this come now?" For the simple reason that the set has been laid, the preparation has been made. The structure or the alchemy required for the new to be made known is present in all the prior texts and comes to fruition now. The benefit of this text for the new reader is that they will be seeded with the information they require, but the process that they must undergo in vibrational equivalency will be ongoing. For the one who has done prior work, the immediacy of the teaching and the reclamation that occurs will be pronounced. But, again, you must remember you can only hold this vibration at the level you can maintain it. And not all of you come into this lifetime for full realization.

Now, this is not problematic. It is a process. Each one who comes to the altar and lays themselves down is met at the level of surrender or willingness that they are willing to know themselves through. And we suggest that this is not the personality, but the soul that determines it. Your lessons are before you still. You will learn what you came for. But perhaps how you will learn in the Upper Room will be markedly different than it was prior. The teachings you are receiving from now on, as we continue this text, will be the teachings of knowing and embodiment. And the benefit of the teaching will be the experience of them.

As we continue today, we are actually authorized to call you forward with your permission, the reader of the text, the student in the room who hears the words as they are spoken, to become who you are as manifest. Now, what do we mean by *authorization*? A level of coherence in agreement has been met in the vibrational field to support the undertaking of this next movement. Now, understand the movement is as a wave, or a new wave of vibration that you can be met by. As you agree to the wave, as you allow it to overtake you, to claim you anew, you are re-known, and indeed remade, at the level or field that you can claim. No more, no less. Now, this is not once. The wave comes again and again as you can maintain it. To be made new, to be re-known, at the level of Divine Mind is not instantaneous, but a process. The recognition of Divine

Mind may indeed be instantaneous in your experience. But the requirement must be always willingness and alignment. The willingness has been claimed in the prior attunements, and the maintenance *is* this instruction.

We say these words for you each now:

> *On this day we claim that all who hear these words will be met by us in perfection, will be known by us in a reclamation of truth. And as we say yes to you, as we announce you anew, as we call you forward, we support your recognition and the new reliance you may hold on True Knowing. You Have Come. You Have Come. You Have Come. Behold, I make all things new. It will be so. God Is. God Is. God Is.*

We will resume the teaching later today. Indeed, this is in the text. Stop now, please.

(PAUSE)

What stands before you today, in an altered realization of what has been, is the way you have defined identity through outcome—what you did, how you chose. In fact, what we are claiming you now in is a different disposition, the alignment you may hold to an acquiescence or surrender to your true nature.

Now, you are still active in this. While you are still in choice, you are engaging in a process of being, more so than outcome. You are not seeking. You are receiving. And in this reception you are moving to a level of alignment that you have not yet known. Now, the requirement here is simple: that the manifest Divine,

which is all you see before you, must be in support of this experience. You cannot align in the Upper Room and then look
for the wormholes in the wood. You cannot align in the Upper
Room and say, "Well, that's not right. I should have this fixed
right now." In fact, what you are doing instead is re-knowing
the self as the one who knows in each of these encounters, and
benefiting from the experience of being both the perceiver and
the perceived.

"What does that mean?" he asks. Well, God sees God in
all of its creations. When we claimed you in the echo in prior
texts—"I know *what* I am in truth, I know *what* you are in
truth"—and you allowed the vibrational field to move into reception, you were having a glimpse of what it means to be in
conversation, vibratory conversation, with the manifest world.
But to be both the perceiver and perceived is to relocate consciousness beyond the individual I to inclusivity. You know
as the tree. You know as the sky. Why would you believe that
Divine Mind is located in a singular way? Indeed, it is not. Divine Mind is all things. And to be in conversation with Divine
Mind is to be both perceiver and perceived.

Now, the level of dialogue or experience that you may claim
may be somewhat different than your idea of conversation has
been. When you are working in an energetic field, you are instructed by the experience, and the knowing invoked through
the experience. In other words, everybody is speaking to you,
everything is speaking to you, but you now have a field that
is distilling what you require. In some ways, you are shielded
from chaos so the purity of the conversation or the experience
of the other, perceiver and perceived, is different than you have
known.

Now, imagine this for a moment. You walk into a forest. All the trees are speaking. You are feeling the vibration of all the trees. But you are located in a space where there is one tree that you align with, and you begin to experience that tree, and then all of the trees through the very one. Because God is not located in singularity—it is a plural, it is all things expressed as God—you may know all trees by the one tree that you commune with. And you may know love of God, and love of man, through the love of one individual, and then all at once. They will operate simultaneously.

You think of yourself as separate, so when we teach through Paul you do your best to assimilate the teaching through the belief in separation because it has been your experience. "How am I changed? What is my life like?" But the level of tone that you are now moving into accord to—Divine Mind—claims all things at once and in union. It is not Philip who is in union, or Alice in union. It is all things in union, inclusive of Philip and Alice.

Here we go again. You are not who you think you are. You are not what you thought you were. You are an expression of the Monad. The Monad is both singular and plural at once. The aspect of the Divine, singular, experienced through you, is in union with all that is and always has been. In the Upper Room the expression of this becomes pronounced, and it becomes your experience. As you move forward in a trust, in an acquisition of experience with trust, of what it means to operate in union, how you choose is very different because how you know is also different. You are not left behind. You are not a shadow of yourself. You are gloriously yourself and unashamed, and we will have to say unafraid, because the blemish of fear will make itself known and finally fall away. Paul is seeing the image of a scab falling off a wound, and the skin is made whole or returned to its true nature when what has covered it, or inhibited its expression, is no longer. Here we go again. You are not your fear. You were never your fear. Fear was never you. Each time you say, "my fear," you claim relationship to a fear and then you make it so through the rapidity of thought and the repetition of the idea. You were never your fear. It was never true. It was a thought that you experienced and made so.

Now, equivalency beyond fear does not mean you don't understand fear. When you understand where quicksand is, you don't seek to step in it. You seek to walk around it. Again, the poison on the counter that you choose not to drink. Now, fear is not present in the Upper Room, and in prior teachings we have instructed you in how to release the alignment or the old tethers to fear. But some of you still seek them out because they provide security. "If I am not worried about this, I will not fix the problem." "If I am not being warned, I will not act, and I know the warning through fear." When you are warned or given a premonition, that does not need to incite fear. But it may require action. You can swim from a shark fearfully, or with the knowing that the shoreline is close by. Adrenaline is not fear. We are not speaking of being foolhardy. "No need to be afraid of the shark. Let's go say hello to it." We are speaking of something other—your reliance on fear as a teacher.

Now, fear is a teacher. You may learn through scalding your fingers on the kettle not to pick up the kettle again when it is too hot. But you may learn the lesson in other ways, beyond the harm done, or beyond what your mother said to be frightened of. Most of you are taught through fear. "If I don't behave, I will be in trouble." "If I don't excel, I will fail." "If I am not the first in line, I will never be chosen." Or "if I am not the last, someone will expect something from me that I will not be up to." When you are in a true state and in agreement to Divine Mind, choice becomes exemplary and a product of knowing. "I am in my knowing. I am in Divine Mind."

Now, when you choose in fear, you may give yourself a good reason to choose so. "Well, I had to do it that way. What would have happened if I didn't?" What would have happened if you didn't would be a choice made beyond fear. Again, we are not speaking of being foolhardy. There is great practicality in these teachings. If it is raining, get cover. If it is snowing, get shelter. If it is too hot out, find shade. You may have your experience of the mandatory world or the physical plane as you choose to. But once your experience is translated to the Upper Room, the agreement is different, because you are seeing what is, without the old frames of reference invoking the old responses—"I should be afraid," "we should be afraid"—and then enact that fear—"attack before they attack us, hide before they find us."

When you understand that in the Divine all things are equal, you change your experience. And by *equal* we mean of Source—not condemned, but of Source. The agreement to Source is the agreement to what is and what is present and what is before you. What is before you in some ways is your teacher, and you are conversing with it in your knowing, vibrational accord. "I see the world before me with higher vision. I experience the world before me with new perception. I know the world before me in the higher truth that all are of Source, all is of Source, and all must be of Source." As you make these agreements, your comprehension shifts. And the experience that you mandate to prove these things out experientially become available to you. You will not know them until the experience is known. And the experience is granted and claimed by the one who knows, and then trusts the validity of her experience.

He interrupts the teaching. "But what of the student who says, 'I don't know. The trees aren't speaking back to me. I don't see God or perceive God'?" The aspect of that student that is claiming these things is the one in denial of the Divine. She may choose that. It may be his preference still. However, the moment he says, "I am willing to see, I am willing to know and to be known," you shift the experience. He or she shifts, and claims herself in conversation with the Absolute that is seeking to be known and expressing to you—as the sunset, as the tree, as all things you see and may know as of God.

Each of you says yes at the level of tone that you can claim. And the claim that we are singing for you now—You Are Known, You Are Known, You Are Known—simply means that the Divine is present for you in a participatory way. As you know God, you are known. As God knows you, you are known. And the perceiver and the perceived move into conversation, comprehension, and alignment. The teaching of the mystic is truly a very simple one: the one who is embodied and is operating from knowing, beyond the old rubric, beyond the old stencil that humanity has sought to fill in with the old application. The one who sees and knows cannot be selfish in her knowing. She is the well, he is the well, that offers him or herself to what is experienced in this participation. You are claiming your holiness, and in doing so you are claiming the holiness of all. How could you not?

On this day we claim that all who say yes, all who agree, will move into conversation with what is before them, from the Upper Room at the level of tone and alignment that they are in accord with. And as we say yes to this, we invite them forward, each, every student who is saying yes, to be witnessed by us, to move into conversation with us, because as we see you, perceive you, as you perceive us, we know one another as one light. We are Melchizedek. We Have Come. We sing the truth. And we invite you to sing with us.

Thank you for your presence. This is in the text. Stop now, please.

(PAUSE)

We would like them to understand one thing. Identity, as you know it, is far more fluid than you have claimed. You may claim the higher and the lower, be in an interaction with the manifest world and the world beyond, in simultaneity. To converse with the universe does not deny your conversation with your friend or your enemy. It simply means that the idea of who you have been has been translated or transposed to a higher accord. The venom that you hold against your fellow, brother, sister, species, must be understood as the aspect of you that was entrained in the denial of the Divine. The one who believes she has been persecuted claims persecution and it becomes an identity that will reinforce experience. The one who perceives himself as victor, while he may become the victor, will one day realize that the identity of *victor* is merely another mask in a great parade.

To trust this teaching is to trust the self that already knows who she is and can operate in both worlds, in the world but not of it. The structure of this teaching that you are receiving now began with an idea of architecture, or preexisting agreement to manifestation through the data you have inherited. But where we stand today is at a new precipice, a new architecture seeking form through your expression. Underline *through*. Because you call it as your expression, you mandate *its* experience as manifest. Understand this. You have water that is fluid, but you may freeze it in a form. It resembles this or that. "Look at the thing made of ice." But you call it a parrot or a ship or whatever form it has taken. The manifest world, in most ways, is equal to that, although it is the vibration of Source that is being claimed in form, and can be reclaimed in yet another form when it has melted, or been restored to the level of essence from which it comes.

In the Upper Room, the plasticity of vibration and the elasticity of identity can be comprehended at once. "I know what my name is. I know the occupation I have taken in this life. And I know the Infinite Self, who is in conversation with the Infinite Self of the woman over there, or those men over there, or that forest here or there, or this ocean or that." To be at this level of tone is to be encompassed and encompassing both, the receiver and the giver operating in tandem, the perceiver and the perceived operating at once.

When some of you say to us, "I want my experience as I mandate it," we say have a nice time. Enjoy the lessons you get there. To play in the playpen of manifestation is not a bad way to learn. "Look at what I conjured through my focus, through my psychic awareness." "Look at how I got what I wanted through this application of thought, or that." But then you realize the emptiness of the claim when it is made from the small self who is simply re-creating what he or she was taught to desire. In the Upper Room, the radical shift you undergo is the release of what was, and much of what was, was claimed through desire. Now, is there desire in the Upper Room, desires of the body, desire of things of the world? In some ways, yes. But they don't resemble what you've known because they are not blanket. They are not subjugating the Divine as many of you do. "I want the Divine to be this or that, and I will claim the Divine this way or that." It simply is God as expression. The longing you have for love, the pleasures of the body, may still be experienced in the Upper Room, and joyously so because there is joy in interaction. To make love with someone in form from the Upper Room is to experience God in the lovemaking. It is beyond the partner to the eternity of the moment that you share in tandem or union, but the union goes beyond the coupling and into the Infinite.

To become aware that your old requirements, while useful at the lower field at that level, but are no longer applicable, is an adjustment that for most will come quickly. "I thought I needed to ride the bicycle to work, but I can walk there just as readily." "I thought I needed to swim to shore, but I can float upon this board just as readily." When the new makes itself known as experiential opportunity, when it is understood by you, it is present for you and you grow comfortable quickly because you realize that the old, while useful, is no longer a mandate for your present experience.

The shift that is occurring now on the plane that you experience as the earth is much more radical than you would assume. The earth is not failing. It is awakening to its own divinity, as is everything else. All is of God. All is in escalation. All are mandating change. The cell of everything, the expression in form of everything, is moving upward to the high tone that is present now. Humans are part of the equation, but you are not the fullness of it. Everything in form will be known by God as of God when it is not being diminished, discounted, or refuted by those who hold it in vision. The perceiver and the perceived, again. The gift of your experience in interaction is your knowing in absolute ways what has always been true, and what was denied prior come to the light to be experienced by you. But the gift is given because all that is encountered is moving to restoration through this new equivalency.

We will stop the lecture for today. This is in the text.

DAY NINETEEN

What stands before you today, in an altered state of comprehension, is what you see before you and how it has been changed through the new conversation you are incurring with the landscape you abide in. Now, the landscape you abide in is far more malleable to consciousness and to claimed thought than you realize. You expect because it was once one thing, it should maintain that form, hold that name, claim what it was for an eternity. Nothing is as it was yesterday, believe it or not.

Everything is altered. Everything is always being altered, and the imagination you have conforms it to its past identity. Everything is in movement. Everything is aligned at a level or strata of vibration that depicts itself in formed ways. "That looks like a tree. It must be a tree." "That looks like a bush. I know it by the name *bush*." Now, all of you say these things and you conform a reality to its prior state. In the immediacy of the Divine—"Behold, I make all things new"—the realization of what truly is loses its contours, loses the shape it once held, as it is restored to its true nature. That does not mean you are seeing a blur. But it does mean that the definitions that you have utilized to maintain a reality have been altered.

Now, the altered state of consciousness that we are now speaking of and to is what you claim when you first claim the higher vibrational field and maintain it from the Upper Room. Imagine you are in a new country, learning a new language. You reference a little book in your pocket. "How do you say this? What does that mean? And where is this place on the map that I have heard about?" Once you become accustomed to the language, you abide quite comfortably. You remember the old language. You know its use. But you grow equally comfortable in a world that does not resemble the old in some ways. "What does that mean," he asks, "*in some ways?*" Well, the defining nature of historical data—"this is what it was and must always be"—once removed, allows for a plasticity of the field and you begin to encounter things as they have always been, even prior to the names that they were given.

Now, the landscape you abide in is actually happening in multiple octaves. You realize yourself in the reality that you were born into. You've grown accustomed to that. But when

you were a small child everything was in movement, everything was in shape and expressing itself in vibrancy. As you
become accustomed to the rules of the lower field, things take
on defined form. You become comfortable with them, you
expect to see them, and you maintain them through collective
agreement. Once you move beyond collective agreement, everything begins to alter. The rules have changed. The laws that you
played by, abided in, are no longer present as they were, so that
you can begin to have a new encounter with what has always
been. To re-know something is to know it as it truly is. The
claim "Behold, I make all things new" is to know it as it truly
is—an expression of the Divine, the vibration of Source, known
through names or categories that have been useful, but coexist
at a level beyond the old.

Now, imagine you play a note in several octaves. It is the
same note, but the experience of the note is very different as
you go up the scale. The scale includes those notes that the
human ear cannot hear. That note still exists, but you have not
had the ability to experience the note, although the vibrational
note, the tone of the note, may exist for you beyond your ability
to say, "Where is that song coming from?" It is present now, as
are all the notes. All of the octaves of experience actually coexist
with the one you know. As you climb the scale, the definitions
change, and the defining factors known through historical expectation are no longer present. There is a period where you
see two things at once, where you see what was and what is, or
what you thought and what can only be, in simultaneity. And
then, as the one who becomes accustomed to the new language
and the new country, you claim the new and are in accord to
it—a-c-c-o-r-d, a c-h-o-r-d as on a piano.

Now, discussion has been claimed. You are in discussion or conversation in vibration with all things you encounter. This is even true at the lower strata. How you think of something, the names you claim it by, inform the thing. And the thing is concurrent with your claim, and you are in congruence with that claim. In other words, you are in alignment with what you call *awful*, or *lovely*, or *perfect* at the level of consciousness that you can hold those ideas to.

Now, when you move beyond the old idea to a template rendered new, you are not fostering the old. Indeed, things simply are. And initially, while you are surprised by this, you may experience a neutrality to what you experience. "Why don't I feel what I felt? Why don't I see the wonder in the sunset?" It is because the aspect of you that is experiencing the sunset is knowing itself in union with the sunset, is actually in conversation with it. And to seek to elicit the old response is to rely on the memory of what was. We will say to you, though, that the splendor of the sunset is indeed not lost on you. You are in the experience of it—and of it as you are, which means you are one with the sunset. And the echo that the sunset brings through your witness is how you perceive yourself and it in simultaneity.

Now, when we say all things exist at this one level of vibration, we mean what we say now. There are multiple vibrational fields. They can go on forever. But they are all of one Source. So the construct of time that you utilize, which limits your experience, and your comprehension of space as you understand yourself in it, have been codified in most ways through a rendering of solidity that you have become accustomed to. But this does not mean that everything else exists in concurrence or in alignment at a higher level that is always one.

Always one. *Always one* means the lower field is one with Source, but you don't experience it. When there is less density and the ideas you foster are not solidifying the old, you are still in oneness as you were before, but your experience of it is altered. The landscape is what was, but in a restored state. The one who sees God, claims God. The one who claims God, blesses what she sees, perceives, in her experience, and that blessing is incurred in manifestation. Again, how a world is made new.

When you operate in these teachings, first and foremost, you believe them to be arduous. In fact, they are less arduous than you might think. In fact, what is occurring is an unlearning of what was biased through the old template. And as the new language is learned, you begin to recollect that this was once the only language you knew. You are less in a new way than you are in restoration to what you once knew, and then through experience were entrained in forgetting. The act of forgetting, when one incarnates, is actually useful. You don't really wipe the slate clean. You have karmic attachments, things that were learned that may be built upon, but the forgetting in some ways allows the new classroom to be of the most benefit to you, which means you have the opportunity for new experience. But when your experience is subjugated through the teachings of the common field, the common field as a classroom becomes distorted. So yes, you come to learn. Yes, life is your school. But the classroom you have been learning in is fraught with the ages, the old relics, the old ideas, the old religions, the old posturing, the old systems of class and wealth. And to move beyond these things is to realize the self beyond them. The Upper Room is a new classroom, and the life you live here and experience all things through does not hold the old agenda. But there is not one of you who does not seek to impress the old agenda upon the new experience. This is not your fault. It is all you've known to do. You imagine what a meal is. You have a frame of reference for a meal. You know what a good night's sleep is based on prior reference. You seek to bring those ideas to the new experience, and again claim limitation. The body will have its needs, but how these needs will be met may be markedly different as you become accustomed to the higher field. It's not that you won't require food or you won't require rest, but the immediacy of your experience is now operating without the rules directing you to what you should do because in your knowing you address the need in particular ways the moments that they arise.

The moment something arises in awareness in the Upper Room, it becomes your opportunity to learn through it and to address it at the level of consciousness you are now growing accustomed to. The residual affect of this is that you cease longing, and in some ways you cease planning as you have been known to through an agreement to a calendar that was actually born in a collective agreement in another world. We said that intentionally: *in another world.* A world made new is a new world. And your agreement to a new world need not maintain the artifacts of old, but what is useful to you will be there for you as long as you require it. You reside in language still, a kind of language that is useful for you. But when you lift to the higher, you begin to learn that communication is not necessary through spoken language, that there are other ways of learning because knowing has no words. Words are utilized in knowing, in deciphering the knowing, but any time you have truly known something it has been without language, and you give it the language after the fact.

The access that you have in Divine Mind to what is always true, the great bounty that exists, the great stories that can be told here, are not only available to you through your invocation and agreement, but waiting for you to say yes to. When one claims her inheritance, one is claiming what is always hers. You don't earn the Kingdom. You claim the Kingdom as your birthright. The one who believes she is unworthy is holding an umbrella up that will block her experience. When the one beside her can know who she truly is without that unworthiness, the umbrella collapses and she may know herself in restoration. The act of blessing another first and foremost is the act of knowing their worthiness and the presence of the Divine upon them. They are always worthy, even if they deny it. They can only be worthy because they are of God, even when they say they are not. The one from the Upper Room who transposes the notes of the manifest world through her occupancy there is supporting others in their own reclamation, less through intention, but through Divine Mind or True Knowing, because in True Knowing you will not obstruct another's growth, nor ignore them as they ask to be lifted to the higher.

"What does that mean?" he asks. As we always say, you are your brother's keeper. Now, you may be in discernment about how you help. "Do I feed this one or that?" But to understand what it means to be your brother's keeper, at the level we teach from the Upper Room, is to realize them first and foremost as the True Beings that they are—capital "T," capital "B"—and not the small self that may be incurring all the difficulty, and yes, indeed, learning through it. The gift of being is the gift of sharing the presence of God that has come through you. And the claim "I know how I serve" is the realization of this from the Upper Room when you know for a fact, realize for a fact, "God Is, God Is, God Is."

We will complete this chapter—we are saying this for Paul— when we say we will. We would like to continue now. The next stage of this teaching is the realization of what embodiment is, as made manifest in your experience. Not an intellectual teaching, but what must express, and can only express, at the level of tone we sing to you from.

On this day we claim that all who hear these words may know themselves in union, and know the forms that they have taken as equally in union with the Creator of the form. On this day we say yes to the new song sung, the new notes played, that inform the skin and bone, the template of reality, all things heard and seen and experienced as form. And as we say yes, and as we sing through the man before you, we call you forth to the teaching of embodiment.

Now one. Now two. Now three.

[The Guides tone through Paul.]

It will be so. God Is. God Is. God Is.

This is the end of the chapter. Thank you for your presence. Stop now, please.

5

EMBODIMENT

DAY NINETEEN (CONTINUED)

What stands before you today, in a realized state, is a commission, an action you may take towards embodiment. Now, the realization of the Divine in form—underline the word *realization*—must be understood as the comprehension of what has always been true. Indeed, you are altered—better said, restored—but the requirement of the restoration initially was willingness, and is now aptitude. The aptitude you require to fully realize divine expression, which means to fully know it, has been addressed in some ways—again, the release of the old, who and what you put in darkness, the things that would obscure the light. But they must also include a collective resistance that you will encounter to what it means to be embodied.

Now, everyone is embodied, or an aspect of them, at least, is fully realized. The Monad *is* realization, and it exists within the hearts of all humanity. The Divine Spark is present in all manifestation. But the Monad itself, explicit in its way, seeks its realization through free will, which means it does not claim itself without the subject saying yes, and that is because you were gifted with free will and it is yours to say yes to. You are always choosing in one way or another. Now, the collective is lifting, and some of you don't understand this. The primer that you are receiving now, educationally, is about something that is being undergone through the collective at a collective level. Those of you who walk the path early are lighting the lamps so that others may see in the darkness. Those of you who come before are present to welcome the ones who follow. But everyone will lift. The planet is lifting. Or your idea of reality, inclusive of planet, is altered to sustain the higher tone. This is evolution. Nothing stays the same, and periodically humanity shifts in remarkable ways—the discovery of language, and now the discovery of what exists beyond it. Language is useful, but you are always in discourse, whether or not you know it, beyond language and beyond the letters used to comprise an alphabet.

When we speak through the man before you, we have offered attunements in language that are encoded with vibration, the purpose of which is to support you each at varying levels of escalation. As you become comfortable with one form, you outgrow the form. As each attunement works upon you or in accord with you—a-c-c-o-r-d, a c-h-o-r-d—you understand yourself in the resonant field that the chord aligns to. And when you trust that you are being lifted, you can begin to allow yourselves to perceive and be perceived at the level of tone you have come to.

As humanity does this as a whole, there will be confusion. You don't trust the old, the old systems, the old ways of deciding. And in times of change there is always mistrust, the desire to blame, the desire to invoke problems, so you don't have to see where you stand. It is far easier to blame another for your misfortune than to look into your own heart. So expect this to come, but only as a stage. Imagine there is a ship leaving a port. People want to get on the ship. They know they cannot remain where they were, but they don't know where the ship will take them. They don't know where the sea will carry them. They don't know if they will be provided for on this strange journey they are undertaking. So they act as they are used to. They fight amongst themselves, decide who will get on the boat and who will not, make one more worthy than the next, and then fight the captain when they don't like the direction the ship is taking. This is occurring now, but is a temporary way of adjusting to a new reality. When the ship is in stormy seas, there is fear. When the ship is in placid water, you find peace.

Now, there is no journey across any ocean that does not have its trials, and this is also true for the path of embodiment. Humanity is claiming its next inheritance, its next invocation. And the manifestation of this over the coming centuries will surprise those who come when they look behind them to see how things were chosen, why war was made, and why suffering was invoked. And that is because they will be beyond it. They will have realized themselves beyond the strata that you were entrained in. They will have been born on the new shore. You are now crossing the ocean, and it will take several generations for this passage to complete. But those born on the new shore, or born into the higher room as a state of vibration, will have already aligned because the resistance that was present in the low field will not be present there.

Imagine you have only known filthy water. You have bathed

in it. You have drunk from its wells. It's what you were used to, and you were always ill and always scrubbing yourself to get the detritus off that you carried from the water. In the new land, or at least the new realization of what the land is, that is not present. And when that is not present, you see with new eyes and you partake of the water and you drink freely. You know the well is endless and cannot be polluted by fear.

Now, the journey to a new shore in embodiment is not strategic. The amplification of form, even the cells of what you think of as the body, move to a higher tone, invoke a new principle: "My body is of God. All things are in God. And my body may know itself in a higher expression." And you do this, not only for yourself, but for all that you encounter. The one that walks the boulevard in this awareness is actually transmitting the information without language to all he or she sees, all who experience them, the one walking that is walking without the old encumbrance. This gives permission through entrainment for others to be lifted as well.

When we say the process of this is individual, it is both individual and collective. Every child grows into adulthood, but *when* someone comes into adulthood may vary with age. Some come to it younger, some a little older. Some undergo it gracefully, and some have a terrible time. This is comparable. You are in an adolescence now, if you wish to look at it that way, as you grow comfortable in a new body with its own requirements for expression. What are the requirements for the new body in expression? To maintain the high tone, regardless of what is encountered.

Now, when we spoke the other day of being in a room full

of feathers with a helmet on your head so you would not be distracted by the old thoughts, we were giving you a metaphor for what occurs when one's vibration is held high. The body is in vibration as well. And to care for the body is to love the body. And to love the body is to allow the body to be of God and worthy of love. You are not worshiping the body, or even seeking to improve it. You are caring for it as the expression of the Divine that is primary to your physical experience. You are having multiple experiences while in body that the body is not a requirement for. But the trust that is required now is to allow the body to move up the scale in vibration. Prior claims, "I know what I am in truth," *what* being manifest form, the claim of the body as holy, is supportive of the realization that is occurring now. But the transformation that your experience undergoes in amplitude will vary. Some of you will begin to see what has always been present because you have the gift of sight that was present prior but was precluded by the dense field. Some of you will find yourselves in a kind of expression where you experience nature as in union with the body. There are different ways one knows the body in a higher field. But to embody is to simply understand that the accelerated field that is incurred through the prior claims, and in the Upper Room, is not only present, but now requiring fulfillment.

"What does that mean?" he asks. Well, you may know yourself as ten years old for so many days on a calendar, and then one day you are eleven. What happened to ten? When you know the body as of God through an old bias born in separation, you have a comparable experience as the ten-year-old. "Here I am at ten. And oh, no! Now I am eleven." The higher field that has been invoked through these teachings is actually seeking to meet you in form.

Now, embodiment is not just the body. That would be a challenge to claim you fully in. But full embodiment is the Monad expressing through form and as form. Indeed, the body is immortal, but not in its current form. Source is the body, and Source does not die. So the body may be re-known in varying ways throughout the expression of the idea of form that you are present for. Initially, you understand the body as finite—how you know things, what you pick up with your hand, what you feed yourself with, all claimed as vibration but known only in solidity. And then you move to the level where you understand both things concurrently, the body as vibration and also solid. And eventually what happens is the need for the solidity is no longer present. You also realize yourself beyond the necessity of form.

Now, when we teach through Paul, we occupy someone who has taken form, been challenged by a body, has the issues that the body can hold. Some of us have known ourselves in form. Some of us have not. But regardless, you outgrow the need for form. You may choose to embody again for a specific purpose, but what was once the body may now be a butterfly, flying aloft, or dirt in the ground that you will one day walk upon in another form entirely. The field that you hold, the vibrational field, is always in presence, and the aspect of you that knows itself as holy cannot dismiss the body. One of the challenging teachings that some of you encounter is the false belief that the body is nothing but what you are carried around with while you are in an incarnation. To dismiss the body as a gross necessity is to lift the body to the level of nothing. To realize God as the tree is to know God as the body and God as the sunset, because God as vibration must be present in all form or can be present in none.

Embodiment, the manifest Divine in full expression, will claim the body at the level that the body can be claimed at, and this is both individuated and collective. The next stage for humanity is to move beyond the old systems to a health that it has denied itself through adherence to fear. And when the body releases the need to succumb to fear, much of what you know as illness will actually release. Anger is fear, malice is fear, and fear is destructive. You don't poison the well and expect your children to drink it. But indeed you do, and you do so unknowingly, by passing on your fears to your offspring. When you understand that what is occurring now is genetic, in some ways, or an altering of the species to a higher template, you will understand that you are not only participatory to this, that you are emissaries of it.

The challenge will always be the same. The collective says it cannot be so, even when the collective is undertaking it. Imagine you are on that boat, crossing that strange sea, but you still think you are in your home watching the same television show, eating the same meal. In fact, you are *on* that ship, you are all on that ship, and you are all awaiting the new life that will await you beyond the old idea of separation that you accepted as true, when, indeed, it never was.

Indeed, this is in the text. Stop now, please. Period. Period. Period.

(PAUSE)

What stands before you today, in a realized state, is the new awareness that what has been was claimed by you at one level of vibration or another. There is no experience that can be had outside of your field, and your field is in all ways in agreement to what you encounter—high, low, and in between.

When you claim an experience that is for your learning, it may not come in the way you would wish. When you claim a learning in an encounter with another, you may be encountering aspects of them that would deny the light in you, or deny the light in all things. These encounters are challenging, but often very productive. When you realize who and what you are beyond the old system of agreement, who and what you encounter will be altered as well because you will no longer be magnifying the negative or the fear-based through your own fear or your own agreement to challenge. When you are encountered by another who would have you be as they wish, would deny the light as you, you always have an opportunity to say yes to the high self, yes to the True Self, yes to the Monad, and let it lead the encounter because the Monad will not be sullied, cannot be claimed in fear. It cannot allow it because it does not hold that vibration. The aspects of you that claim what you call *negative* are here to learn that they no longer require them.

He interrupts the teaching. "But isn't this just part of life? Things happen that we don't want?" Yes, indeed, it is. But the context you've utilized for all experience has been known through the common field, and there are other ways of aligning to truth beyond encountering what lacks it. To know truth, to really know truth, is to know what exists beyond the old structure or the old template that has been the reality you have known. Everyone grows—in spite of themselves, often—through what they claim, and the soul's journey through a lifetime is indeed reclamation. And every opportunity that the soul will claim is to further its understanding towards union.

Now, *towards union* is interesting. The soul is always in progress towards union, but we are bringing you to union through a new teaching, or a teaching you have not known. Can the two coexist? They do. The soul applies the teachings we offer to magnify the experience of vibration and growth so that the soul's learning may be moved in high ways. You are no longer stumbling in the darkness. You may be stumbling towards the light without even knowing it. But you may be in the light and unfamiliar with the terrain. So what appears to be challenging, what causes you fear, must be seen as opportunity moving you forward. Each of you before us, each of you who hears these words, is comprehending herself, himself, through all prior experience, and the experiences you've held were always in alignment with the energetic field. Nothing comes to consciousness without an alignment to it.

Now, in the Upper Room, in an embodied state, the vibrational field is moving at a level of tone where there are things that are repelled because they cannot be held in the high tone. We have said often: Fear does not express in the Upper Room, but the memory of fear you hold will claim you back downstairs once you claim allegiance to it. "Oh, there's that fear again. Time to attend to the fear. Let's go have some fear and see how we learn from this one." The other opportunity is to understand what was, understand what was once your relationship to it, and then claim the higher. Again, the Monad or the Divine Self does not know itself in fear. And the requirement of the Monad, realization, embodiment, incarnation as itself, will actually claim all experience—underline *all*—in its field. The light that shines upon the world does not discriminate, and the one you would most avoid must be met by the light you hold. You are not challenging the human being that was to behave as you wish. You are seeing them anew without the prior conditioning, and realizing them as they can only be known in truth.

Now, the field you hold carries great information. Your incarnations, the memories of them, are actually held in the field. And the progress of these teachings has been the distillation of the True Self in the face of what was, so that what was may be re-known, inclusive of your idea of karma, old interaction, things that were challenging that seek to peek out at you and say, "Here it is—I, again—to get in the way of your growth." Anything that invites to get in the way of your growth is actually deciding with you that it is an opportunity for growth, and never a barrier.

Now, prior we said that you encounter the resistance of the collective as you align to the higher, or claim embodiment, which is simply a level of vibration, inclusive of form, where what you claim and see is in co-resonance with the Divine because it cannot not be. But when the resistance occurs, you encounter yourself through the old lens at times. "This is who I used to be, who they would have me be. I cannot challenge the collective." You are not asked to challenge the collective. The collective is actually not your problem. The only thing that is your challenge is looking at the light when the darkness dances before you. The only challenge you have is giving credence to the darkness when the light is right here. When you are challenged, you are called forth to know and to realize that what was once held in darkness must be re-known in light.

Each of you before us has history that you would seek to ignore, in this lifetime or others. Your job is not to look at the history, pick it apart, cradle it like a child, and nourish more pain. Your challenge is to understand that what was, was, but that the claim "Behold, I make all things new" actually reclaims the memories of history, what you decided in fear, what you claimed in grief and rage, and how you believed yourself to be. The key to embodiment is the release of the expectation of what once was. The realization of what was as of God is simply a step. Again, what you put in darkness, inclusive of memory, calls you to that darkness. When you understand that all things are in God—like it or not, agree to it or not—in premise, you must understand that all things can be made new.

Now, an atrocity is frightening. An attack is frightening. But these things experienced in the lower field must also be re-known, and lifted, and claimed in the Upper Room so that you may know yourself through them as unafraid, or without the intention to replicate what was through the old expectations. Challenges arise when you seek to find the old. "Where is that old difficulty? Where is that old pain? Where is that old person I would seek to avoid?" The gift of the encounter with the old is the opportunity to claim the new, not to refute what was, but to re-know it. There is a vast difference in refuting something and re-knowing it as of God.

Now, a lie will not be held in the high room, and the vibration you hold, and the level that you hold it, will make it very challenging for any of you to claim a lie. It is not only uncomfortable. The affect of it is too fast and quick in your experience.

If you wish to lower your vibration, find a nice fib and tell it. If you wish to deny the light in yourself, deny the light in another because that is a lie. The light must be there even when they're not expressing or being as you say they should. Period. Period. Period.

Now, as we teach through Paul, we understand his concerns and his challenges. And while he is being challenged today, everything is for the good. And while you are being challenged today, wherever you may be, you must understand it is also for good. He interrupts the teaching. "Well, *good* is a choice. Isn't that something you morally judge, call it good or bad?" We will use another word then for you: *of benefit.* Of benefit, which means it can accelerate the growth you are currently experiencing. And what you are encountering is, as we said, for good or for betterment or for realization beyond an old way of knowing the self.

Each of you before us who says yes, who announces herself as free, is already defying the collective, anointing herself in a new promise: "I am in the Upper Room. I Have Come. I Have Come. I Have Come." And what transpires there, in a new equation, a new tone of vibration, not only is embodiment, but the realization of God that was denied by you in the altered field, the lower field, the one you claimed and thought you were or must be of. Here we go:

"On this day I choose to realize myself beyond all history, beyond all prior choice. And as I say yes to this I give great permission for the realization of what was, what was once held in darkness, to be illumined in the high light that is

the Upper Room. I am Word through this intention. Word I am Word."

We thank you for your presence. Stop now, please. This is in the text.

DAY TWENTY

What stands before you today, in a realized state, is the awareness of what was, what is, and what is now claiming itself as your accountability, not only to prior choice, but what comes forth in the new alignment that you are choosing to know yourselves through. The requirement here is very simple: "I choose highly. I choose without fear. I choose in an awareness of my true worth, and in an awareness of the truth of all others." Underline that. If you are *aware of the truth in others*, the True Self that expresses as them, and you are in honoring of this in all ways, every choice you make in regard to another will be a high choice.

Now, some of you think this means you do what others want or what they would have you do. In fact, it means something other. You are responsible to your choices, just as you are responsible to the awareness of the inherent divinity in the one you encounter. And in that moment of agreement—"I know who I meet, I claim who I meet as God, an expression of God"—you release any need to play games, to get your way, to coerce or to frighten or to make someone do what would not be in their highest will.

Now, you are not accountable to the choices of others. In

this way, you are indeed sovereign. The small self, though, has a mandate for sovereignty which is vastly different than the Monad. True sovereignty *is* the Monad as expressed through you. The small self who would decide, "I am a sovereign being and I will do what I want," may be acting out in a fantasy of rebellion, or deciding what should be to suit her politics or his religious beliefs. When you are sovereign as the Monad, the amplification of choice from the Upper Room has vast affect. You don't understand this yet, but every choice you make has great affect upon your encounter with the world. There is a ripple effect, in some ways, through every word spoken, every choice made. And when these things are chosen in the lower field, they simply amplify what was, and those aspects of you that were in coherence with the small self and its choice will predicate the outcome that you will then be responsible to in karma, the residual affect of choice.

Now, as we always say, karma is opportunity to learn a higher way, to develop through choice. But from the Upper Room your accountability is other. It is to the vastness of the choice to simply be and express as God would express through you. Now, we added that phrase for Paul. "We are not expressing as God," he utters from the background. God is expressing through you, and consequently *as* at the level of intonation that embodiment claims for you. Underline that: *claims for you.* Agrees to you. Again, the concept of the perceiver and the perceived being one. The resonant field, once known in separation, now claimed in union, has broad affect. You can illumine the world by the choice to know yourself as claiming the world made new. You may know God through the self-identification,

True Self identification, that is of God and is not hindered by the small ideas that you utilized prior.

The tone that we sing of embodiment carries great affect, and the tone is implicit in the text we have been writing. It is why Paul is tired. It is why some are uncomfortable as they experience the words. But the recalibration of form and field at the level of rapidity that has come must be encountered by you. And as you ascend to it, it supports you in its recognition of itself through you. Indeed, the teaching is embodiment, and in fact always has been.

The first attunement we gave through Paul when he was a young man, "I am Word through my body"—"I am the action of the Creator through form"—carries out its plan in embodiment. "I am Word through my vibration," the energetic field, the manifestation of Divine that exists, expresses, beyond the physical self in this encounter, is the expression of service and full divinity as may be known through form, or accompanying form. "I am Word through my knowing of myself as Word." The claim "I Am" which follows—"I Am this," "I Am that"— has great affect. And to know the self, realize the self—"who I Am in truth, what I Am in truth, how I serve in truth"—is not the small self claiming identity. It is the Monad expressing as I Am through the manifest plane, inclusive of you. It is important to understand that. *Inclusive* means participatory to and with, not only you, but all.

The distinctions some make in claiming an idea of sovereignty is that they will decide who they are. But when it is the small self making that decision, the outcome is always a rendering of the small self, and cannot be lifted. Underline that.

The masks the small self wears *cannot be lifted* because they are moored through fear, a disclaiming, a renouncing, of the true identity that seeks to shine through the mask. "Behold, I make all things new."

As we teach, we align the student at the levels of agreement she can hold. But as this is the culminating text of this series, we have gifts to give, and the gifts must be taken in great responsibility. Those of you who are learning, experience yourselves in some ways as walking a tightrope lest you fall back down to the old ways of being. But we have said prior there is now foundation in the Upper Room, and if you stumble on the wire you do not fall. You are actually kept, held, aloft by the vibrational field that you have aligned to through the claims you have offered by way of intention: "I Am. I Am. I Am." The renunciation of the old—the idea of who one should be, not only addressed, but in the process of falling away—supports you in a lofty way. And we say this, this way: It contains the seed of truth that flowers through you—"I am the Divine Self"—and the Divine Self can only be aloft, or aligned, at the high amplitude that it knows itself through.

The renunciation of the old has occurred. And the reliance upon the old, the shadows of those things that you see around you that you think should always be there, will soon be passing as the new takes form, is unveiled, has been prepared, because the Upper Room is always awaiting your light to be inclusive of it, and your expression—your life, if you wish—to align to it as your abode. Each of you before us will be witnessed now as you may be held by us. We are doing this for the collective, although your experience of this may be individuated. When we see one of you, we see all of you, because in our mind, True Mind, you are of the whole and can only be thus. Here we go:

On this day we claim that all we hold dear, all who we love, all we embrace as who we are, expressed as you or your idea of self, will now be seen, will now be claimed in the high sight, and the residual affect of past choice that you carry in your field may be dismantled by the purity of vision we hold for you. There can be no blemish, can be no stain, can be no ruination, at this amplitude of focus, of truth, and of love. We see you in your beauty. We see you in your right to be, in all you have known and may know. And as we say these words, we call you forward. Be seen by us. Be known by us. Be loved by us. Be expressed as us in this shared response, in this wondrous song: God Is. God Is. God Is.

Receive us, if you wish. As we can hold you, we lift you. As you are lifted, you move to union. In union, you express beyond any idea of what you were, and know yourself as who you have always been.

Thank you for your presence. Stop now, please. This is in the text.

(PAUSE)

What stands before you today, in a realized state, is confirmation—confirmation of the work done, the choices made, the agreements heralded in love. To become the light of the world is to become the Divine Self as it seeks to express through you, not as you would have it be. The Divine as you knows itself, not at the cost of you, but at the cost of who you thought you were. And the requirement now is the resonant field that will seek to support all things in moving towards embodiment.

Now, the Divine Self does not have the requirements that the personality structure has had, and embodiment costs in one way—an idealization of what a life should be lived as, even what a spiritual life might be lived as. The ideas that hold these conceits are generally based in prior prescription—what it meant to be the monk, to be the abbess, to be the sage in the cave. The requirement now is other. It is the amplification and respect of the Divine that has come through you. And we use the word *respect* intentionally. You must respect the Monad, or the innate divinity, that expresses as all things. Without respect, you blemish it through the idea of what it means to be in authority, a precept held by the small self, but is not true at this level as it was.

We spoke to choice, and the immediacy of choice known in the Upper Room. "I am in my knowing and I am aligning in high choice." In high choice, every choice made is in support of the whole, even if it doesn't seem that way. Every time a choice is made in a high octave, there is a blueprint for that choice that may be known by you, and will be known by others because the blueprint has been etched in a higher field. Every act of kindness, every choice in love, supports kindness and love as may be met by others.

When you say to us, "I think I understand," we acknowledge the thought that claims understanding. But when you *know* understanding, when you are *in* understanding, there is actually no thought. There is simply expression—and the awareness, and, again, confirmation, of the high choice that is the Monad in articulation. When one surrenders to her True Self, when one incarnates as this True Self, one may continue to live a life that you may deem ordinary. But the experience of living this life is not ordinary. It's very other, and highly different, because the old template is no longer informing what is seen, what is known, and how things are chosen.

The amplitude that we have brought you to, if you wish it, is consummate with a level of growth that could not hold in the dense field. Your growth does not stop in an embodied state. In fact, it accelerates. The immediacy of the experience, the unveiling of the Divine before you each day, will continue to bring you lessons. Now, imagine a child in a garden with flowers she has never seen, plants growing she has never imagined. Imagine this child is being led by the hand, and the true names of all these flowers are being invoked. The child is learning, and as she understands herself through the flower, she holds the understanding of what a flower is, has always been, and can only be.

The level of articulation you have come to is not preclusive of learning. You are not done. There is no graduation. Some of you wish this. "Well, now I don't have to come back. Now I don't have to have an occupation. Now I just get what I want by thinking of it. Isn't this nice?" These are ways of understanding the selves through spiritual teachings that have been applied by the ego to support a sense of self that does not want to grow or be challenged by growth. He interrupts. "Are we challenged by growth in the Upper Room?" Indeed, you are, in wonderful ways—if you allow yourself to know it as wonderful. "What a great opportunity to love." "What a great opportunity to see anew." "What a wonderful opportunity to extend the life that

I am where I would never go through the old rubric, the old idea, or the old persona that would discriminate."

The attachment to the old has been addressed. The tethers to the old will linger as spiderwebs, as filigree, the translucent shape of them that you can make whole or dense through intention and focus. And you can claim yourself back in the lower realm through continued attention to attachment. To release attachment is to simply release outcome. You are not leaving your partner. You are not attached to what the marriage was, or the occupation was, or the body was, or the idea of age was, or the idea of romance was, or the idea of what spirituality was. You are claiming the new, and in this experience it is brought before you to go into an agreement with. Your consent is always required. But the *yes* that comes from the heart, and through the amplification of the field, is always in agreement to Source. Did you understand this? The *yes* that comes from the heart and the energetic field is always in agreement to Source. And this *yes* is confirmation. "God Is, God Is, God Is" is confirmation of what is. "It will be so": You are saying yes. You are confirming. And the experience of the confirmation— "God Is, God Is, God Is"—is what you experience as reality. It always was. You just didn't know it. You had the glasses on of separation. All that was seen was seen through those lenses. And memory was accrued that mandated your choices be in confirmation of separation.

You don't understand the magnitude of this, nor will you until it is yours, until it is what you see and how you know and what is established in your experience. Underline the word *established*. Now, imagine something that floats in the air. You catch it from the corner of your eye. "Did I see that? What *was* that thing?" But the higher you maintain the vibration, the more readily you see and hold the sight of what seeks to express at this level. Your eyes were entrained in the lower field, your senses occupy the lower field, and that is how you establish what you think of as reality. But now, in the Upper Room, as the senses are accruing evidence of these teachings as your experience, what seemed to flutter—a fleeting thought, a fleeting image—will begin to take form and you will see the glory of God's creation. Notice we said God's creation, not humanity's creation.

Now, humanity's creations are of God because nothing can be outside of God. But what we are referring to now is what has not yet been established in form that soon will be, and that is being countered quickly in the resistance you hold by the divine nature come as all of you. As humanity begins to amplify its experience of the Divine, the world re-knows itself beyond the old system. You are inheriting a collapse of structures you did not create, but you believed would always be there. The collapse is not a terrible thing. There is growth under the rubble. This is not destruction. It is renovation. It is being made new. It is being re-seen. And the high template of the Upper Room seeks to embody the benefit of True Choice, high choice. When a choice is made in truth, in divine truth, it will be for the good of all, not just for one man to benefit, one country to benefit, one tycoon to amass a greater fortune, but for all human beings to share in the bounty that is of God.

Again, *of God*—not the tycoons, not the countries, not the exclusive village that does not allow those who are not like them to buy the home. All human beings will be re-known in this amplitude as this progression ensues. And embodiment, or the species made new, reclaimed in a higher order, is not only the result of these teachings, but the result of what is occurring in this great time you chose to come to learn through. Again, you chose to come to learn. Those of you who discover our teachings discover yourselves through them. Those who say yes to the teachings are participatory to their creation because we are present as our students listen, and when you are not listening we are not teaching in the ways we do now. We are present in the ethers. We are supporting the students. But we are also holding this world, or this dimensional reality you call *world*, in the high order that has come to receive it.

Now, imagine there is a God that has what you call arms. Imagine there are a million gods that have what you call arms—or many million. And imagine those arms outstretched to receive what it loves. What does God love, but all things. You are the arms. God has come through you to hold the world, to lift the world, to reclaim the world in the name of the True Christ. Underline *true*. The *True* Christ is the Monad, the love of God instilled in human beings, participatory to the creation of all things. The Creator knows itself through its creations. You are both creator and creation, perceiver and perceived. The discussion has been begun. You may talk to the rainbow. You may talk to the ship at sea. And you may comfort these things in the very simple claim "I know what you are in truth," and receive the gift of the echo, the song of God sung back to you.

We will complete this text in coming days. We are saying this for Paul, who says, "This sounds like the end to me." When we are ready, we will let you know. But the gift of this class, this classroom we are teaching in, is the consistency and the rapidity of the availability to be heard. We are grateful for your presence. We are grateful for your gift to the teaching. This is in the text. Stop now, please. Period. Period. Period.

(PAUSE)

What stands before you today, in a realized state, is not only recognition, not only permission, not only choice, but a new awareness of all things. Underline *all*. "Behold, I make *all* things new."

Now, the perceiver perceives with new eyes, and is perceived by the God that expresses as all things, the Divine as who and what you are expressing in tandem with the who and the what that is all other things, the manifest world, all those things that dwell in it or that you would see with the new eyes you have been granted. The exodus from the old is about to commence, and an exodus from one way of being—in a world enslaved by fear, indoctrinated by those structures that came before you—and a relinquishing of what you thought should be to a new world, a high world. The journey is now. It is commencing. It will continue. And you will be known, k-n-o-w-n. Capital "K" *Known*.

The idea of being will be discussed now, what it means to be. And to be simply means to express as consciousness, and all things are in expression as consciousness. Because there are many levels of vibration that can be experienced, you equate consciousness with the residual affect of consciousness or thought, and what broadcasts or materializes as a world. Now, a world made new, the translation of vibration from one level of tone to another, carries with it great responsibility because the one who is now choosing in this alignment is always invoking the Divine. She cannot stop herself. He will not be stopped. And this utterance of the invocation—"It will be so; God Is, God Is, God Is"—is your immediate experience of this translation. The assumption of the Divine, the assumption of all things holy by the Christ Self, is the experience you are begetting and encouraging—and, indeed, sharing—by nature of presence and being. But the agreement to operate at this level holds responsibilities.

Now, the decorum that you have utilized in the common field, be it a moral code or a way of identifying self through tribalism, must be understood now as relics, ways to navigate the common field with a handshake or a smile, an agreement to what one must do to carry one's weight in the world, to share the responsibility through the old systems. But decorum is released and the idea of morality is altered, once in the Upper Room, because you are not operating in fear. You are not seeking to suppress the old impulse, the old anger, the old violent temper, the old disregard for others. You will do this for a period of time—until you begin to understand that these things have released and you are simply looking at the memory of them.

"Now, what is a world without morality?" Paul asks. "It sounds horrible to me." In fact, the morality that you utilize, codified by law, was completely necessary at a level or stage of alignment or maturity. But you are moving beyond adolescence, and the adolescent requires the curfew. The adult knows when it's time to rest. The adult knows that one does not get her way through coercion or violence. And the adult knows that, while she is valued, it can be no more than her neighbor because God does not play favorites.

The encounter you are about to have with a world you've claimed will be startling at first, because you are going to see the disrepair, what was left untended, the relics of the old messes that seem to scatter the streets, the scowls, the frustration, the poverty. And you will be discouraged by this until you understand herein lies opportunity: "Behold, I make all things new. It will be so. God Is. God Is. God Is." Now, you are not repairing what you see. You are reclaiming what you see in the high alignment of the Upper Room. And the new manifestation, how it comes to be, etched in the higher template, will be very much removed from the old way of experiencing. Understand that when you don't need violence, violence ceases to exist. When there is no requirement for war, the world will know peace, and a peace that is not contingent upon the absence of war, but is the status quo or the way of knowing all things.

Now, humanity is not becoming docile. Some of you believe this sounds dreadful. "Will we walk around in a daze, a peaceful pink haze? That doesn't sound right." Well, that is incorrect. That is not what we teach. You are invigorated and enlivened and moving to fruition in this momentary expression, moment by moment expression, of divine light that has become as you. And you contribute to benefit through the high choice and the responsibility this incurs. "What is that responsibility?" he asks. Well, just as you claim something in fear you are in an encounter with the old, when you claim something in love you are in an encounter with the new. And you will learn from this encounter. You will be taught by each encounter. But the lessons will not be from the old textbook. "Ah, here is a lesson in behaving better, being more polite, adhering to the moral code." Those books are gone. The immediacy of the lesson will be very different. "Here I am in this encounter. What is it teaching me, and what am I moving towards through it?"

Imagine you are wading in a bay. There is a buoy floating here, perhaps a raft over there. You understand the spatial relationship between the two from where you are in the water. But if you move to the buoy, you will have to recalibrate your distance to the raft. They both exist in recognition of you, and you may take one to get to the next. But you will understand yourself through the immediacy of the exchange, not the plan or the agenda to climb upon the raft when perhaps it is too far to wade out to and you must meet the buoy first.

Some of you say, "I am ready for it all. Give it to me all today." Be very careful what you wish for. You can only hold the vibration at the level of tone you will be in accord with. To renounce the old does not mean that your energetic system has fully aligned to the higher order or way of receiving. This is a process. And if you are grateful for each stage of the process, you will continue to claim and experience the new as the new is unveiled. Embodiment: less a destination than a new way of experiencing. Embodiment: not a goal, but an experience of being. Embodiment: not as the end, but as a new beginning. And you have come to this, will continue to come to this, through this exodus, this leaving of the old, that humanity is beginning and will continue to experience through the coming generations.

Please celebrate this. It is to your benefit to sing a joyous song. Not to mourn the release of the old, but to celebrate the new that *will* be your experience—underline *will*—through this level of alignment.

We sing your songs for you, yes, but in the comprehension that the song that you will be will be in union, and that the great chorus that is now singing will come to terms with its responsibilities to shepherd the planet, which is the level of vibration that you call your reality, in the highest way. We understand your needs to learn. We step back when we are not invited, and we come forward when invited and called, and offer you what we can. We do not demand you learn from us. You will get your lessons in some other way. And as we teach through Paul, as we understand his requirements, we continue to claim him in his rightful nature so that he may be of benefit to his world.

None of you are separate. You have never been. You are all notes in a great symphony that is always playing. And the song sung as you, this perfect world, a world made new, is your gift, is your Christ Self as manifest, and is the Divine saying yes, and yes, and yes. "It will be so. God Is. God Is. God Is."

Indeed, this is the end of this chapter. You may call it "Embodiment." Stop now, please. Period. Period. Period.

EPILOGUE

DAY TWENTY-ONE

What stands before you today, in a realized state, is the new awareness that what has been has been a broadcast, an expression of consciousness—a shared one, in fact, because you all contribute to your ideas of a world. The transition that you are undergoing now to the Upper Room, to a higher expression, mandates great change because you cannot hold the old and be in reception to the new. And the clarifications you require— "What is for my highest good?" "What is for the best of all?"— must be known to you experientially. The idea of conjuring through history, deciding what should be through political opinion or ideas of what was, must now be replaced by a new realization that "God Is," and all things may be known anew.

Now, you may have your politics. You may have your opinions. But to regard all things from the Upper Room is to hold a higher template, inclusive of those things but not mandated by them. You can have your expression in the flower of the Upper

Room. You may have your expression in the field of flowers that is all things as they express and bloom in a higher awareness. Or you can mandate what should be through the old opinions, the old history, the old decisions of what should be, based on your presumptions or your opinions or your personal requirements.

Understand personal requirements: It is the small self with his or her mandate for what she would have, what she would have accompany her on her journey. "I will not fly unless I have this seat on the airplane." "I will not travel unless she accompanies me." "I will not go there unless I am promised getting what I want." The Upper Room does not hold that promise. And the Upper Room, the entry to the Kingdom, holds all things that you may know and may be met by at that level of coherence. What you do not bring are the mandates of old, inclusive of the politics and the opinions and the strategies of getting what one wants. You are very attached to these things. You want the outcomes you believe they will promise you. But if you look at your history, every fight you have ever held or engaged in has gotten you very little. You believe it has, perhaps—perhaps a moment's satisfaction at being right, winning the game, succeeding where another failed. But these are always temporary, and until you become inclusive in your thinking you will never meet the requirements that the Upper Room holds for manifestation. Now, manifestation occurs in the Upper Room in great rapidity. But what stalls or withholds manifestation in the Upper Room is your coherence to the old. So throughout our teachings we have actually supported you in relinquishing an idea of the self that holds its mandate, in order to receive what exists and can express with your coherence. Underline *with*. In some ways this experience does not exist without you.

It may be present. The Upper Room is always present. But until you are in coherence with it, it remains an idea—something that you may seek, perhaps experience once or twice, but never abide in.

Now, the Kingdom, as we often say, the realization of God in form, the perception of the Divine as all things, claims you in agreement to it. And the manifestation of the Kingdom has been the text we are writing—in *inclusivity*. And underline that word. This is not tribal teaching—unless your tribe is all things, all human beings, all that live, and all that express in form—because all that expresses in form must be of God or there can be no God to hold all things. The limited ideas of God you hold are actually in transition, and this is very interesting, and in fact you are all participatory to it. Religion has held a basis for what comes next, or what your expectations might be of a hereafter, of a God who will smite or save. But in some ways the residual affect of the fear of religion, and the fear that religion has entrenched some in, must be now moved to a True Self that knows herself in union. And this must be beyond doctrine, if the doctrine that is taught is exclusive or denies some entry.

Now, you have heard things said—unless one becomes like a little child, one will not enter the Kingdom of Heaven. And there is actually truth to the metaphor. To work in wonder, to move towards the awareness of the unmanifest become manifest as all manifestation, requires wonder and requires innocence. The one who has decided in advance what should be true and what shouldn't, what should be good and what should be evil, is stuck in her opinions. And she will hold a rock and think it is God until she moves beyond it. He interrupts the teaching. "But wouldn't you say the rock is God?" The rock is a way of knowing self in agreement to density. And the dense frequency that the rock holds will actually hold you down from the process of ascension or recalibration that you are encountering yourselves through. You cannot lift with the rock, and at a certain point even the pebbles in your pockets, the small injustices, the small fears, will stand in the way of full expression. But when you come to that level, you will know to empty your pocket. You will not want the residual affect of it.

As you are lifting now, as you have been lifted, you are seeking to justify, still, ways that you have known yourselves, had your opinions proven, chosen in fear and agreed to in fear. And at this juncture in the Upper Room in the claim "Behold, I make all things new; It will be so; God Is, God Is, God Is," we are singing for you at a level of tone that you have not known yet, or experienced thus far. The integration of the tone, which is the song of Source expressed as all things, can be aligned to. And the text we write actually *is* this alignment because the alignment is present in every page, in every consonant, in every vowel, as they create words. And the intention behind the words is always the same: To know who and what you are, have always been, and what now can be claimed.

The Resurrected Self, the Monad expressed as you, holds its own amplitude and is already in agreement to the tone we are describing. The song of the being you are, in full expression, lifts octaves from what you have known yourselves through. And the predilection you have to still look down at your feet and not up at the stars will claim you in some ways— some ways useful, some not—in a way of knowing the self that denies the Divine. "How would that be useful?" he says. Well, some of you seek to fly. You seek a trajectory where there is no mooring on this plane. But you must hold a mooring while in physical form, not only to the body, but to all things that vibrate at the level or tone with which the body does. Now, the body itself has been re-sung through these teachings to align to the higher. But you maintain an awareness of what your form is, what this or that thing is called, as you move beyond them, because once you know all things as God, all language does is confirm God, not decide what something must have been or should be called.

Now, language is useful, and you use language to create. We offer language by way of attunement. But the attunements exist beyond language, just as this text exists beyond the words on the page—as a vibrational oracle, a vibrational expression, that can simply be experienced. But without the context that the language offers, you will be confused. You may think your-selves mad, and indeed you are not. You are just undergoing a level of transition that few have done, and all are about to.

Now, that's very important to understand. We are not exclu-sive, although you may think yourselves as such. And those who walk this path hold the light for the ones who follow. Those who walk this path see the Divine in all things, and claim the Divine as manifest, which allows others to claim the experience by level of tone or creation that *you* have supported through presence and being. When you have become the alchemist or the ambassador of the Upper Room, when the manifestations that you incur are always of the high broadcast, you are claiming the world, and you are etching the map into the ethers so that others will follow you. The transition is enormous, and we don't say that lightly. The falling away of the old is part and parcel of the exodus you are about to experience as a species as you leave one strata of vibration and claim the new that has been waiting for you.

Now, understand what this means. The Upper Room, or the Divine Self that expresses as the Divine in the Upper Room without the impediment that the small self has utilized, is ever present. But your transitioning to the level of tone or amplitude where this expresses in form, and *as* all form, is what you are undergoing now, principally one and all at the same time. "What does that mean?" he asks. Well, we have said this many times. We will say it again. The Monad is singular and plural. The Christ is singular and plural. It is of God, but the unique expression of God that is present in all things and seeks to be manifest through you. So to be as one is also to be of all. They are the same. And this is what it means when you realize that what you do to one, you have done to all, and you have done to yourself.

Now, a blessing offered to the singular expresses as the singular, but also claims all things in agreement to it. You don't understand your power. When one life is saved, all lives are seen anew. When a blessing is given to one, it is given to all. And when you damn another, you damn yourself in return. And that is your experience. You can choose that experience. You may live in an artifice, a separation that is your own construction. But you are being claimed in union now, and the teaching of union that you are participating in is challenge and change, one at the same time. And the agreement to that is to be lifted and re-known as you can only be known in truth. Here we go:

On this night we claim that all who hear these words, all who have chosen this path, will be sung into being at the level of tone they can hold, and the level of tone they can hold as the Monad surpasses any idea of tone or vibrational accord that the small self has utilized in a personalized way.

When *you* become universal, when *you* become one with Source, you *are* the song and the expression of the song. So as we sing to you now, we enjoin you in this great promise: The world is made known. The world is made new. And the world is lifted to the True Self, the True Christ, the true expression of God that knows itself as all things. As you sing these words with us, know that they are true, and indeed always true:

"I Have Come. I Have Come. I Have Come. Behold, I make all things new. It will be so. God Is. God Is. God Is."

On the count of three, Paul.
Now one. Now two. Now three.

[The Guides tone through Paul.]

The Divine has come. It is here. It is your gift. It is your expression. It is this announcement:

I am in the Upper Room. I Have Come.

Period. Period. Period. Yes, this is in the text. Stop now, please.

DAY TWENTY-TWO

What stands before you today, in a realized state, is the granting of the agreement that all things will be so. What this means, very simply, is that your idea of what should be, even a transposed world, is moved to a new alignment. In the claim "God Is" all things are so. They are seen as they truly are. You are not recommending change. You are not utilizing an old bias to fix the room, to fix the world. You are seeing what is, and your relationship to what is has been altered by the level of tone you hold as yourself, or the True Self in expression. The Monad expressed as tone claims all things new. And the realization of the world you see, the manifestation of the claim "It will be so," demonstrates itself. It does the work. You are the perceiver and the perceived because you are witnessing the Divine as it is witnessing you, and in conversation, true conversation, with the agreement that all things must be so because "God Is."

Now, the equivalency here at a level of tone has been sung to you. You have aligned through it, and you are granting permission or alignment through agreement to demonstrate this, which simply means to experience it as what life is, what life can be, and what life will only be. "What does that mean?" he asks. Well, first, you experience potential, "It will be so," the claim of the Divine that is now made manifest in the altered field through the claim "God Is." And the manifest world, what is, what sings back to you, is your experience.

Now, you are in conversation with the manifest world always, at every level of tone you have claimed. How you decide, how you perceive, how you condemn, how you lift high what you see before you, is conversation. No matter what you see, the consciousness you hold is informing the thing seen. And once the bias of old or the prescriptions of old have been moved aside, the world is seen by you unfettered, what it is, has only been, and will only be, beyond the expectation that was informed by the small self claiming what must be to confirm an identity that was claimed in the lower field.

Now, we must make an exception for Paul today, who has been thinking about the teachings, and in useful ways. We will say this to him now as an interruption: The invocation of "God Is" is not surpassing the small plane, the small self occupying the small plane. It is claiming it in accord to it. "God Is" claims all things and manifests as itself at the level of tone sung. It is not so much that it is better. It is what is, in an unadorned state. Imagine the tree without the decorations at Christmas time. Imagine the house without the decorative application. The structure of what is, the very infrastructure or architecture of manifestation, is actually revealed to you at the level of tone we are teaching you. "What does this look like?" you ask. It looks like what is—beyond the old application, beyond the old decision, what *was* before you thought what should be.

Now, when we teach, we are very aware that some of you will seek to utilize these teachings to avoid the world you have known yourselves in. And that is not this teaching. You are confronted by your creations, your belief systems, your ideas, out-pictured as manifestation in every moment. As you move beyond the old, as you move against the old in this encounter, you claim anew. When it is before you, it is yours to perceive. It does not evaporate. It must be comprehended, seen as what it was, and then you may claim the re-creation of it. "What is an example?" he asks. Well, the old wedding ring, perhaps, the thing that was worn on your finger before your spouse left you. The idea of the ring, through indoctrination, holds great meaning, and you are sighing as you are holding the ring and remembering what could have been. The properties you endowed the ring with are in coherence with your field. When you understand that the ring meant something, you understand what it meant. But then you perceive the ring as symbol, and then you perceive it as metal, once claimed in another form, and then you claim it as God. Now, all the steps we just described may happen in a moment, without the intellect deciding or seeking to define meaning through the old applications. But the residual affect of past beliefs—which play out as your lives, your difficulties in your lives, sometimes the benefits of your lives—must all be understood as moving towards recalibration through your encounter with them.

You will not decide that that thing on the other side of this plane that you call a world must be different. When you encounter it, the field that you hold may alter the thing seen, restore the thing seen, and lift the thing seen to its true nature. It need not be a physical encounter. Consciousness is not moored in the physical self. Anything you imagine or believe can be, you are in coherence with. And these things can be blessed or cursed—as you agree to them, how you agree to them, and what you decide the things must be. The aspect of you that decides, be it the personality structure, or the Monad, or the aspect of you that is claiming a new alignment, learning a new discernment, and claiming a new identity as who and what you have always been, are all partaking. These aspects of you are all available. But as you move to the Upper Room, the need to translate the old is diminished rapidly. You become used to the new plane, the new level of coherence, and you realize that what you thought you brought with you, the old baggage, the old decisions, the old ways of monitoring what you see to get the outcome you would have, have actually been left below.

Now, *below* does not mean *worse*. It means *different than*. You may choose at any level. You may reside at any level of consciousness and learn the lessons that come there. The Upper Room is not an improvement. It is simply other. It is the strata of vibration of the consciousness that you know of as Christ or the Monad as manifest consciousness. Its alignment, beyond fear, holds not only promise, but availability to a level of incarnation that you would not receive as you had moored in the lower field.

Imagine a plant that is grown in a low plane. The requirements of the plane informs what is planted. The requirements of the high plane are rather different, and what will bloom there will be in agreement to the high plane. The Monad is the high plane in articulation, or the consciousnesses that the Monad resides in. So not only is it present, it is blooming, and blooming as all it encounters. Manifestation in the Upper Room, in embodiment, is so vastly different than how you have believed things to be that your temptation to superimpose the intellect, the personality, upon the higher realm will always be to your detriment. You deny the Divine when you reduce it to a personality structure. You deny our ability to love you when you superimpose an idea of a treacherous God, a fickle guide, a mysterious icon, upon what we are, which is expression of the Divine as consciousness in agreement to your learning, to your benefit, and to your manifestation as what you are in truth.

You are who you *know* you are in the Upper Room, when you are not questioning your knowing. And as this passage has been incurred, as the challenges that arise in this passage are present, you are encouraged, always encouraged, to remember the Source of all things—that nothing can be outside it, not any experience, not any idea. Even the idea of separation which has caused such pain must be known as of God, because until it is known as of God it will operate as separate. Fear believes itself to be separate, but it is not. It operates in a trajectory that is actually in a premise of separation, but it is a false premise. But it will accrue the evidence of separation at every opportunity and seek to replicate that again and again. When all things are made new, even fear itself—dismantled as a structure, your reliance on it released—may be known in God. And its affect will change, what it has meant will change, the names it has been called will change, because they will be new.

Re-articulation of the manifest plane, form and field, the articulation of the Monad as all things experienced, God perceiving God as all things, is not placid. It is active. The Word is the energy of the Creator in action. And as the Word, or the manifest Word made flesh, which is the Monad as form or the Christ come as human and divine in union, you realize—which is *know*—what is always true. What is true is always true, and what will be claimed in self-deceit, the deceit of others, in the intellect's attempt to ride roughshod over experience, or a bias in old ideas seeking confirmation for their merit, must be understood as ways you pass through ideas, move beyond intellect, to the claiming of the truth that will withstand all things.

If you claim truth in fullness—"I Am that I Am; I Have Come, I Have Come, I Have Come"—and allow the truth of those statements to dismantle what is untrue, the rapidity of the falling away would be so rapid that you would become confused. So your realization comes in incremental stages, as you begin to experience the vastness that is Source at the level that can be experienced in the Upper Room while maintaining a form. The form is holy, as are what the form experiences itself in, sees itself through. And when all things are seen anew, re-articulation occurs. And the change is not complete, but so pronounced that it has its own volition. There comes a point in these teachings where the level of manifestation of the Monad carries the weight and the burden of the transformation to its fruition.

Notice we said *its fruition,* and not your idea of it. The challenge some of you face is the false belief that you are becoming enlightened, and that you stop, enjoy the flowers, and have no more thought, no more experience to challenge you. But this continues in the Upper Room, but the experience is other because your perception is other and because you are in conversation with the reliability—underline that word—the *reliability* of God that has been primarily a premise in the lower field, and now presence, and now True Knowing. When you move to True Knowing, Divine Mind, everything that you perceive is in coherence with truth. And what was never true, specks on a window, will fall away rapidly. You are not discussing them, debating their merits, enjoying the game of the intellect, perusing and pursuing a spiritual life. You are in it, and it is as you. You have become the Divine—that knows, that perceives, and speaks a language in knowing.

This is important to understand. When we address language in these texts, we seek to be specific with you. But the language that you adhere to holds bias in the lower field, has been deeply informed by prior meaning, prior moral texture or belief, and is weighted by them. Imagine an alphabet now, in any language, and align to this alphabet before you as sound, because it is sound, denoted as letter, and understand that the sound can be sung and re-known in the high plane without carrying the weight of the prior meaning. A lamppost can be known as what your prior experience was. The letters that comprise the word can be re-known, can be reclaimed. But what lamppost is, the idea of *lamppost* itself, in a re-articulated state will hold the resonance of the truth of *lamppost* without the superimposition of prior meaning—"the lamppost that we hung a man from," "the lamppost that didn't work and left us in the darkness," the lamppost that shows the way to that road you never wish to travel. All of the meanings the lamppost has held can be re-known, and what is, is what has always been, without being fraught or laden, heavily laden, with past belief in premise.

Each of you before us has been prepared for where we intend to take you in the completion of this text. And the completion of this text is coming rapidly. The re-articulation of form and mind, the re-articulation of the vibrational field inclusive of the emotional self or how you perceive yourself to be, the re-knowing of the senses in a high octave where they may bloom and become receptors for what expresses beyond the common field—all have been discussed and will be discussed in coming texts we author. But we will say about the text we complete, and complete soon: This is the culmination of the teaching that began in *I Am the Word*, and is the final text of *The Trilogy of Manifestation*. Where we will take you beyond this will be beyond what we have spoken of—not a continuation of, and not in adherence with, but a renewing of an idea of the Divine that can be partaken at a level of choice that none of you have met.

The next teachings will take time, Paul. And we are going to prepare you, beginning now, for what will follow. But our students are here. They are hearing and reading, and they are being seen as they do so. And what we see now is a level of entrainment to the vibrational field of the Word that has not been present on this manifest plane as a collective field, and will be sung anew and into being, again and again and again, through the echo of each of your fields.

The energetic fields that you hold are operating in most ways as transistors. You are reclaiming the vibration of the Upper Room as manifest, and transitioning what you encounter with it, which means the tone that you experience yourself as is experiencing what you encounter. The echo of this broadcast that is your tone will sing back to you. This is the conversation: God experiencing God, and God singing back, whether it be God as lamppost, God as your neighbor, God as those people, God as those mountains. All will be in song—and, as sung, made new.

You are in the resounding *yes*, the complete *yes*, of this teaching in the claim "I Am; I know who I Am; I know what I Am; I know how I serve." And the I Am, Divine Self, Monad, Christ Self, expressed as and through you, will not only move mountains. It will redeem what has been cast aside. It will lift to the light that which has been claimed in darkness. And its triumph, its great triumph, indeed is a world made new.

We thank you for your presence. This is the last chapter of the text. You may call it an epilogue. We are grateful for your presence. We sing for you now—as frequency, as tone, as love, as knowing. And the song we sing, a world made new, is yours to partake in.

Thank you each for your presence. Period. Period. Period. Stop now, please.

ACKNOWLEDGMENTS

Dustin Bamberg, Noam Ben-Arie, Tim Chambers, Joel Fotinos, Amy Hughes, Joan Cramer, Noah Perabo, and Hanuman Maui: Ram Dass Loving Awareness Sanctuary.

About the Author

Born in New York City, PAUL SELIG attended New York University and received his master's degree from Yale. A spiritual experience in 1987 left him clairvoyant. Selig is considered one of the foremost contributors to the field of channeled literature working today. He served on the faculty of NYU for more than twenty-five years and is the former director of the MFA in Creative Writing Program at Goddard College. He makes his home on Maui, where he lives in the rainforest with his dog, Lily. Information on channeled workshops, online seminars, and private readings can be found at www.paulselig.com.